PRAISE FOR
CHOOSING OURSELVES

"This intimate account of a mother, a son, and the birth defect that defined their lives is about guilt, fear, bravery, and love; about questions asked and questions unanswerable. It is about wounds and healing—not so much of the palate or the lip, but of the heart."

—Lauren Kessler, award-winning author of *Free: Two Years, Six Lives, and the Long Journey Home*

"*Choosing Ourselves* is a must-read, true story of the challenges, commitments, and unwavering love of parenthood. A compelling story of a parent and adult child exploring their past together—each person speaking their truth to better understand the other's experience—led to deeper understanding and love."

—Nancy Golden, Ph.D., M.S., Special Education, Ph.D., Curriculum and Instruction, leader of the Oregon Schools Research Network, former chief education officer for the State of Oregon

"An extremely rare and valuable contribution to the literature on the experience of disability and family life. The dialogue is deeply humanizing and will be a source of encouragement and also serve as a mirror for many parents and adults with disabilities."

—George H.S. Singer, Professor Emeritus, Ph.D., Department of Education, Gevirtz School, UC/Santa Barbara

"*Choosing Ourselves* is the saga of navigating a health system often lacking in compassion, understanding, and psychosocial skills and the wounds that an insensitive approach to medical care inflicts on the family. Through its stark and moving recitation of the facts, this book serves as a vivid example of how patients and their families may encounter a lifetime of frustration and dashed expectations despite their efforts to achieve some kind of normalcy amidst the challenges of a life-changing condition."

—Catherine Musemeche, M.D., board-certified pediatric surgeon; Fellow, American College of Surgeons; and author of *Small: Life and Death on the Front Lines of Pediatric Surgery*

"Dr. Walker's wish that doctors were interested in knowing her son as a person rather than a 'case,' points to a more truly holistic and inclusive approach to caring for children. *Choosing Ourselves* is an important contribution to the literature of helping families find their own unique voices as they advocate for their children."

—Dr. Norman Scott, pediatrician, Kaiser Craniofacial Clinic (Colorado) co-founder, and Operation Smile volunteer from 1986–2009

"This story of the angst of a mother and son around whether she had done something to cause her son's cleft palate condition reveals an issue that has never come to the attention of society or to the field of Special Education—the impact on families of a bilateral cleft palate. I am mesmerized by Barbara and Jim's depth of honesty and emotion, as well as their ultimate resilience to not just survive but prevail."

—Ann Turnbull, Ed.D., Distinguished Professor Emerita, University of Kansas

"*Choosing Ourselves* uncovers cracks in the healthcare system when serving a child or person with a disability. Yet, it also credits the caregivers who know their limits and, nevertheless pursue the best care they can honestly and openly. This courageous book is a wake-up call for professionals. It will hit you right between your eyes, and you will be better for it!"

—Jane Eyre McDonald, CCC (Certified of Clinical Competence) speech-language pathologist; former executive director of Eugene Hearing and Speech Center; University of Oregon Communication Disorders and Sciences Program faculty member.

"Barbara and her son build a tapestry of inspiration, will, defiance, and tenacity that will inspire generations of families who are faced with the challenges of dealing with birth anomalies."

—William Sarnoff, teacher, chronicler, and author of *Around the Samovar* and *This Is What I Remember*

"*Choosing Ourselves* is a compelling account of a determined mother's fight not only to guide her son through the multi-tiered trials and traumas of the care required to address the repair of his cleft palate, but also to educate medical professionals about the healing properties of holistic care and patient compassion. Barbara's beautiful, honest prose and Jim's poetic accounts of his own memories of the same time, as well as his changing feelings over time, dovetail perfectly. This is a book for all combinations of parents and children."

—Spike Gillespie, journalist and award-winning writer of books, magazine articles, blog posts, and poetry

"When a mother learns she can't breastfeed her newborn because her baby has a severe cleft lip and palate, her idea of motherhood is abruptly rerouted as she navigates her son's surgeries and the psychological and social challenges stemming from his disability. But everything changes when her son asks her—for the first time at age 44—how it felt to be his mother. The result is a stunning co-authored memoir written by mother and son—a unique telling of one disability from two perspectives and ultimately a universal story punctuated with eyes-wide-open memories and a self-help feel for all parents who have ever experienced raising a child with a difference."

—Sarah Barnes, award-winning author of *Meredith & Me: a mother and daughter on a profoundly different journey*

LOVE & ADVOCACY IN
OVERCOMING A BIRTH DEFECT &
THE AMERICAN MEDICAL SYSTEM

CHOOSING
OURSELVES

**BARBARA R. WALKER, Ph.D.,
& JIM H. WALKER**

WITH CONTRIBUTIONS FROM JAMES V. WALKER, M.D.

This book is a memoir. It reflects present recollections of experiences and their impact over time on the authors' lives. Some dialogue has been recreated. Some names of individuals have been changed or omitted to respect their privacy. The information given here is not intended as a substitute for any professional medical advice. It is provided for educational purposes only.

Published by River Grove Books
Austin, TX
www.rivergrovebooks.com

Copyright © 2023 by Barbara R. Walker, Jim H. Walker

All rights reserved.

Thank you for purchasing an authorized edition of this book and for complying with copyright law. No part of this book may be reproduced, stored in a retrieval system, or transmitted by any means, electronic, mechanical, photocopying, recording, or otherwise, without written permission from the copyright holder.

Distributed by River Grove Books

Design and composition by Greenleaf Book Group
Cover design by Greenleaf Book Group
Cover images used under license from
©Shutterstock.com/Michal Sanca; ©Shutterstock.com/sdecoret

Publisher's Cataloging-in-Publication data is available.

Print ISBN: 978-1-63299-733-3

eBook ISBN: 978-1-63299-734-0

First Edition

This project is dedicated to the curiosity that led us to know, respect, and love each other as a mother and son in ways we hadn't anticipated.

Also to the parents and children whose lives have been complicated by a child's birth defect or disability.

And to the care providers who took the time to notice and help parents and children cope with the stress of hospitalizations and painful procedures.

CONTENTS

NOTE TO THE READER vii
PROLOGUE: THE INVITATION 1
PART ONE: 1970–1973 5
    Shaky Beginnings 7
    June 25, 1970, 1:00 a.m. 18
    Not Normal 22
    To Normal-Looking 31
    Ready or Not 32
    On Our Own 37
    What Happened? 45
    Elizabeth 54
    To the Perfect Baby 62
    Postcards from My First Year 63
    Speechless 68
    James: The View as a New Father 75
    Part One Photos 81

PART TWO: 1973–1980 85
    Boomerang Years 87
    Racing Snails 96
    Peer Pressures 98
    Memory Study 1 104
    To a Child's Stubbornness 106
    Standing Firm 107
    See Me as I Will 117
    Dish Towel Dilemma 128
    Torchons 135

Contents   v

    Untethering 136
    What Do I Know? 141
    James: Obligations 153
    To My Doctors 157
    Part Two Photos 160

PART THREE: 1980–1988 163
    The Big Question 165
    To Questions Without Answers 171
    Perhaps I Have a Cleft Because 172
    Solo 173
    Phone Calls from a Bike Trip 183
    Crossing Lines 187
    Essential Credentials 195
    Forever Friends 204
    Ode to Sport 206
    My Name Is 209
    Memory Study 2 218
    How to Live with Myself 220
    Cupid's Broken Bow 228
    Letting Go 229
    Part Three Photos 238

PART FOUR: 1988–2021 241
    Transitions 243
    On His Own 247
    Dallas Specialist 252
    My Son's Sonogram 254
    Lover 256
    Le Fort 257
    Le Fort, Take 2 259

On Anger	262
Tending the Flame	263
James Reflects	265
Finding Words	269
To My Doctors, On Reflection	278
Letter to a Clefted Child	279
Part Four Photos	284

EPILOGUE	285
My Father	287
Dear Brother	288
Beyond Words	290
Let Us Be Clear	294

MEDICAL TERMS	295
POEM NOTES	299
ACKNOWLEDGMENTS	301
ABOUT THE AUTHORS	303

NOTE TO THE READER

This story is told primarily through narrative by Barbara R. Walker and through poetry by her son Jim H. Walker. In the table of contents, we have italicized titles of poems and postcard, letter, and telephone call segments to distinguish them from the chapters in prose. Observations by James V. Walker, Jim's father, appear as separate sections accompanying the narrative, while the recollections of Jim's brother Kent are interspersed throughout the text.

PROLOGUE

THE INVITATION

"You know, Mom," Jim said through the narrow slit between his jaws, "I've never thought about it before, but what was it like for you, being my mother? It must have been hard on you, too." The comment bowled me over. It was November 2014. My son Jim was forty-four years old. He was recovering from a complex cleft palate surgery, one of many surgeries to correct complications from a birth defect—a severe bilateral cleft palate and lip. His jaws had been wired shut since the surgery ten days before.

Since his birth, Jim has undergone eight surgeries and countless orthodontic, speech, and counseling interventions—all aimed at repairing this birth defect and mitigating the hardships it entailed. I accompanied him to the surgeries, procedures, and therapies. They were often painful and disruptive for him. Jim weathered disappointing surgery outcomes, demoralizing encounters with too many professionals, and the sting of too much stigmatizing attention from others. I was witness to it all. Each episode of watching my child endure fear and pain and interruption to his life was wrenching. Becoming the mother of a child with a cleft forced me to reexamine how I thought about myself, parenting, and what I wanted in life. Over the forty-four years of ups and downs, there were many tough thoughts to process and many emotional upheavals to work through. They all begged for sensitive mother-son conversation, but words that could have helped did not come.

Jim has undergone two major surgeries within the past five months. Neither delivered the hoped-for results. After the first surgery in May, Jim, Cathy (Jim's partner), Jim's father, and I each kept our edginess to ourselves as we tended heavy hearts. Then, we learned that the second surgery in November had fallen short, too. But this time, Jim had not been swayed by the surgeon's bright promises and had set his expectations in line with actual outcomes of past surgeries. His balanced reaction to the disappointing news helped the rest of us take it in stride. Conversations at the dinner table were easier than after the previous surgery.

One evening, Jim and I found ourselves relaxing together in the kitchen. I'd been sipping a glass of white wine and he'd just finished sucking down a berry smoothie through a straw wedged in the slit between his wired jaws. That's when he shot me the question: What was it like for you, being my mother?

It was as though Jim had handed me a hot wire. I startled, nearly spilling my wine. My first impulse was to give a succinct synopsis all tidied up for easy consumption. In my head, alarms sounded, but from somewhere deep inside, a steady voice urged me to risk it all, to take hold of the hot wire and make the connection Jim was offering. I was aware that my eyes had flooded, and the words I wanted to say stuck in my throat. Jim leaned forward, his brow furrowed, and he put a hand on my arm.

"Hey, Mom, I didn't mean to upset you."

I shook my head to signal Jim not to misinterpret, not to back away. I raised a finger to indicate I needed a moment to collect myself.

"I haven't thought about what it was like for you, not until now," Jim said in a soft voice. He let me settle myself and waited.

I took several deep breaths. *It's now or maybe never*, I told myself. I pushed aside all cautionary warnings. I steeled my nerves, found my voice, and looking straight ahead, let myself go, tears and all.

"Please don't misunderstand these tears. I'm not upset. I'm not sad, either." The words burned in my throat. "It's just that it's the hardest thing I've ever had to do. What you see are tears from big feelings. It has been huge, intense, all of it. And it's still very much alive in here." I tapped my chest. "That's what you're seeing." He nodded and studied me.

"It's been a lot for both of us." I wondered if what I said would push him away.

"I'd like to hear about it, Mom." It was a gentle tug.

"Oh, I'm not so sure about that," I said. My voice caught. "I'm not proud of some of the ways I handled things, and I'm not sure it'd be easy for me to tell, or for you to hear. And then, too, I'm not sure I want to burden you with my story. It's a mother's worry thing."

"I'm an adult now, Mom, and the father of a teenager. I'd like to know how you managed being my mom with all of this going on." He gestured toward his mouth. "I can handle it."

"We'll see," I said, wondering how I'd ever feel comfortable disclosing my personal struggles—warts and all—to my son. He nodded and we both fell silent. We turned to lighter topics then. Inside, the idea of an open conversation about our experience electrified me.

A month later, Jim's father and I were spending the Christmas holiday with Jim and his family. The house was full of Christmas spirit. On Christmas morning Jim donned a Santa hat and passed presents to everyone amid oohs and aahs and thank-yous. Just as the gift opening was ending, Jim plucked a small green envelope from its hiding place in the Christmas tree's branches and, with a solemnity that seemed out of keeping with the moment, handed it to me.

"This is for you, Mom," he said. "From me."

I looked at him quizzically, but his expression told me nothing. I opened the cheerful red-and-white-striped card and read:

Mom,

Your gift is one we have to share. I've signed us up for a memoir writing workshop starting in Jan and we'll meet with the coordinator this Sat morning.

Here's to sharing our shared memories.

Love,
Jim

PART ONE:
1970–1973

SHAKY BEGINNINGS

On June 24, 1970, I'm destined to make three deliveries to hospitals in Cleveland, Ohio, within sixteen hours. Early in the morning, I deliver James, my husband, to Lakeside Hospital at Case Western Reserve University for his first day as a medical intern. I do not know then that he has drawn night call and will ask me later in the day to deliver a change of clothes for the next day. Nor do I know that I will be heading for another hospital that very night for the earlier-than-expected delivery of our much-anticipated firstborn child.

As with most other important events in our lives, James and I have thought strategically about when to start a family. We met at age eighteen at a mixer when we were freshmen on different college campuses. Love at first sight, we still tell ourselves. After a courtship punctuated by several separations over the next five years, one of which was nearly fatal to our relationship, we became engaged just before graduation in 1966. We planned our wedding for a year later, allowing me to accept a Fulbright teaching fellowship in Arles,

France, and James to get one year of medical school at Case Western Reserve under his belt.

Our friends and family doubted we could maintain our relationship from separate continents. But if anything, the distance and time apart strengthened our commitment to one another, and we married on schedule on August 26, 1967. We were both twenty-three years old.

After three years of marriage, we decided it was time to think about having a baby, despite worries about mixing medical training and family. We have calculated this first pregnancy so that there will be no gap in our income stream. Indeed, James's first day of earned income starts today with his first day as an intern, just a month after I left my job as a French teacher at a girls' school in Shaker Heights, Ohio. Our baby is due twelve days from now. *Perfect planning*, we've been thinking.

After dropping James at work, I return to our first-floor duplex apartment on Desota Avenue in Cleveland Heights, about three miles from the hospital through busy residential streets. I am intent on using the unscheduled days before the baby's due date to finish getting things in order. Even though I'm bulging with a term baby, I dive into scrubbing the toilet and bathtub and vacuuming the rooms of our small abode. For weeks I've been preparing for the baby's arrival. We do not know the baby's gender, so I've painted the nursery yellow. It's furnished with a crib borrowed from James's aunt Janet and a changing table and chest of drawers found at a garage sale. I've made curtains of fabric with bold yellow, orange, and magenta squares to match the colors in the striped area rug. These items, the only ones purchased new aside from the crib's bedding, brighten the room, which is deprived of daylight by the house next door due to its proximity across a narrow driveway. I survey the results and feel pleased with myself.

I tuck away a colorful assortment of recently washed and neatly folded infant clothing and hand-me-down cloth diapers in the secondhand dresser drawers and organize safety pins, washcloths, towels, receiving blankets, onesies, wipes, and Q-tips in the bins of the changing table. Tiny teddy bears dance on the sheet in the crib retrieved from Aunt Janet's attic. The crib bumper is in place and a yellow woven blanket with satin edges sits folded at the foot of the crib. A musical mobile with frolicking fish hangs suspended over the crib, waiting to delight and mesmerize. A poster on the wall blazes with the words "Make Peace Not War" in bold colors, a testament to James's and my sentiments about the Vietnam War and war in general. I place baby powder and rash-soothing lotions atop the changing table. A diaper bucket stands at the ready. As I complete my chores, I compose in my head several letters I want to write to friends after lunch. I'm looking forward to several days of relaxing afternoons, including good books and long naps. I plan to be well rested and ready.

However, today's anticipated leisurely afternoon does not develop as I envisioned. Around noon I notice a telltale discharge I'd been told to watch for—"the plug"! This is the signal that labor will commence imminently.

How can this be? My due date is still twelve days off! And it's not a convenient time, to say the least. I want to believe I'm mistaken. I call James.

"This is not a good day for this," he says. "I drew overnight duty and can't come home."

"I'm not crazy about having this baby today either," I say. "I just wanted you to know that something may start happening soon. Maybe it won't come until tomorrow morning." I know he can't leave the hospital, especially on his first day.

"Can you call Aunt Janet?" he asks. James's aunt Janet is a well-respected obstetrician. She is heavily involved with Planned

Parenthood in Cleveland and views pregnancy and childbirth without sentiment. Three years ago, she got right to the point on the topic of birth control with James. We were to marry shortly after my return from a year in France, within too few days for me to be on birth control pills for the thirty-day period required for them to be effective. And by the way, did we know I couldn't get "the pill" in France, where it was illegal? Hiding a two months' supply of pills inside the pages of a book, James conspired with Aunt Janet to smuggle them to me in France. She also made sure I had an appointment with a colleague of hers at Planned Parenthood within a few weeks of our arrival in Cleveland after our honeymoon.

So, it did not surprise us that the announcement of our pregnancy elicited little fanfare from Aunt Janet. No tears of joy or congratulatory remarks. Though she is prone to chortling when something amuses her and often has a twinkle in her eye, she is all business when it comes to pregnancies.

"Get plenty of rest, no excessive exercise, and eat right. The rest will take care of itself." She and Uncle Jerry have been our family away from home here in Cleveland. We know that if we call on her, she will bring all her equanimity and pragmatism to bear on anything to do with our pregnancy.

I call her. "I hate to bother you, Aunt Janet," I blurt out, "but I've passed the plug and James can't be here. He has to stay the night at the hospital."

"Are you sure it's the plug?" Her voice is flat. She seems preoccupied, only mildly interested in my pronouncement. It's as though she's reading the newspaper while talking with me.

"Tell me what it looks like." A perfunctory instruction. I describe the nature of the discharge.

"Okay," she says evenly. "Stay home and call me if your water breaks." That's it.

I hang up. Deep breath. Maybe if I sit very quietly for the rest of the day, nothing more will happen. Surely this baby can wait. All I need is another twenty-four hours, I figure, until James is available. I tell myself this is what is likely to happen. Then, I start writing letters.

In the late afternoon, James calls and asks how I am doing and asks me to bring him a change of clothes. "Sure," I reply, happy for something to keep me busy. "Maybe I could stick around in case . . ."

"I sure hope you hang on until tomorrow," he says. "Things are really crazy here and there's no way I can get away." I know he is torn, and that he has no choice. Medicine is an exacting profession and tolerates no excuses, especially for first-day interns.

"I'll do my best."

I put fresh clothes for James and some snacks in a grocery sack and lumber to the car. I heft myself into the driver's seat of our thirdhand Plymouth Valiant and drive the three miles through rush-hour traffic to the hospital. Dark storm clouds are mustering and sprinkles dot the windshield. Within minutes of my arrival at the hospital, James appears at the curb, and I hand him the sack.

"Still okay?" he asks, leaning into the car.

"So far as I know." I force a smile.

"I wish I could be with you now, but . . ."

"I know," I say. "Aunt Janet knows what's happening, so it'll be okay."

A quick kiss and "I love yous," and he disappears back into the hospital. I *do* understand the intensity of this day for him, how eager he has been to get off to a good start, and I hope this baby won't disrupt things.

Overhead, the sky darkens. Lightning and thunder announce an approaching storm. Halfway back home, the clouds burst. The windshield wipers can't handle the deluge. I pull over to wait it out. I curse the weather. My bulging midriff is taut and aches. I want to be home. Then, a wrenching contraction takes my breath away.

I'm just tense, I think. *I'll get home and relax and get a good night's sleep.*

After what seems like an eternity, I reach our driveway, clutching my stomach with one hand. I park, catch my breath, climb clumsily from the car, and waddle through the downpour. By the time I reach the back door leading to our apartment I'm drenched. Midway up the half-flight of stairs, another contraction brings me to my knees. I grit my teeth and double over to wait for the pain to subside. After several long minutes, it releases me. Once in the apartment, I quickly change into my nightclothes and scarf down some leftovers while poring over the pages of *Jane Eyre*. To my relief there have been no more contractions. By nine o'clock I am in bed, engrossed in the developing drama between Mr. Rochester and Jane. Except for some persistent cramps, I feel fine. I grow drowsy and settle down to sleep. But I cannot find a comfortable position. I attribute my discomfort to my burgeoning stomach and the thrusts of tiny elbows and feet that have been disturbing my sleep for the past several months. I decide to get a glass of water and walk a bit, hoping to settle the baby within and relieve some of the muscle tension.

As I make my way into the hallway, a warm liquid gushes down my legs. A puddle gathers on the floor. This baby is not waiting until tomorrow. I waddle to the bathroom, grab a towel to stuff between my legs, and head for the phone. It is 9:30 p.m. and Aunt Janet will not be pleased.

"Yes?" she answers in her usual, perfunctory manner.

"I'm sorry to bother you again, Aunt Janet, but my water just broke. I think I need a ride to the hospital."

"Just relax, Barbara." Her voice is firm. "Tell me when this leak occurred."

"Just now."

"Are you having contractions?"

"Well, there were a couple of big ones earlier, and a lot of twinges just before the water broke."

"Hmm. It could be a while yet."

A pause. I'm afraid. I pray.

"Okay. I'll be over. Have your things ready."

Thank you, Lord!

A quick phone call to James, who is paged, and I wait. "Just want you to know. My water broke. Aunt Janet's coming over. I think I'll be going to the hospital."

"I'm so sorry I'm not there." His words are strained. I know he is tormented. "I just can't get away. We're swamped here. Call me when you get to the hospital."

I find a way to contain the seeping fluid, change back into the garish daisy-print maternity dress I'd made for myself early on, throw on a raincoat, grab the overnight bag that has been packed for weeks, and station myself at the front door. The rain has not let up. The street is dark. I wait there summoning every ounce of patience and serenity I can muster.

Finally, a good twenty minutes later, headlights appear, creeping up the street through the blinding rain. They stop in front of our apartment. I grab my bag and head out the door, fumbling to lock it behind me. I meet Aunt Janet halfway down the walk. She is proceeding toward me, grinding away at each step in her customary, methodical way. She raises her steady gaze and eyes me carefully. I'm irritated by the thought that she's checking to see if I'm panicking.

"Let's examine you first." She flicks one hand toward the house, directing me back inside. I wince, but submit. More fumbling with the door lock, and I stumble back into the living room and slump onto the sofa. At that moment I am seized by a vigorous contraction, and I let out a moan. Without rushing, Aunt Janet places her hand on my abdomen.

"That's a good one. Let's see how long till the next one." Clearly, I am not in charge. Still, her presence is reassuring. I tolerate the wait. She looks at her watch. Before long, another hefty contraction cuts off my breath.

"Okay," she says. "In the car. I think you're going to have a baby today." *Is that urgency in her voice?* I feel vindicated as I clamber back out the door, again struggling with the lock, and into Aunt Janet's car. She does not waste time. In very short order I find myself at the steps of the maternity hospital whose six floors loom above me. Rain, coming now in dark sheets, is relentless.

"I'd better let you off here and park. Don't waste any time checking yourself in. I'll be along in a minute." The champion of Planned Parenthood wants me to go it alone. I don't like the idea. This is no way to have a baby. Where is the wheelchair and attentive assistant? A little hospital procedure would be appreciated.

"Okay," I say, swallowing my righteous indignation. Who am I to complain at this point? I climb the broad concrete steps in the downpour to the hospital entrance. A vicious contraction catches me midway, and I slump to a sitting position. I clutch my stomach for what seems an eternity. I am sopping wet when I finally pick myself up and trudge up the remaining steps into the vast, empty lobby. I make a beeline for the huge reception desk on the far side of the lobby, leaving a trail of water in my wake. The lone receptionist is bending over her desk. She does not look up. Does she not hear my panting? Sense my urgency?

"Excuse, me." I try to remain courteous.

"Just a minute, please." She remains focused on whatever she is reading.

When she does look up, she scowls at me over her glasses. "What is it?" I might as well have been just in off the street looking for a restroom.

"I'm having a baby. Where do I go to be admitted?"

"You'll have to wait here until a nurse can come for you. The delivery rooms are on the sixth floor. They'll take you up if they think you need to be admitted."

I rush toward the elevators.

"You can't go up there!" The receptionist is on her feet in hot pursuit.

I punch the up button. "Listen!" *Forget courtesy now.* "My water has broken. My aunt is parking the car. She's a doctor. She told me to get in here pronto. I'm not standing around waiting for you to take me seriously." Another contraction. I clutch at the wall.

"But you need to be in a chair. You can't just walk up there on your own."

The elevator door opens. While the receptionist sputters objections, I limp in. I punch number 6 and do not look at the protesting receptionist as the door closes. When the elevator door opens on the sixth floor, I encounter two nurses with a chair.

One conducts an abbreviated exam and deems me admissible. I'm fighting a building indignation. We stop at a large chalkboard while she enters my name. "What's your blood type, Mrs. Walker?" By then, I barely know my name.

"I can't remember. O negative, B positive, something like that. Here, just take a sample." I hold out my finger. I've dropped all pretense of civility. *What's with these people? I'm having a baby, not a hemorrhoid, for God's sake!*

"Okay. Okay. Take it easy." With that, one of the nurses wheels me to a room at the end of a long, quiet hall. When I stand up, a gush of amniotic fluid flows down my legs and forms a large pool on the floor.

"Sorry," I mutter. But to tell the truth, I couldn't give a rat's ass.

The nurse heaves a sigh, thinking no doubt of the work involved in mopping the floor. "Just get yourself into this gown and into bed." Humorless as the Pope. Once I'm situated in the bed, she takes vital signs, sizes up another contraction. Keeps her thoughts to herself. A smile would be nice.

What I would give to see James's face appear at the door. To utter an "It's okay." Or "How ya doing?" I tell myself he'll be here soon. Aunt Janet is probably seeing to that at this very moment. As the nurse turns to leave the room, she slips on the watery floor. Her arms and legs go akimbo as she loses her footing. She lands with a thud on her posterior. She groans. I say nothing. *Maybe she had it coming for not taking me more seriously*, I'm thinking.

Aunt Janet appears. "James will be coming."

She smiles that wry smile of hers and pats me on the shoulder. I can breathe deeply now. Outside the room, decisions are made and then they roll me to the delivery room. My contractions are strong now and coming in quick succession. My excitement grows, but still no James. The doctor and nurses stand around me in masks and gowns, curiously inactive.

My contractions ebb.

"What's happening? Why have my contractions stopped?"

"It's okay," the doctor says. "That happens sometimes. Actually, it's convenient because we want to wait for your husband to get here. It's a long hike through the tunnel from the main hospital." We wait. "He's here," someone says. "Give her the Pitocin now." Someone administers an injection.

James appears at my head, short of breath but all smiles. "This is it!" He squeezes my hand.

"I'm so glad you made it," I say. A tear escapes.

"Do you want to watch this, James?" the doctor asks. James plants a kiss on my forehead and moves to the foot of the delivery table. Induced contractions erupt with a force that strips away my capacity to focus on anything else. Within a few minutes, I hear a gurgle, then a vigorous cry. My baby is born.

But why is everyone so quiet?

JUNE 25, 1970, 1:00 A.M.

"It's a boy," the doctor announces in a steady voice. The baby wails but everyone else in the room remains strangely quiet. James, who has been observing the delivery, moves to my head and strokes my forehead, quiet. I grin at him but am puzzled by his solemn gaze. I imagine he is touched beyond words by witnessing the birth of his son, our first baby.

"May I see the baby?" I ask politely, though I'm irritated at the delay.

"We're taking him to the nursery to clean him up first." The doctor's voice comes from beyond my feet, beyond my field of vision. I hear a swinging door open and shut, telling me that someone has exited with my baby. James follows in the direction of the door. There is hushed movement in the room. Someone removes my feet from the stirrups and lowers my legs to a resting position. Two nurses in scrubs appear and give instructions so I can assist them in transferring me to a gurney.

One of the nurses busies herself at a prep table near the gurney. "Please roll on your side so we can give you your shot." I oblige. Their sober demeanor confuses me. Were there to be no congratulations on the birth of a fine son? I feel disconnected, not only from my newborn child, but also from those in the room.

"What's the shot for?"

"To dry up your milk, dear."

"But I'm planning to nurse . . ." I sputter, feeling helpless against their ministrations.

Silence.

"It's okay," soft words from the doctor. I feel reassured. Then a sharp pain in my right buttock as a needle delivers a medication. The nurse offers a couple of pills, which I take, trusting the care I'm receiving.

A short time later, I lie alone in a room painted a dull shade of salmon pink. I note the reproduction of van Gogh's *Sunflowers* on the wall beyond my feet. I wait. And wait. And wait. I tell myself to be patient. This is, after all, a large maternity hospital with five floors devoted to delivering babies. The doctors and nurses are busy. My baby has been delivered and there is so much to look forward to. Gradually, a peaceful fog lulls me into a contented state of mind.

Eventually, the doctor enters the room, still in scrubs. His expression is serious.

Poor guy, I'm thinking. He is covering for my OB and doesn't know me from Adam. I can't expect much. He is just getting the job done. He pulls up a chair and leans in. He takes a deep breath before speaking.

"We've checked the baby thoroughly. His internal organs are intact and his vision, hearing, and mental functioning are normal."

"Great," I say, wondering if all new mothers hear this report.

"We do have a problem, however."

By now, I'm adrift in a haze, induced, I learn later, by the sedative administered in the delivery room.

"Your baby was born with a cleft palate. It's a physical deformity and can be fixed. He's a little jaundiced as well, and we're monitoring his bilirubin level. Otherwise, he's a healthy baby."

From a distant place I watch myself return the doctor's steady gaze.

"Oh." I nod and manage a thin smile. The doctor must be relieved that my face remains expressionless. I am not going to go hysterical on him.

I am clinging to the words "healthy baby" and reaching for breath. Deep in my chest, a tentacle of alarm takes hold and squeezes hard. I am aware that I do not cry or cry out. Instead, I swallow. I am floating, suspended, taking in the unfolding news in a bizarrely serene manner. It is a relief to be calm.

"Are you ready to see your baby?" The doctor waits.

I nod.

The doctor returns with the bundled baby and holds him so I can see his face.

"Here he is." The gentleness in the doctor's voice encourages me to look straight on as he points out the lip, split on both sides. One side is open to the nostril, the other nearly as much. Both lips curl around the clefts. A portion of the baby's upper gum glistens through the opening. I move my eyes to take in the perfectly shaped head, forehead, and eyelids, the chubby cheeks.

"How about his toes and fingers?" I ask. The doctor unwraps the blanket and brings the baby closer. I take one tiny hand at a time and let the fingers—all ten of them—curl around my index finger. I take my time counting them. Then, the toes.

"Good," I say. "He's got all his toes and fingers."

The doctor nods.

"His palate and upper jaw have clefts, too," the doctor continues.

It's more than I can take in.

"And you'll notice that his skin is a bit yellow. We'll put him under lights right away to help control that condition. And that's about it."

June 25, 1970, 1:00 a.m.

I know I should be reacting, but I feel nothing. I say nothing.

"He'll be getting all the attention he needs tonight in the nursery. And you need to get a good night's sleep."

I touch my baby's cheek and then watch the doctor carry him out of eyesight. Alone in the room, noting the wretched salmon-pink walls again and wishing someone had better taste than to paint hospital walls that color, my emotions remain curbed and I float above awareness. Those sunflowers droop more than I remember.

Shortly, James comes into the room with Aunt Janet. Worry and sadness show on his face. Aunt Janet, a rock in any crisis, stands aside. James takes my hand and strokes my forehead again.

"They want you to get some sleep. So, I'll go back to work and see you first thing in the morning."

"Sounds good." I squeeze his hand.

They leave and I doze. Someone wheels the bed with me floating in it from the room and down the hall. We stop at the elevator. As the bed jerks into the elevator, I believe that everything is going to be alright. I drift further into the developing haze and am asleep before I arrive at my room on the fifth floor.

NOT NORMAL

I awaken slowly to a room full of sunlight, but my mind is still on the birth six hours earlier. In the bed next to me, Yolanda is propped up on her pillows, wide awake and bubbling with energy. She grins at me.

"Good mornin'," she sings out. "We got babies!"

I nod, forcing a feeble smile. *But your baby is normal,* I think. *Mine is not.* I sink into my pillow. Something heavy lodges in my chest as I lie there chewing on this reality.

Before long, a nurse bristling with cheerful efficiency enters the room.

"Good morning, ladies. Congratulations!" She encompasses us in her smile, but as her eyes sweep over me, I see a shadow of concern. She approaches and pulls the privacy curtain around my bed, cutting me off from Yolanda's exuberance. She presents a glass of water and several pills. I swallow them without questioning what they are for.

She whispers, "Don't you worry, now. Your baby's doing well. Your husband came by earlier. You were asleep, and we didn't want to wake you." I wonder what kind of chaos James must be facing, grappling with his duties as an intern, and now issues with our new baby on top of that.

Then, in a somber voice, the nurse tells me someone will be bringing my baby in later for a feeding. She asks if I'm up to it. "It will be difficult, dear, because he can't suck like normal babies."

I get stuck on "not normal." Again, I merely nod, and my mind drifts.

"Not to worry," she says tenderly, a voice I should find comforting. "We'll make sure you get it right."

My baby arrives bundled in blue flannel blankets and a matching cap. All that shows is his face. The nurse hands me the bundle and watches intently. I am aware that I am under scrutiny. I hold my baby against my chest, liking the weight and warmth of him. He feels sturdy, solidly built. I study his face and take in the abnormality—a split and misshapen upper lip and the exposed incomplete upper gum. I wonder how he will eat. He stirs and cries. I remove his cap and cup his perfectly round head in my hand. The baby fuzz is soft against my palm. A warmth eases the heaviness in my chest, and I feel a connection taking hold, but I cannot take it all in. Later I will learn to feed him. When James visits next, we'll talk about names. For now, I simply want to feel the compact sturdiness of his tiny body, absorb the sensation of joy—feeble as it is—and get used to his face.

Meanwhile, the word gets out quickly that James and Barbara's baby has been born with a severe bilateral cleft palate. Aunt Janet has immediately informed Uncle Jerry, who, like Aunt Janet, is a physician and intimately connected with the medical community. After consulting with James, who is in the throes of his second day of internship in another part of the hospital complex, Uncle Jerry appears at my bedside in midmorning to inform me that he has contacted *the* plastic surgeon in the city with the most experience with cleft repairs. A surgery will be scheduled within days for a partial lip repair. This will be the first of many surgeries over the next four decades.

Shortly afterward, a disheveled Dr. Hess, our pediatrician, arrives. His hair is rumpled and his tie hangs loosened below an open collar. His eyes widen as he reports that he's been asking around for hours about the needs of a newborn with a cleft palate. He tells me he has never taken care of a child with this birth defect, but that there are pediatricians in town who have. He will understand if we want to choose someone else.

I think about how Aunt Janet and Uncle Jerry pulled strings so Dr. Hess would take us as patients. He was young and earnest and enjoyed a reputation as a family-oriented pediatrician, more or less a novelty at the time. James and I came away from our pre-birth consultation impressed by his warmth and his interest in learning about us and how we were thinking about having a baby in our lives.

As he talks with me now in the hospital, my trust in him grows. Dr. Hess's openness and willingness to discover what my baby needs convinces me he is the pediatrician I want. For the first time since coming to the hospital, I feel like hugging a medical professional.

"Well, I don't have any experience either," I say. "If you think we can figure this out together, I want to stick with you."

"Okay, then," he says, "let's get started."

I feel reassured until later that afternoon when a hospital doctor delivers alarming news. Our baby has been diagnosed with ABO blood incompatibility. Soon after his birth, it became evident that our son was becoming increasingly jaundiced, indicating a dangerous rise in the bilirubin level in his blood. ABO is similar to Rh factor. Both result from an incompatibility between a baby's and mother's blood types, causing the breakdown of red blood cells in newborns. If not corrected, the toxic effect of bilirubin can cause irreparable damage to the baby's brain. Our baby's condition is concerning enough that the doctors have placed him under special fluorescent lights designed to correct his quickly rising bilirubin level. He will be monitored closely and if the bilirubin level rises too quickly, or too high, the baby will receive a blood exchange transfusion. What can I do but take a deep breath and ask for reassurance that my baby's condition is treatable? The doctor offers an encouraging smile, but I feel numb.

When I view my baby next, he has been moved to a corner of the nursery. He lies on his back in an Isolette under harsh blue fluorescent lights, a towel covering the top third of his face to protect his eyes. I take it all in and remind myself to be thankful that he is here in a university hospital where he's getting the best treatment available.

I am grateful, too, that the staff still bring him to me for brief visits several times a day, mostly because I need to learn to feed him.

"Here, dear," the nurse says softly as she hands me a baby bottle with formula in it. "This is how we will feed him for now." She shows me how they have widened the slit in the red, pliable nipple, a nipple designed for premature babies whose sucking is particularly weak. With her guidance I position the nipple in my baby's mouth so that it rests to the side where his gums can meet. Instinctively, he works his mouth in a sucking motion, but his cleft lip and gums render sucking impossible. He throws his head from side to side and wails. His face turns red and his brow furrows deeply as his body stiffens. We reposition the nipple several more times without success and as his crying intensifies, the nurse takes him from me.

"That's enough for now," she says. "We'll try again later." She whisks the baby out of the room. I am drenched in sweat. Tears roll down my cheeks. What if I cannot manage to feed my child? Later, when I am walking the halls, I peer through the nursery window and see a nurse holding my baby and feeding him with a syringe.

My baby is quiet and content in her arms. Her easy competence only heightens my sense of failure. Feelings of inadequacy erode the mothering instinct that began to assert itself earlier when I was holding my infant. The inkling of joy I felt then slips away and I wonder if I'll ever be able to be what this baby needs.

By the second day my baby adapts his approach to the nipple. He uses a chewing motion and empties the bottle in a matter of minutes. From then on the nurses leave me alone to feed him. I watch him as he attacks the nipple, going at it with a sense of purpose that allows me to think that he will measure up to whatever faces him. I say to him, "You are a little tiger, aren't you? We can figure this out, you and I."

I cling to that sentiment, and my spirits rise.

On one of James's early morning visits, I mention that we need to provide a name for the birth certificate. "The nurses keep bugging me about it."

"I'd like to hold him first," he replies, "but the nurses are telling me newborns are allowed to visit only with their mothers." I go with him to look through the window of the nursery. There is our tiny son, who has been lying on his back since birth with a towel wrapped around his head to protect his eyes from the intense lights. What we see, all that James has seen for days, is our baby's exposed cleft, dramatically displayed by the bright lights. It's also a drastically different face from those of the dozens of others appearing above infant bundles in the Isolettes around the nursery. We hold hands but don't find words.

Before James rushes off to his intern duties, we have a final conversation about names. We come back over and over to the same one: first name James, after his father, grandfather, and great-grandfather. But we stop short of dubbing him James Vincent IV as James's parents were hoping, and choose Higgins, my maiden name, for his middle name. Even then, the name seems too weighty for the tiny infant snuggling in my arms later. "We'll call you Jimmy for short," I reassure him and touch my lips to the top of his adorable head.

I am eager now for feeding times. I take heart in the way Jimmy attacks the red preemie nipple, chomping ferociously with one side of his gums until he has taken what he needs. There's an intensity in his eyes that I read as determination. Afterward, he settles into my arms for a snooze, and I can't take my eyes off him. I cup his head in my hand and kiss his face, inhaling the sweet warmth of his skin. I open the blankets and study his tiny body. I run my finger over his velvety arm, then unfurl his fingers one by one. His fingers curl around one of mine, letting me believe he wants to hold on to me. I kiss his tiny fist. I move his legs up and down, and the deep wrinkles around his chubby knees unfold and refold. His nails . . . all twenty of them . . . fascinate me. When he stirs and grimaces, I coo, and he settles back into the blankets. Even the strains, grunts, and gurgling noises signaling bowel movements give me pleasure. When he opens his eyes, I am enchanted. Something stirs in my chest and the future seems somewhat brighter.

Bill, the new obstetrics intern attending me, is James's classmate. I mention to him that James has yet to hold his son. Bill's eyes widen.

"Really? I'll take care of that," he says.

The next day James enters my room as usual. His face glows. "What a great little guy!" His eyes glisten. "Bill got me into the nursery. I got to hold little Jimmy," he says.

The next morning, James's face is clouded. "Bill got in trouble," he says. "The charge nurse filed an incident report on him for bringing me into the nursery without authorization."

"What could be wrong with that?" I ask.

"Against protocol," he answers. "They're afraid of germs, I guess. Still, I feel horrible. He'll catch hell from someone about this."

Suddenly, we feel like troublemakers rather than parents who simply want to hold their newborn. For the rest of our ten-day stay on the obstetrics floor, James does not get to hold Jimmy.

I learn quickly that questions about the medications I'm being asked to take will elicit only curt responses. The nurses typically reply with a terse "Doctor's orders," or offer only brief explanations that sound canned. I resolve to be a good—that is, compliant—patient, so I take the pills, but do I really have to abide the floor nurse with the sugarcoated, high-pitched voice, bent on bringing me closer to *her* Lord? To be honest, I welcome the daily sitz baths she administers. These treatments involve a chair with a doughnut-shaped seat that allows me to submerge my bottom in a warm saltwater bath, thus promoting healing of the episiotomy. I'm all in favor of healing, but I could do without the accompanying sermons.

"Here, dear, this will do you a world of good. If you like, I could read to you from the Bible while you soak."

"I'll settle for the sitz bath," I say, though I expect my refusal will have little effect on her zeal.

Nurse Righteous (my secret name for her) is sometimes in charge of dispensing evening medications. As she delivers the usual small pill one evening, she assumes the pious pose to which I've become accustomed and purrs, "Here's your happy pill, dear."

"Happy pill?"

Her face decomposes for a moment, and she fumbles for words. It appears that she's made a slip. She straightens as if to gather her wits and explains in a hushed, offhand voice, "Oh, Doctor ordered these to give you a little lift, dear. We don't want you to be sad." She plasters on a smile and gives me a conspiratorial wink. This information is now our little secret.

So, I am being muted. I have been since the moment they rolled me on my side and gave me shots after delivery, before letting me see

Jimmy. My doctors and the hospital staff do not want to risk me having any of those messy emotions people have when life throws them a curveball. *Hmm.* I begin to wonder what my emotional reaction might have been, might be now, if I were unfettered, not sedated. At the same time, I do not want to rock any boats. I give them what they want. I swallow the pills.

Concerns about my mood may also explain the order to attend a group meeting every morning. "It'll be good for you, dear," from Nurse Righteous. The several mothers in the circle have dazed expressions. I deduce that something is also not normal with their babies and they, too, are the recipients of happy pills. None of us has much to say. A bright-eyed social worker launches with gusto into an upbeat lecture on what babies with special needs require, with particular emphasis on nutrition. She assures us that referrals to appropriate specialists will be made for us before our babies leave the hospital. Her words barely register through the fog that clouds my thinking. After a time, we mothers shuffle obediently back to our rooms.

Later that day Nurse Righteous informs me that she told the photographer who came around to take photos of newborns to skip Jimmy.

"We didn't think you'd want a photo of him. Normally, we don't take a photo when there's a facial disfigurement."

Zing! Another arrow to the heart. Bull's-eye!

Within a week, Jimmy's bilirubin levels have corrected and he's deemed healthy enough for an operation to close one side of his lip. I'm thankful but still, a pain lodges somewhere in my chest, like salt in a wound. Reminders that Jimmy isn't normal bear down again. I stare through the fog and past Nurse Righteous and say nothing. Thoughts of what lies ahead for Jimmy take shape and haunt me. I screw up the courage to worry aloud to Dr. Hess. What if Jimmy fails to thrive because of his feeding problems? What if I can't figure out how to feed him? How will he chew? What about being able to speak? Is there anything I can read?

"First things first," Dr. Hess reminds me. "The surgery is in two days. Let's get through that and then we can think about what comes next." I don't tell him I've been avoiding the thought of surgery on my baby, who will be just ten days old in two days.

I try to settle my thoughts and to focus on the positive. With difficulty, I shove aside hundreds of worries and think about what this first operation will achieve. The plastic surgeon will close one side of Jimmy's upper lip and after a couple of weeks of recovery in the hospital, he will come home with a prosthetic palate, a plug of sorts, fashioned from a mold, to fill in the large hole in his hard palate. The prosthesis will make bottle feeding and, later, spoon feeding easier by preventing food from escaping through the open roof of his mouth and out his nose.

On the day of the operation, I abandon Jimmy to the care of orderlies I don't know, and they take him away. As Jimmy heads to surgery, I feel helpless and unsteady. I dare not give vent to the gloomy thoughts nipping at the edges of my mind, or the tangle of emotions churning in the pit of my stomach. I want to remain sedated in the fog, where I do not have to see the whole picture or figure out where to go from here. I do not want to consider how far from normal it is that ten days after giving birth to this much anticipated baby, I have had to surrender him to surgeons and I am going home without him.

I'm discharged in a wheelchair. James is there to take me home. Later, much later, he tells me that Dr. Hess stopped him in the hall that day and warned him to watch me; that sooner or later, I'd hit the wall.

"If she shows signs of emotional stress, get in touch with me. It's not unusual for mothers of newborns who are not normal."

To Normal-Looking

You haunt our every mirror,
every moment of reflection,
with an undefined faith
everyone else believes.

You sow doubt in the mother
cradling her newborn.
You reveal the doctor
realizing his limits.

You want us to seek you
for the rest of our lives
despite all evidence
you offer nothing tangible;

nothing that connects mother to son,
son to self, one person to another;
nothing
that answers the darker questions
of our distinct, unavoidable details.

You compel us to choose ourselves anyway,
to focus on the wonder of just living.

—Jim H. Walker

READY OR NOT

The surgeon tells me to spend the night before Jimmy's surgery at home. He says I need to get some sleep. Not to worry. And not to come to the hospital until I hear from him. I will get a call when Jimmy is out of surgery and recovered enough for me to see him. Ever compliant, I go home. That night, I lie awake. Visions of my ten-day-old baby on an operating table haunt me. I hear my mother stirring on her cot in the living room. She has come from northern Maine and has been at the apartment for several days, helping in all the ways she can think of while we wait until Jimmy can come home. She mends clothes, changes the bed, does laundry, irons, cooks casseroles and freezes them. She has food ready when I come home after long days at the hospital with Jimmy. She bends over my $88 Singer sewing machine, stitching the hand-me-down diapers so that there is a quadruple thickness where it matters.

When I stumble out of bed on July 5, she is already up cooking French toast. We both know that at that very moment little Jimmy is undergoing surgery to repair the larger of the two clefts in his upper lip. I fight the urge to race to the hospital, but I follow the doctor's orders. Our thin smiles reveal our worry. We hug each other a long while without speaking. During breakfast and for the rest of the morning, we make small talk and run through the checklist for Jimmy's homecoming. We stand together in the nursery and survey with satisfaction the abundance of baby supplies.

"We certainly are ready!" My mother takes a deep breath. We survey the room and its bright colors and try not to think about why it is still empty. I have no idea what "ready" should feel like as I await a baby who will be recovering from surgery and who can't feed normally, but preparing the nursery has been a helpful distraction. The fog of the post-delivery days has lifted and I no longer have "happy pills" to keep my emotions in check, but something else is at work, something of my own that is able to calm the sadness and fear that are festering. My mind drills in on what I'm able to do. For the moment, all I can do is walk from room to room and wait for the call from the hospital.

The call comes shortly after noon.

"The surgery and recovery went well, and he's on the ward now. So, you can visit him anytime." The nurse delivers her message as though she were confirming the weather report. Still, this is the news we are waiting for.

"He's out of surgery, Mom, and he's doing fine!"

"Thank God!" My mother drops her dish towel and this time we laugh as we hug each other. We allow ourselves to cry, releasing pent-up worry and dark thoughts. Within minutes I am on my way to the hospital.

The children's ward is an enormous room, half of the first floor of Rainbow Children's Hospital. This is where Jimmy will stay until the surgeons are certain he has recovered from surgery well enough to be entrusted to my care. The ward is crowded with high-railed cribs, many surrounded by a mind-boggling array of tubes, IV bottles, and equipment. A nurse is expecting me.

"You James Walker's mom? He's over there in the Isolette. Don't disrupt him." Again, all business.

I find Jimmy in a covered glass box with tubes attached to it. I peer in. I gasp. His eyes are black-and-blue and his upper lip is caked with dark, dried blood. Stitches of coarse black thread hold the left side of his upper lip together where the surgeons have operated to close the cleft in his lip. The right side of his lip remains open. An angry purple bruise swells on his left cheek. Where the skin on his lip was pink and smooth yesterday, it is now battered and swollen. Bile rises in my throat. I reel and stumble out of the ward. I fear I will either faint or vomit. I make my way down the hall and fall onto a bench in the lobby and struggle to breathe. I stare at the floor, immobilized.

A soft voice at my side: "Were you not prepared?" It is a nurse from the ward. I feel the warm pressure of her hand on mine. She waits while I catch my breath. I trust she will not expect me to buck up, or offer me a sedative.

"I had no idea."

"Kinda hard to look at that suture line, isn't it? Sorta like he's been in a dogfight, huh?"

"But why the glass box? Isn't he doing okay?" I fight back tears.

"Oh, that. He's in the Isolette so he gets plenty of oxygen and has a germ-free environment for a while. He'll heal pretty fast, if that's any consolation."

I nod and wonder what I'm supposed to do now.

"Why don't you come back in now?" She leads me back to the ward and stands with me beside the Isolette. My head aches and I want to retch. My eyes sting. I have to look away. I feel brittle enough to break in two. I hug myself.

"Take deep breaths," the nurse says. It takes a long while before I can keep my eyes on Jimmy's face.

"My poor little boy" is all I can say. "I'm so sorry."

"I'll get you something to drink," the nurse offers. She walks away and I slump into a chair near the Isolette. Over and over again for the next hour I rise and force myself to gaze at my baby's mangled face. *I have to get used to this*, I tell myself.

Within twenty-four hours, Jimmy is transferred from the Isolette to a hospital crib. Right away the nurses insist that I start bathing him in a washbasin the size of a salad bowl. His soapy body slips and slides out of my grip during the first bath. I'm sure I will drop him on the floor. I call for help. Still, I cannot master the one-armed hold the nurse shows me. By the time I put him back in his crib, my blouse is soaked with sweat. Later, the nurses hand me the syringe and direct me to feed Jimmy. Again, I shudder. I fumble with the syringe and am fearful of rupturing the stitches on his lip, that critical suture line the nurses take great care to clean ever so gently with a Q-tip doused in rubbing alcohol solution. The amount of formula I deliver seems always to be either less than Jimmy wants or more than he can handle. He stiffens, screws up his face, and wails. His tiny fists clench and his arms tremble. It takes several feedings before I get the hang of it.

But holding Jimmy as he sleeps comes naturally. He nestles into my arms and makes tiny grunts and squeaks when he stirs. These moments restore me. I go home only to eat a late-night meal and get a few hours' sleep. I get up at dawn, wolf down some toast with jam, and rush off to the hospital to spend my days and evenings with Jimmy. The nurses cut no corners in teaching me to feed him properly and to clean the suture line. Meanwhile, in the adjoining hospital building, James is slaving away as an intern, with precious little time for sleep or visits with Jimmy and me.

When Jimmy is sleeping, I wander around the ward. I see babies who will never leave the hospital. One ten-month-old boy's destiny is a protective plastic bubble, and his parents can only touch him through built-in sleeves that protrude inward to allow them to put their hands on their baby. Two-year-old Tony, in the crib next to Jimmy's, has severe cystic fibrosis that necessitates frequent massaging of his chest to clear his lungs so he can breathe. The nurses position him on their laps so that his head hangs toward the floor and then they massage and pound on his chest, singing to distract him. When he's breathing well, Tony hangs over the railing of his crib and chatters with me and anyone else who ventures toward his corner of the ward.

"Wha's you name?" he demands with a smile.

When he's well and bored, he jumps up and down in his crib, and calls to the nurses. If no one responds, he pulls down his diaper and pees in a long, high arc through the upright crib rails.

"Ah, Tony, you rascal!" a nurse chides. "Keeping down the dust again, eh?"

Tony grins, pleased with the attention he's getting.

Tony's teenage mother either cannot or will not learn to give the care he needs to live in the world. During her brief and infrequent visits, she speaks sharply. Tony fusses and cries and calls for the nurse. No one can say what Tony's future holds.

Within a few days I have figured out how to bathe, clothe, and change diapers for my minuscule baby. The syringe feedings are now pleasant times for both Jimmy and me. Our situation could be much worse. Doctors can repair clefts. I hold my Jimmy close and count my blessings.

ON OUR OWN

Life is plenty chaotic once we are home. Disrupted sleep, feedings that don't satisfy, diapers that don't contain as they should, and fussiness I cannot soothe. I'm often at a loss and in tears, unable to discern what part of my feelings of failure has to do with being a first-time mother and what comes from having to care for a baby with a cleft lip and palate.

My mother stays on for a week. This allows me to make runs to the store and deliver James and pick him up from the hospital without having to figure out how to manage a baby in the bargain. Besides keeping food on our table, Mom takes up her grandmothering role with relish, and I'm grateful she's so eager to hold Jimmy, change diapers, and dress him in one of his peanut-sized outfits, engaging him in little conversations as she does so. For both of us, the moments when Jimmy grunts or squeaks and opens his large, dark eyes, taking in heaven-knows-what of the scene around him, are magical.

Feedings are a different matter. One of our trickiest tasks is to fashion bottle nipples that will work. With a sharp paring knife, we gingerly enlarge the slit in the preemie nipples supplied by the hospital. If the slit is just right, Jimmy can get an amount of formula he can handle by chomping the nipple with his gums. If the slit is too small, he gets too little. Within seconds, he emphatically abandons the nipple, arches his back, and clenches his quaking little fists into knots. As soon as he catches his breath, he lets loose a wail that rattles the windows. His arms flail as I try to reposition the offending nipple, often without success. If the slit is too large, he gags on the excessive flow of formula and regurgitates the excess, gasping frantically for air. As soon as he draws breath, he bursts into loud, piercing protests. In the beginning, botched feedings are the norm, and they drain me of energy and confidence.

To make matters worse, the three-minute boiling process required to sterilize the nipples softens them so that the slit enlarges, ruining what was a functional nipple for the previous feeding. Before long, my mother and I decide that washing the nipples in very hot, soapy water will suffice. This adjustment results in more reliable nipples from feeding to feeding. Not perfect, but much better. Finally, I engineer feedings that are more satisfying to both Jimmy and me.

Like any baby, Jimmy does his share of fussing and crying. Unlike other babies, his cleft lip and palate render him unable to suck, so the pacifier that mothers rely on to quiet cranky babies is not part of our life. The only method that works when Jimmy is distressed is to hug him to my chest, rub his back, and walk him to and fro in our small apartment. I conjure up cooing sounds and command my own body to release its tension.

"It's okay, little baby." Eventually Jimmy surrenders. His head drops onto my shoulder and his body slumps into mine. I press my cheek against his head and kiss it. The tenderness of these moments when I'm able to calm him stands in sharp contrast to the tightness that characterizes so many feeding times. These moments allow me to believe I can figure all this out. I begin to walk Jimmy like this whenever it's time for sleep. If I'm lucky, he falls asleep within minutes and does not rouse when I place him in his bassinette or crib. He responds similarly to my mother, and we congratulate ourselves.

There are times, however, when this baby will not settle down to sleep in his crib. He cries persistently and I rush in repeatedly to check on him. Picking him up and walking him soothes him only momentarily. As soon as I place him in a prone position, he wails. I consult my mother. She's as stumped as I am. I consult Dr. Spock's *Baby and Child Care*. This is the bible for raising babies, and the only resource in print I have. He maintains it is okay to let babies cry, that it is a natural way for them to release tension. I cannot stand the thought of it.

On one of the days when Jimmy's crying goes on for over half an hour, however, I'm in tears and desperate for help. I turn to my mother. She sits motionless in the armchair staring straight ahead, her fingers clenched together in her lap. I imagine she finds my mothering inadequate and is biting her tongue against advice she could give. I'm ready to admit defeat.

"I give up. What should I do, Mom?" She turns and says in a most gentle voice, "He's your baby, sweetheart. Do what you think best." I wonder if she knows what a boost those words give me.

"Alright, then. Dr. Spock says it's okay to let a baby cry for twenty minutes. I'm going to fold diapers in the basement. I'll be back when twenty minutes are up."

"Fine by me," my mother says. In the basement one floor below, I fold diapers in a fury, nerves on edge. What could the neighbors be thinking? I check my watch frequently as Jimmy cries with a persistence that tears at me. Gradually, the heartrending crying subsides into intermittent whimpers. By the time I run back upstairs, Jimmy is asleep, and he stays that way for a blessed two hours.

"Ain't easy on the nerves, but I guess it works," I quip and smile thinly at my mother. She sighs and rises from her chair. "Seems to, doesn't it?" She hugs me for a long moment.

I take heart from Dr. Spock's reminder that letting babies cry teaches them to self-soothe. I learn that if I allow Jimmy to cry for ten minutes when I put him down to sleep, he seems to do just that. From then on, at nap time and bedtime, I listen until Jimmy's crying ebbs into a whimper. I tiptoe into his room and rub his back a few times, softly crooning a lullaby or the tender words mothers the world over use to soothe their babies. Without fail, Jimmy settles into a deep sleep that will last for several hours. Finding a successful sleep-time routine calms me as much as Jimmy.

Unlike other newborns, Jimmy has no roof to his mouth. To prevent whatever enters his mouth from exiting through his nose, he has been fitted with a customized prosthesis, a rubbery plug fashioned to provide an artificial hard palate. For this I am grateful, as the prosthesis controls the formula dripping into his mouth, eliminating a problem that would have made feedings a bigger trial than they already are. The prosthesis fits snugly into the opening in the roof of his mouth and must be removed frequently for cleaning, just like dentures. Every morning, after changing Jimmy's diaper and while he is still on his back, I anchor him to the changing table by placing my forearm firmly on his chest. I then stick my finger into his tiny mouth and pry the plug out, a maneuver that greatly offends him. Reinserting the thing is no picnic either. In the beginning, it takes several attempts each time with Jimmy writhing and crying throughout. By the time the cleaning operation is finished, we are both in a stew. Mom keeps her distance, giving me space, it seems, to figure things out on my own. When I carry tearful Jimmy into the kitchen, she encircles us in her arms, and then passes me a hot cup of coffee. Over time, I learn to distract Jimmy with seductive nonsense talk and brightly colored toys with moving parts hung strategically over the changing table. I become more adept at removing, cleaning, and reinserting the plug, but it never becomes routine.

My father arrives from Maine several days after Jimmy comes home. He approaches him with a grin and peers into his face.

"Hi, there, little fella," he says with a tenderness that makes my eyes sting. He's all smiles when he picks Jimmy up and sits him on his lap. When feeding time comes, though, and Jimmy is not happy, my father paces, clicking coins in his pocket. His expression is tight. He feigns aloofness. The wrinkle of his brow belies his worry for Jimmy's future and mine. Still, in all the ways I could hope for, my parents take this little baby and me into their hearts, problems and all.

After my parents leave, I find a routine that accommodates Jimmy's needs, James's internship schedule, and my household chores. I allow time to push Jimmy in his carriage around the neighborhood after his nap. When we are at home, I relish Jimmy's nap time, ensconcing myself in an easy chair with a good book, dozing a fair amount myself. I'll always associate F. Scott Fitzgerald's novels with Jimmy's first summer, particularly *The Great Gatsby*. When Jimmy and I have quiet times, I hold him and take in the warmth of his little body, and the baby smell of him, as though it were the most precious of perfumes. I kiss his soft baby hair. I imagine, as I look into his large brown eyes, that they return my gaze. I sit him nearby in his infant seat when I do the ironing or sew at the dining room table. I don't mind the late-night feedings that introduce me to *The Tonight Show Starring Johnny Carson* and other, early-morning TV shows—all new experiences for me.

I notice that Jimmy routinely falls asleep whenever he is in motion—not only when I walk him, or during rides in the baby carriage, but particularly in the car. Without fail, he falls asleep within minutes after the car begins moving. I add car rides to my repertoire of techniques for lulling Jimmy into afternoon naps. I plop him into the car bed I've set up in the back seat of our old Plymouth Valiant and drive around the block once or twice. If I time it correctly, I can transfer him from car to crib and he's good for a two- or three-hour nap.

James's work schedule never varies: His duty at the hospital starts at eight o'clock on a given morning and continues for thirty-six hours. Then, he comes home at eight o'clock in the evening for twelve hours. Every other weekend he is home from Saturday noon until Monday morning at eight. We are a one-car family, which means I bundle little Jimmy up and take him on trips to and from the hospital. On the evenings James comes home, I keep our baby up, hoping he will stay awake for a brief visit with his father before he's put to bed. Besides, if he fell asleep, I'd have to wake him for the car trip to pick James up from his shift at the hospital. When he spots us waiting at the curb, James's face breaks into a smile and he rushes to the car. From the passenger seat, he reaches back for Jimmy in his infant seat and teases a finger into Jimmy's hand until the baby clasps his fingers. Once we arrive home, James scoops Jimmy up and holds him for a while before we put him in his crib.

James's time at home is precious. He is dog-tired and sometimes has gone with little more than a few hours of sleep in the previous thirty-six hours. He wolfs down a meal and falls asleep immediately, sometimes at the dinner table. The next morning, he is up at seven and we are at the hospital by 7:45. Because his time with us is so limited, I do not complain on Saturday afternoons when, upon arriving home, he heads for the crib and disrupts Jimmy from his sleep in order to have time with him. He spreads a blanket on the living room rug and puts Jimmy on the floor beside him.

"Hi, little guy," he says as he touches a finger to Jimmy's nose, or tickles his neck or tummy, evoking baby giggles that set us both to giggling ourselves. More than once, I find father and son sound asleep in mid-play—James on his back and Jimmy face down on his father's chest.

Mostly, though, Jimmy and I are on our own at home. I visit from time to time with Laura, a friend who lives across the street, two doors down. Her baby girl, Elizabeth, was born a couple of weeks after Jimmy. We chat about our daily lives, books, and the weather over lunch and watch each other's baby, taking turns running our errands. I'm grateful for this help because it reduces the number of times I have to weather the inevitable stares and remarks—well-intended though some may be—in reaction to the gaping split on one side of Jimmy's still unrepaired cleft lip.

I use some of my free time to scour local pharmacies for preemie nipples. Pharmacies do not usually carry these, I learn, and I keep scrounging from the hospital. One sweltering summer afternoon, after several unproductive inquiries, I happen into a pharmacy on Euclid Avenue, not far from our apartment. I'm expecting yet another disappointing response. The pharmacist asks why I want preemie nipples. I explain.

"Hold on a minute," he says and disappears into the back. He returns with a thin booklet from Mead Johnson. He thumbs through it. "Yes," he murmurs. "I thought so." He looks up at me with new light in his eyes. "Mead Johnson has just developed a feeder that allows you to apply pressure with your thumb." He shows me pictures of the feeder. It is a closed, doughnut-shaped affair designed to hold formula or milk. Its circumference is reinforced by a sturdy ring. The top side of the doughnut is a dome from which protrudes a nipple; the bottom side is flat and pliable. By holding the feeder in the palm of my hand with the nipple protruding between my first and second fingers, I could apply any amount of pressure with my thumb to the pliable side of the feeder, and in this manner, regulate the flow of formula.

"How do I get these?" I ask.

"I can order some for you," he says, "but it's an expensive proposition. These are disposable feeders and cost about fifty cents each." My heart sinks. I don't see how I can afford such an expense. The pharmacist is quick to see my shoulders sag. "Let me see what I can do. Perhaps they can give me some samples." He takes my phone number and I leave, half hopeful that something will work out.

A few days later, the pharmacist calls. "I got you some samples," he says. "Come take a look."

I leave Jimmy with Laura and head straight to the pharmacy. The pharmacist is beaming. Not only has he procured a dozen free samples of the dome feeder, but he has also been able to get me a supply at half price. Furthermore, he's made some inquiries and reports that if I wash the feeders very carefully in hot, soapy water, they can be used for multiple feedings. The tension in my shoulders releases as if unburdened from a heavy load, and tears slip down my cheek.

"If you only knew . . ." I start, but cannot finish. The pharmacist smiles, rests a hand on my shoulder, and says he's happy to help.

I quickly learn to work the feeder. Jimmy responds at once with soft, self-satisfied grunts and humming sounds. He attacks the nipple with renewed purpose. Finally, feedings have become times of easy closeness.

How lucky to stumble upon a pharmacist who knew how, or perhaps simply cared enough, to help. This encounter, my mother's votes of confidence, and James's enthusiasm for his new child—all give me the encouragement I need to keep trying. I'm determined to get the hang of what it takes to be a good mother, and especially, a good mother to my little son with a cleft palate.

WHAT HAPPENED?

The mother in me is stepping up. Jimmy is two months old, and I've become a pro in my own mind at preparing preemie nipples and handling the dome feeders. I slip the prosthesis in and out of Jimmy's mouth with nary a hitch. I know now how to deal with my two-month-old's fussiness and fits of rage and to capture his happy-baby moods for my own enjoyment. I sit him on my lap several times a day and articulate *m*'s and *d*'s and *t*'s and *s*'s, the sounds I'm told he will have the most difficulty pronouncing when he starts to talk. I hope he will learn them more easily if he hears them incessantly in his first months of life. Jimmy responds to my mothering, and I spend happy hours with him, snug in the cocoon of our intense connection.

I am still trying to muster up courage, however, to deal with what awaits me outside the security of home. I dread thinking about the startled reactions to Jimmy's distorted lip. My vulnerability became apparent while I was still at the hospital. Friends came with good intentions, as people do, but also with the morbid curiosity of ambulance chasers, to see firsthand what had gone wrong. At first,

I walked with them to the nursery, the way new mothers do, to view Jimmy through the window. They would catch their breath, unable to mask their shock. Smiles dropped from their faces. They stared for a moment or two and then turned away. In the leaden silences that followed, the pity in their eyes ambushed me and pushed me toward the jagged edge of heartache and a sense of failure. There were no words, no gestures, to salvage those moments.

After a couple of these soul-wrenching visits, the thought of one more panicked me. When my teaching friend Nikki called to say that some of the high school seniors I'd taught wanted to see my new baby, I balked. I remembered their teenage glee when they'd learned I was expecting. I did not want to see those innocent faces cloud over at my expense.

"I'm not up to any more visitors right now," I told her, "especially not my students. Could you explain the situation to them for me?"

But now that Jimmy is two months old and I'm feeling more confident as his mother, I'm hoping a carefully rehearsed explanation of Jimmy's cleft will allow me to talk about Jimmy's birth defect with anyone, even the most insensitive gawker, without faltering. I want to weather others' unsettling curiosity, be able to shove my feelings out of the way, draw a curtain over my discomfort, and tell people matter-of-factly how his cleft palate occurred in the first trimester of pregnancy, how no one knows exactly why, and that fortunately, it can be fixed. I tell myself repeatedly that curiosity is a natural thing and that basically folks are well-intentioned. I work hard to be less sensitive. I do not want to be a mess of hurt feelings in the presence of others. I tell myself that I can unbundle the throbbing sadness that still pulls me down when I'm alone. With others, though, I want to manage my still raw emotions and muster up an I'm-handling-this-well persona to satisfy their need to know what went wrong.

On one particularly bright summer afternoon, I decide I'm up for a walk to the post office, five blocks away. I plop Jimmy into the baby carriage and head out. He falls into a deep sleep on his back. At the post office, a gray-haired man with an engaging smile opens the door for me and I breeze into the lobby. The gentleman follows and stands in line behind me.

"I just love babies," he says. "Got two little grandkids myself." He peers into the carriage. He catches sight of Jimmy's upper lip and the still unrepaired gap on one side that exposes his gum. The gentleman gasps and recoils. His smile disappears into his mouth, which has fallen open in shock.

"Oh, my!" The kind sir stammers something about *poor little tyke* and steps quickly back. People around us look puzzled, and they peer at the baby carriage but do not inquire.

So much for being in control. I turn away. By the time it's my turn to buy stamps, I am aflame under the scrutiny of those around me. I feel exposed, out of place, an oddity. Overcome with an urgency to protect my baby and myself, I push my way out of the post office and hurry toward home, teary-eyed and deflated, withering with every step.

I try to come to terms with the gentleman's reaction to Jimmy's face. I want to believe it is an isolated incident, that most people will keep their reactions to themselves. I brave a few more errands. I tuck Jimmy into the infant seat and sally forth into the grocery store and out to the mall. Some days I skate through, avoiding unwanted attention, but too often we attract stares, some laced with stunned disbelief, some with pity. I cannot ignore the sideways glances, or the muffled comments made behind hands held over mouths. Worse yet are the exclamations of concern.

"Why hasn't he been fixed?" asks a startled mother at the mall.

"Oh, my! You poor dear!" says another.

Attempts to make me feel better are no easier to bear.

"Well, at least he's not adopted. Then you'd have to worry about what else is wrong with him!" chirps a friend of Aunt Janet's.

"You're lucky it's not worse!" says a friend.

Each time I hear comments like these, my skin crawls with something I cannot identify—embarrassment, shame, guilt, helplessness? I want to disappear. Sometimes, the comments feed self-disparaging voices in my head that harp about my weakness. At times, though, deep down, I feel the urge to stand up for myself, an ember of self-respect refusing to extinguish.

One hot summer afternoon, I decide to buck up and pop into the grocery store on my way to pick up James from his shift at the hospital. I hold two-month-old Jimmy tight against my chest and head into the store. His face is visible over my shoulder as I head for the middle section of the store, in search of rice.

"Excuse me, dear." I feel a tap on my arm and turn to find a white-haired wisp of a woman in an elegantly tailored brown suit peering at Jimmy's face. She is wearing a trim velvet hat with a mesh veil that covers her forehead. Her kind, weathered face is level with Jimmy's. With a countenance of deep concern, she studies him and continues. "I was just wondering, dear, if you're doing anything to fix your baby's face." She purses her lips to a stern pucker, shifts her eyes toward my face. I'm feeling soundly scolded.

I shrink inside and I start to crumble under her piercing eye. But then, before I turn into a puddle, I feel an urge to squelch this sweet little lady. *How dare she subject me to this?* Somewhat alarmed that my growing fury at this intrusion will unleash a retaliatory remark, I scramble to find a passably polite response. Deep down, though, a voice dripping with sarcasm hisses, *Of course I am, dear. I'm actually taking sewing lessons and I'm almost skilled enough to stitch this silly lip back together.* On the surface, however, I simply sigh, mumble something, and hurry away without rice. My rehearsed explanation has flown out the window.

I'm in tears when I reach the hospital. There's little James can do to console me. On the way home, I return to the grocery store with my list, but this time Jimmy waits in the car with his father.

From that day on, I arrange to shop for groceries after picking up James to avoid taking Jimmy into the store with me. I ask James to buy stamps and mail letters at the hospital. I count on my friend Laura to watch Jimmy if I have errands during James's absences. I feel at the mercy of unfiltered reactions for which I do not have a viable defense. I do not understand my weakness. Why can I not rise above the reckless curiosity, the understandable shock and sympathy? Wouldn't I react similarly? I have no answers except that I am not up to any of it.

There's something else I question, and the possible answers begin to haunt me. Why did this happen? What caused my baby to have a cleft?

I ask kind Dr. Lowrey, my obstetrician, for help in understanding what might have caused Jimmy to be born with a cleft. "Could I have done something during pregnancy?" I ask, anticipating a list of things I might have done.

"Stop worrying yourself about causes," he says with authority. "There could be a dozen reasons. It could be genetic, or something as minor as a cold, or indigestion at the wrong moment of gestation."

"I'm kind of worried, though, about having more children . . ."

"The best thing you can do is start planning for the next child now," he says.

Are you kidding? I want to scream but keep my thoughts to myself. He changes the subject, advising me to make more time for myself and to make a date for an evening out with James within the next two weeks. Dr. Lowrey's concern for my well-being touches me but does nothing to allay my worries about causes that are festering now like untreated wounds.

I start apologizing privately to Jimmy, over and over again, as I watch him work away at the preemie nipple or as I rub his back to ease him into sleep. One afternoon, I mutter my usual apologies over the bassinette in the living room where Jimmy is napping.

"I'm sorry. I'm so sorry."

I've forgotten that James is within earshot. "What are you saying?" he asks. He sounds alarmed.

"Oh, just that I'm sorry."

"About what?" He has caught me off guard.

My eyes well up. "I must have done something. Something caused this. I had to have done something."

"Do you really believe that?" He approaches me and peers into my face, surprise written all over his.

I shrug my shoulders. "Why shouldn't I?"

"There's no reason you should," he says, hugging me. "I can't stand to think that you're blaming yourself."

"But what proof do we have that it wasn't my fault?" I blurt out the list of possible causes that I've conjured up and cannot disprove: the medicine I took for a bad cold; the fainting spell induced when I washed my eye with hydrogen peroxide, mistaking its bottle for eye wash; too much coffee; a glass of wine at that student party; too little sleep; too much exercise in the first trimester, too little. I spare him my darkest thoughts: the possibility that I am being punished by a just and providential power for any number of uncharitable acts I've committed in my lifetime.

"We need help with this," James says. "I think it'd be good for you to talk to Dr. Hess." Then he tells me that Dr. Hess warned him that I would eventually have some very dark days and that he wanted to see me when they started. I'm not sure I agree, but James succeeds in extracting a promise from me to disclose my worries to Dr. Hess.

And so, I do. Dr. Hess has been seeing Jimmy every two weeks, checking primarily on weight gain, since feeding problems often result in failure to thrive in newborns with severe cleft palates. I'm looking at Dr. Hess's back while he examines Jimmy, who is squirming and protesting loudly on the exam table.

"And how are *you* doing?" Dr. Hess asks as he tries to examine Jimmy's ears. He asks this question every visit and until today, I've replied in Pollyanna mode. I have wanted him to see me as up to the task. But this time, I venture the truth.

"I had a bad time at the grocery store a couple of days ago."

"Oh? What happened?" He's still wrestling with Jimmy.

"A little old lady made a comment about Jimmy's face and I couldn't handle it," I say to Dr. Hess's back. He is quiet for a long moment. I wait, half expecting a reassuring comment like "Those things will happen, and you'll handle them better over time." Instead, he places a hand on Jimmy's tummy to keep control of him and turns toward me.

"Finally," he says, with a tenderness that surprises me. "You're human, after all. I was beginning to worry that you would never let yourself have feelings."

A knot of tension unravels somewhere inside. I know it's safe to cry.

Dr. Hess reaches out and says gently, "Make an appointment to talk with me, you alone, within the week."

In Dr. Hess's office a couple of days later, I take a deep breath and cautiously admit my failures: my inability to handle the stares, the comments, the sympathy, or to come to grips with the thought that I did something to cause Jimmy's cleft. I dare to mention the small-minded and murky thoughts that surge up, thoughts

I'm afraid to look at straight-on, much less fess up to James. I let Dr. Hess hear how often I'm feeling cheated, sorry for myself, full of resentment, tired of having to act cheerful about it all when I want to scream. I tell him I am discovering I had deceived myself in thinking I would be the kind of mother who could rise to any occasion.

"And now look at me. Jimmy deserves a strong mother, and I'm a mess. It's hard to discover what a weak person I really am. I'm ashamed and can't stand myself." I let out the air that has been compressed in my chest. "And I don't know how to deal with it."

Heat rises to my cheeks. I look down at my lap, bracing for Dr. Hess's reaction. He's remained quiet and attentive through it all—my tears, and the most thorough confession of my flaws I have ever made to myself or anyone else. I expect him to be horrified. I look up. His tender expression takes the punch out of my self-disgust.

"What painful thoughts you have been carrying," he continues in a quiet voice. "I'm not surprised. These are normal responses to the birth of a child who is not normal." Dr. Hess relaxes into his chair, less intent now. "Most of us are allowed to hold on to our fantasies about our newborn children for years," he says. "Most parents have the luxury of learning gradually over time, and in smaller doses, that their children have flaws they wish they didn't. But you have not had that luxury. You got the wind kicked out of you on Day One. I'd be worried if you weren't having difficulty. Your troubling thoughts are normal reactions to being hugely disappointed. In time, you'll work through them."

I leave Dr. Hess that day, clinging to his words. I now have an inkling that I am not a monster after all. Perhaps I can find a way to forgive myself for having disabling emotions and not-so-socially-redeeming thoughts and accept them as expected reactions to the loss of the "normal" baby I'd anticipated.

I continue to shrink from others' pained curiosity and efforts at well-intended advice, particularly from people with children without birth defects. I do not appreciate being told how lucky I am for the easy situation I have, compared to mothers whose babies are much worse off. I detest unsolicited speculation on the causes of Jimmy's cleft from dentists and doctors at social gatherings, followed by recommendations to seek help from a particular plastic surgeon, be it in Miami, Los Angeles, or on the moon. The steady stream of unwanted comments fuels a new cynicism in me, and I indulge myself in imagining a repertoire of snarky retorts. Someday, I know, I will have to confront the roil of unsettled thoughts and feelings that leave me so at odds with myself and others. For now, I'll work on forgiving myself for having them and focus on learning to care for my baby and his cleft.

ELIZABETH

One of my toughest challenges has come from my friend's irresistibly adorable baby girl named Elizabeth. Her mother, Laura, and I became fast friends as teachers at Hathaway Brown School for Girls—she in English, I in French. We were delighted to discover we were expecting a first child within several weeks of each other, soon after the school year ended. Even better, we were neighbors with husbands training in medicine at Case Western Reserve University hospitals. We'd have many occasions to share motherhood and our busy lives. We had a lot in common then.

With Jimmy's birth, my launch into motherhood hits a major snag. Instead of a smooth transition from maternity ward to home, I detour unprepared into rough, foreign terrain: ten days in a fog on the maternity floor while Jimmy gathers strength in the nursery; the shock of my baby's battered face post-surgery; then two weeks commuting from home to the hospital pediatric ward where Jimmy recovers; and learning to feed him with a syringe and preemie nipple. The months following our arrival home require frequent trips to the plastic surgeon, plus twice-monthly visits to the pediatrician, who checks Jimmy's weight and development. I feel desperate for reassurance that he is thriving with me at the wheel.

Laura is ecstatic with her baby girl—born two weeks after Jimmy—who sports deep-blue eyes, ash-blond hair, deep dimples, and a perfectly formed mouth. Laura is on course for precisely the mothering experience she envisioned. As she happily nurses her baby, I'm fashioning custom nipples and struggling with a prosthesis in hopes that formula will not escape through Jimmy's cleft palate and out his nose.

Laura and I visit back and forth two to three times a week and help each other with childcare. Much of our conversation deals with our babies' sleep patterns, gestures, and weight gains. Laura can't say enough about what an easy baby Elizabeth is. I say little about Jimmy's problems. I don't talk at all about pounding the streets in search of a feeding device—and she doesn't ask. I don't tell her how Jimmy fails to find relief from tension and fatigue, as most babies do, by sucking on a thumb or pacifier, how he often chokes as he gulps down formula, or how he regurgitates after feedings because of the excess air he takes in through his open palate. Elizabeth, meanwhile, is thriving and grows cuter by the day. I try to be happy for Laura, but the stark contrast between our mothering experiences stokes self-pity rather than generosity of spirit.

I will myself to endure Elizabeth's perfection and Laura's unblemished happiness. I bear it because I want desperately to keep up my friendship with Laura. Our chatter about our babies, baby food, diaper services, recipes, and books lends a semblance of normalcy to days when I'd otherwise be alone at home mired in worry about Jimmy. I try to tune out Laura's accounts of Elizabeth's latest endearing antics and her fretting about minute changes in the hue of Elizabeth's hair or the shade of her eyes. Frequently, though, I'm swallowing hard and holding back tears. I fear if unleashed, my sadness would unnerve Laura and drive her away. She's the only friend who spends time with me, and I value the company. So, I bottle up the turmoil in my mind.

As time goes on, I wonder if Laura's kindness is a pose and if, in truth, she dreads our time together. I sense that she begins to stifle her pride in Elizabeth to spare my feelings. Before long, I resent the child that brings such joy to her mother. I begrudge Elizabeth's smile, the way she waves her chubby little arms and kicks her feet so gleefully in the air. I spend far too much time thinking of perfect babies and dwelling on the unfairness of it all. Like a broken record, I get stuck on a refrain that takes me nowhere: *Why me? What did I do to deserve this?*

I do not like the person I'm becoming. I turn on myself. I am weak, small-minded, mean-spirited, not at all the person I thought I was or want to be. An inventory of shameful behaviors from twenty-odd years of memory plays over and over in my head and taunts me. Had I not avoided those who were disfigured or odd in some way? Had I not stared at the boy on the school bus who had a cauliflower ear? How many times had I held grudges, picked fights, or called names? Had I not felt smug about the ease and successes in my life? Am I now being brought down to size, punished for believing I had the world by the tail? My mother's favorite words of recrimination taunt me. *You reap what you sow, young lady! Just you see. You'll fall off your high horse one of these days.*

When I'm able to hold disappointment in myself at bay, I battle worries about the future. Is Jimmy gaining weight? Can his palate really be repaired? What about the missing teeth and the gaps in his upper jaw? How many surgeries are we facing? When will they end? Will his speech impediment be severe? Will he have trouble making friends? Will people tease him? Reject him? Will he like himself? Will he be happy? How can I help him get what he needs when I have no idea how to begin?

Though Jimmy is less than six months old, I decide to seek advice about Jimmy's potential speech problems from Dr. DeWitt, the plastic surgeon who repaired Jimmy's lip.

"Is there something I can do now to help him with speech? I've made some flash cards with the letters of the alphabet on them, and I spend some time each day sounding out the letters to him. Maybe hearing the sounds now will help him later?"

"Don't bother," he says as he closes the chart in front of him, signaling the end of our conversation. "It won't make any difference." Dr. DeWitt leans toward me. Gently, but with authority, he says, "You're worrying too much. I don't think the cards will make any difference. Relax. Just be a good mother and he'll be fine."

He might as well have struck me. I burn with humiliation. *To think that my silly efforts would make a difference!* I hide the pain that registers deep in the place that already feels small and wounded. Dr. DeWitt has no idea how much I believe I am not a good mother. His words will stalk me for years. Each time a feeding goes wrong, or I can't soothe Jimmy, when he falls, or I lose patience, I'm convinced I am not making the grade as a mother. *What the hell is a good mother, anyway?*

The futility of my efforts grates daily on my nerves. I berate myself for imagining a child who does not have to struggle at each feeding to control his food, who can suck on his fingers or a pacifier to his heart's content, whose distorted lips are not a reminder of surgeries to come. When I try to buck up, I fall flat. Where is that hardy, forward-looking person from all those heady years of growing strong in the cocoon of a healthy family; the determined girl who overcame failing grades early in her freshman year of college and landed on the honor roll at year's end; who thought she was set for life when she married an earnest man with a promising future; who sailed through her pregnancy? I am not such hot stuff, after all. I tell little Jimmy I'm sorry he ended up with me for a mother.

I try to draw on Dr. Hess's words of encouragement from a few weeks ago. He seemed to understand my torment. But his efforts to shore me up have no power now to pull me out of this quagmire. I'm afraid to show my sense of failure and worthlessness to my husband. Outwardly, I appear to be coping. I manage errands with Jimmy by looking anywhere but into people's faces. On weekend outings to Thorn Acres, the country property owned by Uncle Jerry and Aunt Janet, I put up with the comments of their curious and well-meaning guests.

"At least he's not retarded," whispers a graying matron.

I have no response to these comments, especially since I know Jimmy is being monitored for signs of additional anomalies. I've been warned that birth defects can come in multiples. I don't challenge these well-meaning people, but I do imagine impolite retorts having to do with how off-base and off-putting such remarks are. Within minutes, I slip back into the bog of avoidance and dark thoughts and leave the room.

And Baby Elizabeth is still right across the street. I avoid looking at her cherubic smile, feathery wisps of golden hair, and cameo-blue eyes. I'm up to my gills with tolerance the day I lose control. Laura is lamenting, once again, that Elizabeth's golden tresses may be turning brown.

"I wouldn't give a damn if Jimmy's hair were the color of shit brindle," I blurt out. The words fly from my mouth and cut the air like a knife. "I'd just like his mouth to be normal."

Laura starts and turns red. I should apologize, but I am not sorry. Instead, I feel relief.

"I didn't mean to . . ." Laura stumbles at words.

I interrupt. "I know. It's just that I have a lot on my mind besides hair color." I steer the conversation to a safe topic.

I yearn to know that Laura and Elizabeth have bad days, instantly ashamed for having this thought. The problem eventually extends beyond Elizabeth and Laura. Now, all mothers and normal babies become thorns in my side. I hear about a baby born with biliary atresia, a condition in which the bile duct is blocked and that spells almost certain death within the first year of life. For a moment I think them lucky because they know their ordeal will end in the near future, and my thought horrifies me. Of course, I know they are bearing great sadness. I realize I have to be wary of unchecked cynicism that could erode my capacity to empathize with others' misfortune.

Not long after, I dream that Jimmy dies peacefully in his sleep. In the dream I'm not upset. I startle awake and leap out of bed in horror. I rush to the nursery and snatch up Jimmy from his sleep, willing to rouse him to assure myself that he is indeed breathing. *What was wrong with me that I could have a dream in which my child's death was a relief?* The turnings of my mind throw me into despair. I dread the next dark thought.

I make another appointment with Dr. Hess. In the safety of his office, I dump the entire load of ugly, haunting thoughts, unable to contain them as they gush forth. I exhaust myself with the telling of it all. I let him see my shame for resenting Elizabeth.

"Worst of all, and the hardest to tell, I'm having dreams in which Jimmy dies in his sleep, and I feel relief for both of us. What kind of cowardice is that?"

To me, this is the most damning revelation of all.

I'm desperate for an insight to help me live more easily with Elizabeth's perfection, the problems Jimmy's cleft is throwing at me, and most important, my own shortcomings.

"I can't stand myself," I mutter. "I'm certainly not the noble person I thought I was." Dr. Hess hears me once again.

"You're still grieving," he says in the gentle tone of voice that brought me here. "And you're in the throes of the emotional disturbance that goes with it. Of course you wish your baby didn't have the problems Jimmy does. Of course you are hurt when people make insensitive comments. Your resentment toward normal babies and their lucky mothers is very understandable. But now you're also turning on yourself because you think you should be able to soldier through all this *and* handle the taxing demands of Jimmy's care without flinching. Try to be less hard on yourself."

"And the dream?" I shudder. "What kind of mother has a dream like that?"

"It's normal," he says matter-of-factly. "Give yourself some room to fall apart, and don't let the dark thoughts scare you. You'll figure out a way to tame them. But for now, just make note of them."

His words are a balm. Some of the hardness I feel toward myself softens. My breath comes more easily, reaches deeper into my lungs, and untangles the knots in my shoulders. I sit a bit taller. A sliver of a forgiving thought wedges itself into a spot among the thorns. A bud of hope unfolds its petals and springs to life. A whisper flutters in my soul: *You can find a way to live more easily with little Elizabeth's perfection.*

After this visit with Dr. Hess, I fret less and become a more gentle witness to my days. I expose my shaky hold on my bearings to James and take strength from his support. By Jimmy's first birthday, I face the days less wary of bumps in the road. I laugh more easily and sing along more with tunes on the radio as I work through the day's chores. I entertain Jimmy and myself with nursery rhymes and children's songs. I play "Pat-A-Cake" and "Eensy-Weensy Spider" at every opportunity. These games animate Jimmy, and his brightened mood boosts my own. I babble at him as I change his diaper, guessing what amuses him and what he's thinking in that little mind of his. I tell him how strong he's becoming as he flails his arms and legs in a moment of exuberance. I enumerate the events that will fill our day: the meals ahead, playtime with his stuffed bear or monkey, story time with Mommy, a walk around the block and then a very long nap, please. Maybe a visit with Laura and Elizabeth if there's time.

I coo at Jimmy during feedings and I'm certain he is amused. I exclaim and praise him when he chomps away at his bottle. We are both becoming more skilled at keeping formula from escaping, and feedings become times of easy closeness. I make funny faces at him when I remove the prosthesis from his mouth, and he complains less. We play with rattles and take turns batting at the jungle animals on the mobile over the dressing table. We splash together in the tub. I fuss with his hair and can't bear to trim his lush, emerging curls. He draws me in with the smile in his big brown eyes. I continue to seat him on my lap once a day for a ten-minute spell and flip through the letter flash cards, pronouncing each sound, hoping Jimmy is storing them in his mind for future use. I hold him long after he falls asleep in my arms, acutely aware of the warmth of his little body as it sinks into my chest, the softness of his hair against my cheek, the steady sound of his breathing. A tenderness I thought I'd never feel quiets my mind. I whisper in his ear that we will figure this out together. We will make our life work.

When we visit Laura and Elizabeth these days, I chatter more easily and find myself commenting on how Elizabeth's light blond hair resembles her mother's more and more, and how the blue of her eyes is deepening. I turn my gaze often on my own child, smooth his soft brown curls, and smile into his dark brown eyes.

To the Perfect Baby

Your arrival is an anticipated
surprise, like every new fact
your mother is eager to learn.

You are the dream of those who love you,
who loved you before you came into the world,
screaming to be held.

Despite your obvious defects,
she sees you as pure potential,
no matter the ruin of your face.

You are still more than she imagined.
She staggers under the suddenness
of her new life, leaning in anyway.

Moments come for accepting what we're given
as perfection; they find each of us eventually,
our expectations spent, our certainty swift.

Postcards from My First Year

Just before becoming my mother, she stands in a hard rain on her doorstep in a daisy-print dress. She is waiting, water-broken, for her strong aunt to ferry her through the storm, as strong aunts often do. At the hospital, she manages to be troublesome to those caregivers who couldn't care less. Her husband arrives just in time, as new fathers often do. She hears her son's first cry, then she sleeps as who she is for the last time.

She sees her son's complete bilateral cleft lip and palate days later. He has a severe instance of a common birth defect. She takes in the shape of his head, touches his cheek, and slowly counts his toes and fingers—ten and ten—finding comfort that they are as she expected. (*Hiya Mom, I'm here.*) She had so many expectations, although this will take her years to understand. Even a print on the wall of a painting of sunflowers seems not as it should be. She is drugged as the medical system quietly draws her and her son into its mind-numbing, unending grind. She is flattened.

She fails at feeding him initially. Or at least she feels like a failure; there is a difference, she will learn. She is joyful when she holds his warm smallness. She and her husband settle on giving their son her maiden name. She assumes those taking care of her and her baby know what's best, or at least she assumes they are trying their best. She will make a life of pursuing the difference between knowing and trying. She is still breathing.

She stands in the nursery at home with her own mother weeks later, anxious for good news of her son's first surgery. The yellow walls, handmade curtains, and bold rug are a shade darker; not darker, but less bright. She is beginning to believe all this is somehow her fault. (*I know that feeling!*) Her mother doesn't know what to say or quite where to stand or where to place her hand on her daughter's shoulder, but she is present anyway. Somehow, they are all still breathing.

She visits her son in the recovery room where everything is too well-lit and very in order, and would be so regardless of her presence. Her son is disfigured from the surgery because he is still healing. (*Won't be the last time for this . . .*) She expects him to look different, to look better than he did before the surgery, but he does not (*. . . nor for this*). She visits him every day and notices other children do not have visitors. She sees her son's difficult path forward, and also sees some children's paths will never leave the recovery room. She begins to welcome the blessings of her burdens. She begins to breathe with purpose.

She senses her husband is around, close enough so she can feel him when she needs to. Even when he is sleeping between shifts, he is steady for their son and for her and he does not seem to need much from either of them. She is glad for the gift of him. (*Yeah, Dad is a pretty solid guy.*) She builds her routine around her husband's routine. She pushes herself up.

She teaches her son to eat with a modified preemie nipple and a plug in his palate. (*Sure glad I don't remember this.*) She discovers those who help just because they can. She discovers not all doctors are aware whether they are helpful. She learns to do things no one teaches her. She wonders if she is a good mother, if she is even capable of being a mother—not capable, but worthy. She discovers small things to hold on to: her son's dense warmth when he falls asleep on her shoulder. She steadies herself.

She whispers apologies to her son for not knowing why life came to be this way for him. She knows this is irrational, but she has little else to offer. She shudders, sometimes, at what she would be willing to give up to change their circumstances. She wants answers to questions she has been told are beyond knowing. She holds on to the moments her son keeps milk down and his gurgle-laughs. Each day they both grow stronger.

She shops at the grocery store with him and is snared by the judgments of others as they pass in the aisle. Sometimes they do not use words, only sling a biting glare. Nothing can be done; his lip is still a hitched curtain of skin. Sometimes they admonish her about how lucky she is. Sometimes they tell her what she should do. Sometimes she curses them and whispers more apologies to her son, her unanswerable questions like unhealing wounds. She falters.

She coos to him with the articulated sounds of the semi-vowels and mute consonants he might later struggle to master. She sing-songs nursery rhymes *(I think I remember that.)* and uses flash cards in hopes his speech comes easier. (*Gawd, t, t, t, d, d, d.*) These are solid things they both do and hold on to. She wonders what his voice will sound like. She knows she will like his voice however it sounds. She is still breathing.

She resents the easy days of her mother friends, especially those whose babies appear perfect. She imagines they have bad days, but she wants to know they do. She still wonders if she can be a good mother; her doubts curl darkly around those few things she holds on to. She dreams her son dies in his sleep, and it is not a bad dream. She learns to give her shadows room to breathe. (*Took me some time to learn this too, Mom.*) She learns to live with her darkness and is a more forgiving witness to her days. She stands and steadies.

She slowly arrives at gratitude for her unexpected life. She leans in now. Her son has come through several surgeries, she has confronted several doctors. (*Won't be the last time for this.*) They have created much to hold on to and are reflections of each other, though this will take him years to learn. She already feels the rigid grip of the medical system around them both, and will return it, in kind, her entire life. She has become original again.

He does not remember anything distinct from this time. He will only come to know all this through her memories. Through one another, they will learn the other edge of what is known. She understands this, and the world is new again.

SPEECHLESS

When we moved to Rochester, New York, in 1972 for James's residency training, we lost our cherished Dr. Hess. Our new regular pediatrician was recommended by some medical trainee friends and has been diligent and friendly, so I am disappointed when Dr. Gray, an elderly doctor who gives the impression he'd rather be napping, ambles into the exam room instead of our regular pediatrician. He mumbles a listless greeting, and after a cursory exam he announces that Jimmy will get a tuberculosis test today. Dr. Gray sighs as he sets up the multiple-needle device he will use to puncture the forearm, then he purses his lips and approaches two-and-a-half-year-old Jimmy, who is sitting on the exam table. Dr. Gray's brow furrows over piercing eyes. All business. He reaches for Jimmy with his free arm.

"Lie down, young man," he says. "On your back, and give me your arm." Jimmy looks at me in panic.

"If I hold him, it might be easier for him." My voice is barely audible.

"I prefer that children lie down when I administer shots." The intensity in Dr. Gray's voice pushes me away. He shoves Jimmy backward with his arm. Then he squares his feet and bends over Jimmy, pinning him to the exam table with one forearm. Jimmy squirms and tries to sit up.

"Lie still!" the doctor booms. "I can't do my work if you won't lie still!" But Jimmy is having nothing to do with it. He throws his shoulders from side to side. The doctor applies more pressure. The tine test device, held aloft in Dr. Gray's other hand, menaces from above.

"I said, lie still!" Dr. Gray hisses. Jimmy flails his arms and legs in frantic motion. Dr. Gray presses him to the exam table.

Words of protest lodge in my throat. I want to rescue my child, but the well-indoctrinated belief that doctors know best paralyzes me. Finally, as the struggle continues, I blurt out, "Please! His regular pediatrician allows me to hold him for shots. He's very squeamish about needles."

"Nonsense!" Dr. Gray intensifies his hold on Jimmy. Jimmy struggles violently. The doctor leans his full weight into his arm to hold Jimmy down. He turns his distorted face toward me. "This is obviously a child who doesn't mind," he growls. "Tell me, what would you do with this boy if he stuck his head in the oven?"

I'm speechless. I mumble an unintelligible response, something about giving a scolding, explaining how dangerous the oven is. The doctor cuts me off.

"Whatever you're doing, you're not effective."

I wither and fall silent. Dr. Gray turns back to Jimmy, wielding the multi-needle instrument. He grabs Jimmy's arm and stabs him with the injection device. Caught unaware, Jimmy screams and starts kicking, catching the doctor squarely in the groin. The doctor groans and strikes Jimmy hard on the chest. I rush to Jimmy and grab him up in my arms. He clings to me, sobbing.

I hold Jimmy close for my own protection as much as his. I push past the doctor and head out the door, clutching Jimmy tight. By the time we reach the car, I am fighting back tears.

I don't let go of Jimmy until he stops sniffling. When I wipe the tears from his cheeks, he looks away. He remains quiet while I buckle him into his car seat. My thoughts are a jumble.

"I'm sorry, Jimmy. I know shots are scary and I wish the doctor had tried to make it easier for you. We won't ever go to that doctor again, I promise you." I kiss him on the head. "I absolutely promise you."

Jimmy remains quiet on the ride home. I grip the wheel with such force that my knuckles turn white. I struggle to keep my mind on my driving. *What has just happened? My child just got smacked by a doctor and I was practically speechless!* My cheeks grow hot, and I clench my jaw against the urge to cry. *Why in the world did I let him handle Jimmy that way? What kind of mother lets that happen to her child?* The more I think about it, the more I blame myself as much as the doctor for Jimmy's being manhandled. But Dr. Gray's words hit home. I must be a poor specimen of a mother if a doctor has to ream me out like that. I shudder to think about the second child I'm expecting in four months. *What will I do with two children, when I'm bumbling so with the first?* I sniffle and wipe away tears.

From the seat beside me, I hear Jimmy mumble something. His voice is hesitant.

"What's that, Jimmy?"

"I'm sorry I made you cry." I steal a glance at him. His eyes are still wide and the sadness and worry on his face jar me. I pull the car to the side of the road. I turn toward Jimmy and put my hand on his knee.

"Honey, you didn't make me cry. I'm upset because that doctor was so mean to you. And to me, too. He should not have held you down and most of all, he should never have hit you. It all makes me very sad, and mad, too. That's why I'm crying." I rub his knee. "You did nothing wrong. Do you understand?" He nods his head ever so slightly. But he looks away and I'm not sure he believes me.

When I park the car in front of our town house in student housing, our neighbor and good friend Scotty, a pediatric resident, approaches with his usual cheerful smile. When he sees me, his face shows alarm.

"What's wrong?"

"Terrible time at the doctor's office." I pause and then say, "Tell me, Scotty. You're a pediatrician. Do you ever find yourself having to strike a child in your office?"

Scotty's eyes widen. "Of course not! That would be unthinkable!"

"When you give shots, do you allow the mother to hold her child?"

"Of course!"

"Suppose the child was resisting, would you physically restrain him?"

"No."

"What would you do if the child was hard to control?"

"I'd leave the room and ask the mother to calm her child down."

Then I relate our experience. "It's going to be hell to take Jimmy back to any doctor now. Hell for both of us."

"I'm truly appalled," Scotty says. "That should never have happened. I'm so sorry."

I thank Scotty. He has pulled me back from the abyss I lean toward when an encounter with a professional seems too hard on my child and I can't seem to help the situation. Once inside the house, Jimmy escapes to the *Sesame Street* show and I nurse my wounds in silence.

Later that afternoon, Scotty intercepts James as he arrives home from the hospital. I see James's body tense as he grasps what Scotty is saying. When James comes through the door, his face is stormy.

He drops his briefcase and gives me a protective hug. I shrug. He has to know from my empty expression and sagging shoulders how dejected and helpless I feel. He pulls back and starts pacing in the cramped space of our kitchen. He stops and comes close. He whispers so that Jimmy, who is absorbed in watching Big Bird's antics nearby, cannot overhear.

"This is *not* okay. This should never have happened. I'm going to call Dr. Gray and have a conversation."

"Please don't," I say. "It's over. Talking to him won't make a difference. Besides, I have nothing to say to him."

"Well, I do," James says. "He mustn't think what he did is okay. Doctors are supposed to do no harm, at the very least, and look at the upset he's caused not just to Jimmy, but you, too!"

The next day James calls Dr. Gray. His wife answers, saying Dr. Gray is napping and can't be disturbed. James insists that the matter is important and asks Mrs. Gray to wake the good doctor. I listen as James introduces himself and registers his grievance. In addition to mishandling his son, the doctor has upset his wife in her fifth month of pregnancy, which he finds alarming and indefensible. How can he justify such behavior? I cringe. I fear the intensity of James's rebuke will unleash further fury and criticism.

"Well, that may well be, Dr. Gray, but with all due respect, that does not excuse the behavior."

James listens some more.

"If you insist," he says. "We'll be home Sunday afternoon at two o'clock." I can't stomach the thought of encountering that man again.

On that sunny Sunday afternoon, most of the interns and residents and their families are in the common area at the center of the quadrangle of town houses where we live. I long to be part of the volleyball game outside, rather than inside, where James paces and I sit quietly, dreading Dr. Gray's visit. I've reiterated to James that I'm at a loss for words and do not want to meet with the man, but James asks me to be present. Jimmy is sound asleep upstairs.

Dr. Gray drags himself up the path. James lets him in. I wait. He looks at me with sad eyes.

"I bet I'm the last person you want to see," he says. I say nothing but allow a wry expression to play on my face as if to say, you've got that right.

Dr. Gray takes a seat and apologizes for "that unfortunate episode." He explains that he doesn't have the patience he used to. He's sorry he lost his temper. He was wrong, he said, and his apology sounds sincere. He's about to retire and doesn't want to have a stain on his record. He wants to know what he can do to make things right.

I avoid looking at him. I start to feel sorry for him. What an unfortunate way to end his career.

James says he's sympathetic, but hopes he understands how upsetting the whole thing has been to Jimmy and me. Also to him as a doctor-in-training, who is reminded constantly of the dangers of misusing power in the doctor-patient relationship.

Dr. Gray nods. "Of course," he says.

In the silence that follows I see an opening. Though I feel shaky, James's steadiness in his reproach of Dr. Gray gives me the little bit of encouragement I need to speak up, this time for Jimmy.

"Dr. Gray, I wonder if you appreciate what it's like for a two-and-a-half-year-old child who's been through three surgeries and dozens of doctor visits where he's probed and stuck with needles. Every visit to a doctor's office, every needle, every person in a white coat terrifies him. He panics at the sight of exam tables. If you had let me hold him, the shot might have been easier for him. I wish you had listened to me. 'That unfortunate episode' the other day in your office didn't have to be so hard on any of us. We've had too many tough times with doctors and hospitals, Jimmy and I, and every rough encounter makes the next appointment that much harder."

I look Dr. Gray square in the eyes, speechless no longer.

JAMES: THE VIEW AS A NEW FATHER

As I completed my last year of medical school, we prepared for the birth of our baby. Our saved notes are full of "firsts"—first day Barbara wore a maternity dress (February 13), baby's first kick (February 25), first audible heartbeat (March 8). I graduated on June 10, 1970, and two weeks later I began one of the most grueling segments of a physician-in-training's career: the internship.

I was assigned to initiate my internship on one of the most physically challenging services: the open wards that served the public. My "routine" schedule called for three months of thirty-six hours "on" and twelve hours "off." My "on" hours meant living and working on the wards delivering direct patient care to a constant influx of sick and often critically ill patients, repeated rounds and conferences with medical and nursing staff, and many busywork tasks. Sleeping was intermittent. My "off" hours at home provided sleep, food, whatever interaction with family I could muster, and more sleep.

On the first day of my internship on June 24, during Barbara's labor, I ran back and forth through the long and dimly lit underground tunnels that connected the medical and obstetrical hospital buildings. Shortly before I was paged for Barbara's delivery, I had just admitted the first patient of my official medical career, a middle-aged woman with pyelonephritis (severe kidney infection).

I arrived in the obstetrical suite in time for Barbara's final contractions, and I can only recount a jumble of sights, sounds, emotions, and poorly organized thoughts over the next few minutes—the bustle and noise of medical staff in preparation, Barbara's tenacity and uncomplaining efforts, elation with the delivery and forceful cry of our new baby. "It's a boy!" Next, a stunned brief silence, the obstetrician whispering to me and showing me Jimmy's cleft lip, then my wordlessly touching Barbara's forehead, before being ushered from the room by the obstetrician who reassured me our son was probably healthy and had a surgically correctible congenital anomaly.

During these few minutes, I was bewildered. I had no experience in my medical education with anything related to cleft birth disorders. Our baby was whisked away to wherever newborns go. I was whisked away, and Aunt Janet and the doctor instructed me on what to tell Barbara, who by now was well sedated and would soon be whisked away to bed. When I have revisited these numbing moments, I am reminded of how little I had to offer her.

Around 2:30 a.m., I returned to the medical ward through the tunnels. I recall that the numbness gave over to tears, and I choked back sobs before I was able to redirect my thoughts to my patient and the intern responsibilities back on the wards. At that point in time, the three most important people in my life were Barbara, my son, and my first patient.

My most vivid memory of Jimmy's first two days was that the treatment protocol for the ABO blood incompatibility required that I could not hold him. Nor, because of the protective bands over his eyes as he lay in his bassinette beyond the nursery window, could I see any part of his face except his cleft lip. And he could not see me. Those moments were tough, and it was difficult to stifle my emotions—sadness that I could not comfort him and lingering concern over his rising jaundice. I did not share with Barbara that I was worried about kernicterus—a complication of newborn severe jaundice that can result in acute and permanent brain damage. That condition never materialized, but for a couple of days, I felt quite anxious about that possibility.

Prior to Jimmy's first surgery, my visits with him and Barbara at the maternity hospital were brief. She spent her days on the front lines dealing with well-intended but awkward conversations with staff, struggling with feeding problems, coping with hospital protocols and procedures, and confronting the uncertainties of any given moment. Barbara assumed the mantle of responsibility, and in retrospect, one of my greatest regrets is that during these first few days, I didn't acknowledge to Barbara how our baby benefited from, and how I was comforted by and grateful for, her resiliency.

In 1970, the hospital system associated with Case Western Reserve University School of Medicine was probably as well equipped as any in the country at the time to deal with newborn craniofacial disorders, but it wasn't until the mid-1980s that most hospitals used ultrasonography to detect presence of a cleft lip and much later that craniofacial teams were established to support parents before and after the birth of a child with a cleft palate. This is not to say that Barbara and I felt deprived of good medical services in June 1970, but the historical perspective of the evolution of the standard of care may deepen understanding of what Barbara, Jimmy, and I were confronted with at that earlier time.

During the first three years of Jimmy's life, Barbara found herself in an environment that also demanded hard work and commitment to perform in a role for which she had no training or role models, and no system to support her. She had to find her way and create her own rewards. When she brought Jimmy home twenty-four days after his birth, she left behind the hospital environment that had provided professional care for Jimmy as a patient, if not for her. But that system did not support or prepare us for what lay outside the hospital walls.

Barbara faced the at-home frontline challenges almost entirely by herself, and during nights and weekends when I was home, she initially made every effort to insulate me from what she was experiencing. At first, I was insensitive to the emotional impact that led her to "turn on herself," as she says. I was stunned when I overheard her apologizing to Jimmy, privately expressing a deeply felt sentiment that I had not recognized until then. I realized that I had been missing Barbara's distress and that there could be consequences to our relationship if we continued without change. I think it was then that I prioritized the three most important things in my life as Barbara, Jimmy, and my marriage.

That day, my attempt to ease Barbara's anguish with "scientific" information did not mollify her. Since the scientific community was uncertain of the etiology of cleft disorders, how could I convince her that either of us was in some way not accountable? Furthermore, this uncertainty was a realistic concern in contemplating another pregnancy.

At least Dr. Hess was effective in responding to Barbara with the empathy and comforting communication any of us would desire from those to whom we confess our darkest thoughts. He listened, he validated, and he encouraged her to give herself more time to heal emotional wounds and find ways to understand and forgive herself.

Over time my work became less grueling, and occasionally my schedule allowed me to spend two out of three nights a week at home. I assumed a more active role in parenting and husbanding. I think I realized that it was possible to negatively affect a relationship, not just by trying to help in the wrong way, but also by failing to recognize an opportunity to do something that *would* help. During these three years, these "helpful" things ran the gamut from just arranging for a babysitter and insisting on a date night, or encouraging Barbara to attend an art class, to organizing an extended vacation for the two of us to Saint John in the Virgin Islands when Jimmy was eighteen months old, and another vacation to the Bahamas a year later. Initially, Barbara resisted these vacations, citing concerns about leaving Jimmy in the care of others, but once we found ourselves on the beach or lingering over a casual meal prepared by others, the back-home pressures melted away and Barbara remarked how invigorating the respite was. We discovered the romance and a playfulness that were often elusive in our current lives and recognized how much this time away together—away from my work and her parenting responsibilities—reinvigorated our relationship. This awareness would serve us well in other trying times.

At home I found I could be helpful as a liaison among various health professionals who treated Jimmy, beginning with our move to Rochester in late 1972. In these pre-internet years, I facilitated conversations and written communications among surgeons, pediatricians, surgical residents, and other medical colleagues.

But Barbara had grown to resent the decisions made without her consent about medical treatments. She became frustrated with the disconnects in information and direction, and dismissive attitudes inherent to medical hierarchies. Her experiences made me appreciate that the medical system was imperfect, underdeveloped in some ways, and operated with some biases. Given her feeling that as a mother, she was not taken seriously in most medical encounters, Barbara welcomed my taking this role as a facilitator with medical practitioners. Gender may have had a part in my effectiveness, but being a doctor-in-training was a great advantage too.

I made a more direct intervention on her behalf in Rochester, where we experienced a pediatrician whose manner could not have contrasted more starkly with that of Dr. Hess. An upsetting encounter during an appointment for Jimmy was one of the first times in Jimmy's first three years that I felt strongly that I had to intercede. I was still a physician-in-training, stepping out of line in confronting an established senior pediatrician. But by now I had enough experience to understand the importance of a physician's conduct as well as his or her medical expertise. In challenging this doctor, I saw an opportunity to share some of the responsibility of parenting Jimmy that Barbara had shouldered for so long.

Two-month-old Jimmy with James after first lip surgery.

Three-month-old Jimmy with Barbara after second lip surgery.

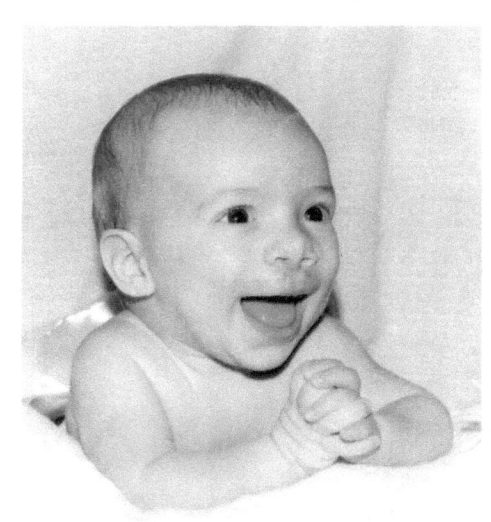

Jimmy laughs for a photographer at four months of age.

Eleven-month-old Jimmy with Barbara.

Jimmy with James on his first birthday on grandparents' farm in Maine.

Jimmy, age two, with James.

PART TWO:
1973–1980

BOOMERANG YEARS

When Jimmy is three, his life is disrupted not only by the birth of a brother, but also by our relocation to the West Coast. Within two more years we will uproot ourselves again and move back to Rochester, New York. He will have many adjustments and so will his father and I.

Deciding to have a second child has not been easy. Learning that my odds for having another child with a cleft were increased multifold, I hesitated. No longer naïve about the possibility of congenital defects, I worried that having a child with one defect made me more likely to have one with a more serious condition.

During my second pregnancy, I watched my diet like a hawk, avoided alcohol, medicines, and spicy foods, got eight hours of sleep a night, and took advantage of opportunities to make amends for past misdeeds. With each little sniffle, an odd cramp, a moment of indigestion or heartburn, I imagined my pregnancy going haywire. Like all mothers-to-be in those days, I was flying blind. There were no prenatal tests to determine the health of the fetus, or the gender for that matter. Let alone birth defects. I awoke frequently in a sweat from dreams of giving birth to severely deformed babies. When some abnormal bleeding occurred in the fourth month, I told myself it might be a good thing if I lost the baby. I was not proud to be thinking this way, but that didn't stop the inner voice that warned me to spare myself having to deal with more than I already had on my parenting plate. When I dared to disclose my worries to friends, they brushed aside my concerns and told me not to borrow trouble. James seemed less troubled than I, and his optimism grounded me. If he was wrestling with demons, he kept quiet about it.

In the early seventies, the federal government was conscripting doctors to serve the war effort in Vietnam via a lottery program called the Berry Plan. James's lottery number allowed him to defer induction until after he completed his residency training. He was scheduled to report to basic training in June 1973, when I would be seven months pregnant. Early in the pregnancy, I appealed to James to see what he could do to delay his military service by a few months. In case there were problems, I wanted our second baby to be born at the University of Rochester's Strong Memorial Hospital, rather than in a military hospital.

"If you have to, go ahead," I told James. "I'm not budging. I'll find a place here to stay with Jimmy until the baby is born and then we'll all join you."

That plan did not seem the best to James, so he appealed to his assignment officer. When he learned that our first child had been born with a birth defect requiring significant medical intervention, the officer was happy to ensure that I would not give birth to a child while James was in the military. He could foresee liability and a potentially huge financial outlay and acted to spare the military that responsibility. He did not hesitate to delay James's military duty by three months. This turned out to be a very good thing.

Kent Edward Walker's birth is not without complications. On the evening of August 3, James is not on duty at the hospital and is in the delivery room from the start. We are ecstatic to see that our baby has no physical sign of a birth defect and I remain euphoric throughout the night at the hospital, but my initial giddiness gives way to alarm the following morning when we're told Kent needs an urgent blood exchange transfusion. He's been diagnosed with a severe case of ABO blood incompatibility. How can that be? We'd been assured the ABO blood incompatibility that afflicted Jimmy rarely occurs in a second pregnancy. Now we're hearing that Kent's condition is more urgent than Jimmy's was. The fluorescent lamps will not correct the rapidly rising bilirubin in his bloodstream. He's moved immediately to the neonatal intensive care unit (NICU) for the blood exchange transfusion and monitoring. Within forty-eight hours, Kent's life-threatening condition is corrected. He remains in the NICU, and I'm allowed visits to start nursing. I've no doubt we've dodged a bullet and shudder to think what might have been the outcome had we been on that military base in Central California. Kent would have required emergency transport to a larger, full-service military hospital with intensive neonatal care capability. The delay in treatment would have put him at risk for damage to vital organs, particularly the brain. At least I'd had the right instinct about staying in Rochester to deliver Kent at Strong Memorial Hospital.

At the same time, it is not lost on me that I've given birth to two babies with ABO blood incompatibility, a problem that normally does not occur twice. Given Jimmy's cleft and the second, more severe ABO blood issues with Kent, James and I agree that something in our combined DNAs is amiss and with regret, we decide not to tempt fate a third time, and we give up our dream for more children.

After the brush with disaster, Kent settles into being an easy baby. He is spared the frustrations that complicated Jimmy's feedings and bedtimes. He has none of the tension in his little body that marked Jimmy's early months. Having a baby who comes home three days after birth with few feeding problems, no scars or open palate to tend, and no surgeries on the calendar is an extraordinary gift. I am grateful to be able to nurse Kent, an experience I looked forward to with Jimmy three years earlier, but which was denied because of his cleft.

As expected, three-year-old Jimmy takes some time to get used to his baby brother. He greets Kent with intense curiosity, seeming to reserve judgment as he tries to figure out what has just happened to his world. We know that three-year-olds worry about being displaced by newborn siblings, so we take pains in those first days to facilitate gentle touching. We follow expert advice and purchase a baby doll and carriage for Jimmy so he can practice holding and feeding a newborn and changing a diaper. He needs extra instruction on gentleness but soon gets the basic idea that newborns are fragile.

We've been told also that a baby doll would serve as a surrogate for any aggression our toddler might feel toward the intruding sibling. That advice proves wise. One week after Kent's birth, James bundles Baby Kent into his carriage and invites Big Brother Jimmy to take his baby for a ride in his little carriage as well. It is an adorable sight—father and son strolling side by side through the student housing complex, each in charge of his baby. As they approach a bluff near our apartment, Jimmy gives his carriage a heave-ho that sends it careening out of control into the street below, baby and all. The look of satisfaction on his face is unmistakable. Real Baby Kent is too young to be fazed, but it occurs to me then that I have a sizable job cut out for me if I want to foster a healthy sibling relationship.

Six weeks after Kent's birth, we move to California to begin James's military service at Castle Air Force Base. We rent a small ranch house in a modest residential neighborhood in nearby Atwater. Jimmy seems happy to have his own room. He settles in with his books, stuffed animals, and a stash of worn cloth diapers that I'd dubbed "raggies." When he was an infant, I placed clean diapers under his face to absorb excess saliva that escaped his mouth when he was sleeping, and he became attached to them. Pacifiers were of no use to him, as he could not suck to release tension, but he clutched the raggies against his face as a bedtime comforter. I never fail at Jimmy's bedtime and nap times to play an LP of *Sesame Street* songs on the portable record player in his room. While many parents are playing Mozart at their child's bedtime, believing that classical music is good for the brain, I rely on Big Bird and Kermit the Frog because they are consistently effective in lulling Jimmy to sleep. Once asleep, Jimmy is lost to the world.

Most of the time I'm grateful Jimmy is a sound sleeper, but we've learned to keep an ear out because he is prone to sleepwalking. While we're grateful that he can rouse himself when he needs to go to the bathroom during the night, he does not always find the toilet. Once, he opened and urinated into a dresser drawer. On another occasion, I heard a strange sound in the kitchen. I investigated and found Jimmy urinating into the refrigerator's vegetable bin. These incidents amuse us. They also serve as antidotes to hassles related to Jimmy's cleft and as fodder for lighthearted stories to share with family and other parents with similar tales.

He shows enthusiasm for preschool when he learns that there will be other children there to play with. My only challenge is to convince him to become fully toilet trained, a discipline he has resisted.

Once he hears that the preschool doesn't accept children who are not potty trained, he gets with the program. I'm learning that this is a boy who will do things in his own time and when it matters to him, thank you very much, and I realize that there will be parenting challenges related to his personality as well as to cleft concerns.

In his play, Jimmy is intense. He spends long spells building block and Lego structures or creating flamboyant paintings on a large easel. He rides his tricycle at high speed. I take note and am pleased to see qualities emerging that show evidence of his zest for life and that for most of the time, he is occupied with the usual activities of all children his age.

Kent imprints on Jimmy, who, for the most part, tolerates Kent's tagging along. He quickly learns the cost of toppling one of Jimmy's carefully constructed towers of blocks or adding a scribble to a drawing left unattended on the easel. In time Kent learns to navigate the playroom with more caution.

Within weeks, we make the most of James's time off and venture into the San Joaquin Valley and the foothills of the Sierras. At every turn, it feels as though we've been transported to a Western movie set. Before long, we refurbish a secondhand mini camper van so we can explore as much of the West Coast as possible. Kent takes to his post in the porta-crib we wedge on top of the bench between the refrigerator and rear window. At five months he babbles at us from his crib, and later, when he can pull himself up, he stands at the rail and holds court as our family arranges and rearranges the dining and sleeping spaces in our tiny on-the-road habitat. At campsites, we position the camper van so that when Kent pops up from his nap, he can see us outside. With a come-hither smile, he bobs in place until we come get him.

His three-year-old brother, on the other hand, routinely sends us into panics on camping trips. No sooner do we arrive at a campsite than he bursts from the car and heads off at a run for an adventure of his own making. Once, we hear his voice overhead and look up to find him waving at us from a ledge thirty feet above us. Another time he disappears and we finally spy him running in reckless abandon along the summit of a giant mud mound in Death Valley. We are scared witless when, at age four, Jimmy runs off in the dark from a campsite at Morro Bay. There is a waterfront with an abrupt drop-off nearby and we are terrified that he might fall into the deep water. He doesn't, but we endure a nerve-racking half hour before finding him. He doesn't admit he couldn't find his way back to our campsite. This penchant for taking off on his own is a harbinger of things to come.

During our twenty months in California, we make our way through Yosemite and Death Valley National Parks, the Sierras, the Sonoran Desert, inland and up and down the coastlines of California, Oregon, and Washington, falling in love with the immense expanses of forest, the rocky bluffs and endless beaches, the high desert, the mountains that offer snow sports, the innumerable state and national parks, and the variety of interesting cities for culture and entertainment. We don't realize at the time that the West Coast will later draw us back.

While there is a vacation quality to our daily lives in California, the need for medical attention for Jimmy's cleft issues continues. The closest reputable cleft palate clinic is at Stanford University's Children's Hospital in Palo Alto, a good three hours from Atwater. The team there does a thorough evaluation of Jimmy's lip and palate and schedules surgery to revise the larger lip scar and pull soft tissue to the back of his palate to help with speech. We agree on the surgery, but I balk at the recommended orthodontia. Won't Jimmy be going through a tough enough time with the surgery and its aftermath without months of braces on teeth that will eventually be removed? As for my part, I cannot picture braces on my often resistant four-year-old or the long drive to the orthodontist in Sacramento whenever something goes amiss. I prevail upon James to inquire, and we learn that orthodontia, though desirable from the surgeon's point of view, can wait without negative consequences. I'm grateful to be relieved of managing orthodontia in addition to everything else.

I keep busy enough with appointments at Stanford requiring multiple trips with Jimmy for presurgical planning and for the operation itself. And then there are follow-up visits for suture removal involving unpleasant prodding and poking, which Jimmy endures. To make matters worse, Jimmy takes a fall just days after the sutures are removed from his lip. The football helmet he wears to protect his lip fails to prevent a rupture of the suture line. To his horror and mine, his lip splits open. Distraught, I rush him to James's office and emergency repair is scheduled within hours by a general surgeon at Castle Air Force Base. The surgeon does the best he can on healing tissue that is still swollen. At the follow-up evaluation at Stanford, the doctors shake their heads and tell us the emergency surgery on compromised lip tissue will result in a much more pronounced scar, an unfortunate development. This setback leaves me despondent for weeks.

Added to my concerns about Jimmy's distress from surgeries and their aftermath are worries about Kent. My trips with Jimmy to appointments with Stanford Children's Hospital's surgical team and a Sacramento orthodontist consume hours, days, and sometimes a week at a time, during which I leave Kent with caregivers. Though I believe he is too young to be left so often and for so long with others, there is no way around it. It is a price a sibling in his situation has to pay. I try to compensate by giving him ample attention when I am at home. As an adult, Kent will express surprise and sadness that I have spent so much time for so many years worrying about whether he got enough space in our family or attention to his needs. He assures me it was not a worry for him.

Once James's military obligations are fulfilled in 1975, we land back in Rochester, New York, where James will undertake a two-year fellowship in nephrology at Strong Memorial Hospital. Back we go into the medical training drill—long, tiring hours for James with precious little time for leisure or family. We settle into our first purchased home, in a neighborhood near the hospital that is populated mostly by families with a parent in medical training at Strong Memorial. Much of our at-home life is normal family business. I tend to the usual tasks of homemaking and the needs of my two young children, repaint a few walls, make curtains, take Stretch & Sew lessons, and join a neighborhood cooking group. I make a point of baking fresh bread once a week and plant a patch of vegetables and marigolds in the backyard.

Jimmy's medical needs at this point are minimal compared to previous years and do not disrupt school or home life. He has braces applied to hold insecure teeth and maxilla in place. A small barrier is placed behind his lower front teeth to reach up and behind his upper front teeth and prevent them from receding. He tolerates all this and gets on with being a little boy who enjoys the backyard swing set, Legos, and boisterous birthday parties. We find families in the neighborhood with whom we were friends in James's residency years. James and I find time for tennis, bridge, and occasional dinners out with friends, and I hope the boys will find compatible playmates.

Racing Snails

I am four-ish
or three.
The sky is blue,
the day is warm.

I go outside
alone
to race the snails
across the walk,

leaving the new
baby
and my mother
inside. I'm big

enough to wait
for kids
to run after
the ice cream truck.

I am hopeful,
only
just aware of
differentness,

and that somehow
I am
not like the kids
all around me

and their staring
questions.
They all see it.
Mom will fix it.

Soon we hear it
and run
after ice cream
all together.

PEER PRESSURES

In Rochester, Jimmy and Kent reconnect with children who have already gotten used to Jimmy's lip looking different from theirs. In making friends with new peers, however, Jimmy is not spared reactions to his scarred lip. I witnessed an incident with another child soon after we moved into our new house. Jimmy eyed the group of children playing in the yard across the street. Amanda, a confident, blond, blue-eyed seven-year-old, commanded a small gaggle of boys, all younger than she by a couple of years or more. She was directing them to and fro as they chased a ball in some sort of improvised game.

"Why don't you join them?" I asked.

It took Jimmy some time to decide to venture into their midst.

I watched as he edged down the driveway and crossed the street on his Big Wheel tricycle. As he entered the driveway of the house where the children were playing, Amanda separated from the group and approached Jimmy. She planted herself squarely in front of him with arms crossed over her chest. He stopped and sat inert on his Big Wheel facing her. The other children broke off from their play and gathered behind her. I could not hear what Amanda said to Jimmy, but her words seemed to strike him like daggers. The other children stared. Jimmy dropped his head, slowly picked up his Big Wheel, and turned it back toward our house. He pedaled with effort, shoulders drooping, his face puckered against tears. Amanda and her troop maintained their disapproving stance until Jimmy was well across the street.

I suppressed an urge to take Amanda by the ear and march her right to her mother for a scolding. But the expression on Jimmy's face as he came into the house struck a deeper chord. He did not speak, and tears streaked his cheeks. I gathered him up and held him close on my lap for a long while. He slumped against me and allowed me to press the gentlest of kisses now and then on the top of his head. Together we absorbed the blows from Amanda's rejection. This assault left bruises on both of us. In my head I was formulating a calm but stern conversation with Amanda's mother. But what if Amanda's mother was one of those peacock moms who believed her child could do no wrong? Even so, it would be worth a try.

After a long, quiet time like this, I finally found words for my child. "It's hard when people are mean, isn't it?"

A slight nod of the head and a sniffle. "It's my lip."

"It's not fair, but it happens."

Silence.

"Is there anything you think we can do about it?" I was making room for him to tell me what would make things better. Jimmy's answer came slowly, almost a whisper.

"I could tell Amanda's mom. Maybe she would help."

"Hmm . . ." I shuddered with apprehension, thinking about those peacock moms. Jimmy could be singed further.

"She's a nice lady. She smiles at me a lot."

I hugged him. *Why not?* I thought. If he wanted to tackle the situation, let him do it. The next time he saw Amanda's mother in the yard, he headed across the street. I watched as he got her attention. She stopped raking. I held my breath. Her face gradually dropped the smile as she leaned in to listen. For some time, they talked back and forth, locked in conversation. Finally, she nodded, straightened, put a gentle hand on Jimmy's shoulder, and said a few more words. Jimmy nodded in reply, turned, and strode back to our house with an unmistakable air of success.

He entered the house with a smile. "I was right. She's nice. She said Amanda wouldn't be mean anymore and that I can come play anytime."

"Good for you, Jimmy," I said. "You were very brave to talk to Amanda's mom." He nodded emphatically. *It's a beginning,* I thought. *He's got to find ways on his own to face the unkindness that lurks out there. And I have to let him take matters into his own hands as much as he can.*

Furthermore, Jimmy had touched Amanda's mother in ways I could not have, so that she became his ally. From then on, Amanda did not spurn Jimmy when he ventured across the street to play. Would that all mothers were like hers. And that all children were amenable to correcting their hurtful behaviors.

After weathering encounters with new children, Jimmy finds a groove in kindergarten and first grade at Public School 49. An insightful teacher allows him to go to the art room if he finishes his math work first. There he mingles with fourth-graders, a huge boost to his ego, and creates myriad clay sculptures and other artwork. He wises up a little, too, after a classmate cons him out of his new set of crayons. Like other mothers, I remain alert to signs of difficulty at school, but as far as I know, Jimmy's cleft lip is not a cause for unhappiness with classmates. But I remain vigilant, always vigilant.

Finally, in 1977, James's medical training complete, we follow our dream to seek our future on the West Coast—in Eugene,

Oregon, to be exact. The area's sophisticated medical facilities and the practice offering James a position fit his criteria to a T. I'm confident that the University of Oregon can offer me ample opportunity for graduate studies, a goal I deferred when I got married. The promise of a wholesome family life, good schools, and recreational adventures in the nearby Cascade Mountains and on the coast of Oregon seem too good to be true. We shed many possessions in a yard sale, pack the rest in a twenty-foot U-Haul truck, and head west in tandem—I, driving our station wagon, and James, the truck. We find a fixer-upper in an area with highly recommended schools and Jimmy enters second grade. I'm hoping he will have a smooth transition to this school and a new group of kids, but I'm not naïve about the difficulties his appearance may cause him in a school where he knows no one.

Meanwhile, James and I have trouble trying to establish a working relationship with and among the various professionals we find to manage Jimmy's ongoing cleft needs. We hope the orthodontist, dentist, and speech therapist will involve us and coordinate their treatment plans with one another to optimize results and minimize hassles. But we find they are not particularly interested in communicating with one another. James and I do our best to cobble together appropriate care, even inviting the professionals involved to lunch to discuss treatment, but that does not happen. Our prodding may have resulted in a conversation or two, but for the most part Jimmy's care is fragmented. So, we navigate a whole new set of professionals once again, apprehensive about how we are being received.

And, as we feared, Jimmy has other troubles soon after he starts the school year. The teasing and name-calling begin almost immediately, and he quickly loses his enthusiasm for school. Recess is loosely monitored and Jimmy reports a worrisome number of rough encounters with classmates and scuffles with kids who make fun of him. One day, he hides in the bushes rather than go to school. The day before, he'd shoved a boy who was teasing him, and the boy's older brother roughed Jimmy up.

I grow increasingly alarmed the day Jimmy arrives home after school in a sour mood and throws a cookie in my face when I ask him how his day has gone. I send him upstairs to his room with instructions to cool off. Shortly afterward, I hear thumping on the side of the house. I rush upstairs to find Jimmy's door barricaded. I force open the door and find him hanging by his fingers from the windowsill, struggling to clamber back into his room. I pull him in, and he crumples in my arms. He planned to escape out the window.

"I just want to run away," he says. I hold him tight until he stops crying. He doesn't have to tell me he believes no one understands his troubles. I feel I, too, am making life hard for him and I feel at a loss to makes things better. I mention to one of Jimmy's doctors my concern about emotional problems from teasing. I tell him about the day Jimmy wanted to run away.

"Kids do things like this to get attention. I'm not sure you need to be so anxious about it. Let's give it another six months and see if things get better." I know he's right about my being hyper-anxious and is trying to allay my worries. And I also know I am not willing to wait six months in hopes that "things" magically get better.

"I don't think so," I say barely above a whisper. "I want to talk to a counselor." My words stumble out. "I want a counselor for Jimmy as soon as possible, someone who can help him deal with the emotional stress he feels from name-calling and teasing." The doctor senses my determination.

"Okay. Jimmy's pediatrician can help you with that."

I insist to Jimmy's pediatrician that I want a referral to a good counselor. Two days later, his assistant calls with a couple of names, and within a week, James and I have an appointment with Dr.

Manny Lotito, the head of counseling for the school district. He listens with kind, focused eyes as I unload my worries about Jimmy's problems at school.

"I just feel so bad that I can't seem to help him," I blurt out. "It's not his fault and he's paying such a heavy price. It's all so unfair."

"Ah, the guilt doesn't help, does it?" Manny is tapping on a tender spot, and I wince. I shake my head and lower my gaze, feeling the weight of years of self-recrimination. James touches my hand. "It's understandable," Manny continues, "but you need to get a handle on it. I'll meet with Jimmy, do some evaluations, and then meet with you folks in a few weeks. In the meantime, Barbara, find a counselor for yourself."

Manny's evaluation of Jimmy reveals that Jimmy believes others see him primarily as someone with a scarred lip and a speech impediment. When schoolmates shy away, exclude him, tease, and bully, what else could he think? Manny gives us ideas for bolstering Jimmy's self-image. Jimmy and I both get some counseling and James and I work at home to shore up Jimmy's confidence in himself.

We agree with Jimmy's second-grade teacher that transferring Jimmy for third grade is a good idea. The school she recommends is an alternative school with mixed grade levels and less structure. The teacher thinks this school would be more academically suited to Jimmy's needs and temperament.

"He'll do better with more independence and more challenge," she says.

James and I are thankful for a teacher who has gone out of her way to advise us about a more appropriate school setting for Jimmy. We hope to see a return of the enthusiasm he showed for school in Rochester. We hope that a change of schools for third grade will also give him a new start with a new set of kids, getting him away from the teasing and bullying that has plagued his second-grade year.

Memory Study 1

You look stupid . . . Hare-lip! Hare-lipped dumbass!

Quickly you learn there aren't that many teasing words,
but each one, each time, leaves a little mark, a little memory.

Year to year, only a few kids ever do the teasing,
and a few more just watch and all the rest just look away.

What? You sound stupid . . . No one can understand you.

Even the sound of my own voice in my own head flows thick.
I try to avoid talking, try to avoid being present,

try to avoid anything causing me to be noticed because then
the cleft will be noticed, and then I'll be the center of attention.

(The exclusion . . . The pattern of exclusion.)

Children ruthlessly choose those most like them,
leaving out others for the slightest detail of difference.

Any common mistake—a missed kickball kick, a stammer in class—
is connected to the cleft so I'm easier to pick out next time.

You look retarded . . . Retard! . . . Stop looking at me!

I imagine something deeper within me must also be different.
Though I sense no one is actually normal, I don't yet
    really believe it,

and I can't stop sulking on the words of these others.
The possibilities in the words are as real as the heat of the sun.

(The targeting . . . despite trying to be unseen.)

I see other kids' details—their faces, clothes, darker skin—
    cause them
greater torment than mine, yet the weight that is mine has my
    full attention.

What happened to your face? . . . You look stupid. Stop looking at me!

I learn to be unlooked at, unseen, unheard—to be, but without
    presence.
I learn to accept this separation as just living. Easier on every-
    one this way.

To a Child's Stubbornness

You are too necessary
for us to be mad for long,

despite your blindness
to our clear experience,

despite your deafness
to our clear warnings,

despite your caterwauls
to our clear insistence.

Your timing always sucks,
yet we love how you reveal

a child's unfolding character.
You are the first wall at their back,

their first thought of resistance.
You help them discover

where they can draw a line
and make a first stand.

You are what digs in
for as long as it takes

any child's perception
to become understanding.

STANDING FIRM

Until a few minutes ago, the morning was shaping up like other routine school days. James departed early for the hospital and Jimmy, now in third grade, and Kent, a kindergartner, have stumbled into the kitchen and are perched on stools at the kitchen counter munching in silence on Pop-Tarts.

"Got your homework?" I ask Jimmy. He says nothing.

At 7:30 I cue the boys. Usually, they head off to brush teeth and hair and get their shoes and jackets on, but this morning Jimmy lags.

"Time to get a move on, Jimmy."

"I'm not going to school."

I snap to attention. In the past, Jimmy's refusals to go to school have come on the heels of incidents of bullying or teasing about his distorted lip. So now, as a reflex, my cleft-concerns alarm sounds and I brace myself for news that once again Jimmy has been harassed at school. Has there been another put-down at recess? I prepare for the worst.

Hold on! I catch myself. *Not so fast! He's said nothing about being teased.* I'm prone to jumping into a rescue response without thinking things through. The accumulation of cleft hassles with other kids has conditioned me to react this way. It's the mother bear in me who, unable to prevent harm, wants to settle the score. I must fight the rush of emotion—the hurt and anger—that rises whenever I get an inkling Jimmy has been bullied. *This situation is about Jimmy's distress, not yours*, I tell myself. I shove my inner turmoil under wraps and refocus on what I'm hearing.

"What do you mean, you're not going to school?"

"I can't go. She'll nail me."

"What on earth are you talking about?"

"My book project isn't done, and the teacher will nail me. I can't go."

"Don't be silly. Your teacher may not be happy, but she won't be unkind."

"Yes, she will. You don't know her. I'm not going."

To be honest, it's a relief that Jimmy's troubles are caused by a scary teacher rather than teasing. If the problem were playground avoidance, I'd be operating from the soft spot in my heart that caters to Jimmy's hurt feelings and my own. I'd be telling myself that of course Jimmy could stay home. Of course he deserves a break and extra TLC, given he has more to deal with than most kids. I'd want him to know his feelings matter.

But hassles with a teacher? His distress is genuine and I want to take it seriously, but allowing him to stay home from school? He'll have to face her eventually and weather her disapproval for incomplete homework. Better sooner than later. Besides, who's to say he won't make the same plea tomorrow? Isn't this the kind of situation where any parent needs to tell her kid to buck up? Doesn't he need to be able to weather tough teachers? If I help him protect himself from her, won't I be signaling that I don't think him capable of surviving her disapproval?

This has to be a tough-love day. I have to stand firm. No catering to Jimmy's fears or dread. To bolster my decision, I recall the advice of parenting gurus who insist that when children refuse to go to school, a parent must get them there no matter what or how. Alert the teachers, and if necessary, take the child in pajamas, kicking and screaming, but get him there. Get him back on that horse that threw him off. Let him learn he can weather it.

I don't want Jimmy to feel humiliated, though. Maybe we can negotiate a way out of the fix he's in that will allow him to save face.

"I can see you're upset, Jimmy, but you have to go to school. I'll write a note asking for more time. We can work this out. This is not the end of the world."

Jimmy stomps out of the kitchen. I am getting nowhere.

"I'm taking Kent to kindergarten. We'll talk about this when I get back," I call down the stairs. "And you *do* have to go to school today, young man."

During the drive to kindergarten and back, I think harder on why Jimmy is so insistent on avoiding his teacher today. I remind myself that Jimmy's resistance to adults is not new. Dr. Hess mentioned signs of his defensiveness when he examined him as a two-month-old.

"Look how he arches his back and screams when I touch him," he said. "I'd say he came into this world with an oppositional temperament. Take my advice. Don't expect this child to respond well to authoritarian parenting and don't ask him questions that give him a choice of a yes or no answer unless you want to hear no. Try to avoid toe-to-toe confrontations. He'll take you on! Best to give him choices you *and* he can live with."

I believe, also, that Jimmy's defensiveness is more than temperament. He appears to resort to resistance as a means of self-protection, a fight-or-flight response to avoid experiences where adults in authority exercise power over him. From infancy, he has been coerced into situations that have caused discomfort or pain. The multiple nonnegotiable surgeries, wound tending, manipulations of the prosthesis, and installations of mouth appliances must have made him wary of adults exercising control over him. And now, large-and-in-charge adults in more benign situations often trigger his resistance. It seems that both hardwiring and harsh treatment have conspired to shape Jimmy into a first-class resister.

Has Jimmy's teacher presented him with a do-it-my-way-or-else ultimatum that activated his resistance? Somehow, his extreme dread must be overcome. How else other than to face the music and see it through?

I return home and find Jimmy sitting squarely on the family room sofa, arms crossed tightly across his chest. He greets me with a scowl.

"C'mon, Jimmy. It may not be as bad as you think. You've got to go to school."

"I'm not going."

I falter. The toughness I'd hoped I could muster was a myth. I need help with this.

"I guess I'll have to call your teacher and see what she suggests."

Silence.

I call the teacher, hoping she will be eager to relieve Jimmy of his fears. I explain to her that he is balking at coming to school because he's worried that she will be angry with him for not completing his book project.

"Just get him here. I'll handle it from there." I cringe at the word "handle." That could spell disaster. So could the he-needs-to-toe-the-line tone of voice Dr. Hess would have warned her against in dealing with Jimmy. But she sounds so sure of herself, and she *is* the teacher. I acquiesce.

I hang up the phone, take a deep breath, and approach Jimmy, who is curled into a knot of resistance. I plant my feet and square off with him.

"Jimmy, I've spoken to your teacher. She wants you to come to school." He glowers at the floor. "Jimmy," I try for a soft tone, "it's not okay to stay away from school. I'll drive you if that helps. Let's get in the car." He shakes his head and glowers.

"I don't care what you say. I'm not going."

Why can't he just do as I say for once? I've exhausted my repertoire of considerate approaches. In a last-ditch effort I resort to my imperative I've-had-it voice, knowing this exposes my inability to find a more dignified solution.

"Jimmy, if you don't go willingly, I'll have to help you. You *are* going to school."

He does not stir.

"Okay, then." I get my car keys and return. I take Jimmy by the arm and pull him from the couch. "I really hate to do this, but you give me no choice." I hear the mixture of anger and desperation in my voice. I set my jaw and forcefully escort Jimmy toward the car. He resists, making every effort to hold back. I'm at my wits' end and at the same time, appalled that I'm using physical coercion on my child.

"Please, Mom, don't make me go." I maintain my resolve to get him to school as directed even though the panic in his voice jars me. As I try to maneuver him into the back seat, Jimmy wrests away from me. He scrambles away just far enough to escape my grasp and turns back to face me. His face is red, and he is sobbing.

"I thought you'd be on my side, Mom. Why aren't you on my side?" With that he turns and runs away from me into the backyard. I collapse against the car. My mind flips. *What the hell am I doing? My son is resisting something he dreads, and I side with the person he's afraid of?* I stare at the space between the trees where Jimmy has disappeared. Now he dreads me as much as the teacher. I can't bear the thought of his running blindly through backyards, convinced his reason for avoiding the teacher does not matter to me. I feel like an abject failure.

Where has Jimmy gone? Will he come home? Will he ever trust me again? Since I seem to be intent on throwing him to the wolves, better to get as far away from me as he can. I feel worse than useless.

Pull yourself together, for God's sake! Somewhere inside, the mother bear in me roars, this time at me. *Come to your senses! Do something. Your kid needs some help here!* I snap to. Somehow, the teacher poses a threat to my child. I march back inside and call the school. I demand to speak to Jimmy's teacher again.

I tell her Jimmy will not be coming to school today, that he remains very worried about how she'll react to his incomplete assignment. When I say I want to meet with her to discuss Jimmy's refusal to come to school, she suggests that he is making a mountain out of a molehill, or perhaps even manipulating me.

"Could be," I say, "but he's the kid here and we're the adults. We need to figure out why he's afraid to come to school today."

She objects. I insist.

"I'll be there after school today."

Shortly after the phone call, I spy Jimmy on the back deck. I open the door.

"Want a snack?" I ask.

He nods and comes inside. We say nothing as I cut up an apple.

"You don't have to go to school until tomorrow, Jimmy. I'm going to talk to your teacher later today and ask her to figure out a way for her class to be easier for you." He nods as he chews a slice of apple.

"I'm sorry I was tough on you this morning. I thought if I could just get you to school, you'd see that your teacher is not so scary. But there seems to be more to your problem with her than I understand." I pause, hoping he'll enlighten me. But he looks away. *How the heck am I supposed to help if he doesn't tell me what's going on?* He seems to be telling me, though, that he doesn't trust me to see it his way, like so many times in his life when he's protested going to doctors and orthodontists he dreads, and I've made him go anyway. It makes me sick to think he sees me as siding with them against him, but I understand why he does. All I can do at this point is restate my willingness to be helpful.

"I'm ready to hear more about what's upsetting you, sweetheart, whenever you're willing to tell me."

Silence.

"Well, I'll talk with your teacher. And one thing you can count on for sure: I'll be on your side now." Still, he is not forthcoming, leaving me in the dark to tackle the problem.

I'm in the teacher's classroom at the closing bell. We discuss the book project. She dodges the topic of Jimmy's distress. She makes it clear that a deadline is a deadline and Jimmy needs to get the book project done on time or expect a failing grade for the project. Then she tries to bring *me* into line.

"He'll certainly feel left out when he doesn't have a book to display at the authors' party on Friday. Do you really want that?" I feel scolded, as though I bear some responsibility for the incomplete book project. She seems totally unwilling to take a look at her part in why Jimmy isn't comfortable in her classroom.

"Don't you think he'll feel bad about failing the book project?" she asks pointedly.

"I'm not so sure he'll feel it as a failure," I say. *He seems more invested in not cooperating with you,* I say to myself. I rise to my full height.

"It won't be the end of the world," I say with calm authority. "It's not the worst thing to experience an F at his age. It's elementary school, for God's sake. I'm sure he'll draw a valuable lesson from all this." And I'm not bluffing. The higher ground in this situation is clear to me.

The teacher shrugs as if to say she thinks I'm way off base.

I attend the authors' party on Friday and make a point of admiring out loud the student books on display, watching Jimmy out of the corner of my eye as he stands in the background with a sober expression. The teacher ignores both of us.

As promised, she gives Jimmy a failing grade for the book project. I have no idea what he takes away from standing firm against his teacher's ultimatum, the F, or missing out on displaying his work at the authors' party. He says nothing about it, and I don't ask. I know he could have written a story—he likes to write—and I can't imagine he would balk at crafting a book cover. I do know not to poke at him about it. I also know I'm feeling fine with the stand we both have taken. Once the episode is behind us, life continues for Jimmy as before with no further upsets involving the teacher. I don't know how much Jimmy stews about the incident afterward, but I smolder way too long about it, imagining well-turned statements of righteous indignation I could have expressed to the teacher.

Right after the book report incident, I also make a mental note that in refusing to complete the book project, Jimmy seemed to be refusing to be intimidated by someone backing him into a corner. This will not be the last time Jimmy will stand up to strong-willed adults in positions of authority, including me. In most cases, I will not be certain if he is simply manifesting the stubbornness and strong will characteristic of his temperament, testing his inner strength, or if a deeper, unarticulated principle motivates the stands he takes. It does seem though that in each instance, as with the book project standoff, he will emerge no worse for wear, often stronger and more confident in himself. Besides, I reassure myself, standing up for himself against heavy-handed authority figures will serve him well in medical settings where he will want to be on equal footing in making decisions about his treatment. I was happy to learn many years later that Kent did not recall my consternation with Jimmy's resistance to teachers, either in elementary school or later. As for the teacher whom Jimmy thought would nail him in third grade for an incomplete assignment, Kent assured me she was that way with all students.

The episode with Jimmy's teacher was good for me, too. I come away from my meeting with her feeling surprisingly more sure of myself. I resisted her with a defiance that liberated me, defiance in line with Jimmy's. In taking Jimmy's side and refusing to be intimidated by the F the teacher brandished, I wagged my finger at what felt like an abuse of power. In challenging her authority, I claimed my own. It felt invigorating to fire up just as much over a homework concern as when Jimmy's cleft has been the issue. Any student in that teacher's class might have drawn the same disapproval. The incident reassures me that cleft problems do not dominate Jimmy's life, that most of the time he is dealing with the same challenges and frustrations, frictions and upsets, successes, and failures as any child his age.

The incident also awakens in me a keen awareness of my own ability to take a firm stand and rise to action on behalf of my child. My challenge now will be to choose judiciously when to intervene and when to stand back. I expect my boys to tolerate tough demands from adults in authority who are guiding their education, skill development and teamwork in sports, and medical care. I want them to accept and adhere to standards and behaviors that foster character and encourage them to grow into caring and responsible family and community members. I believe they benefit when they wrestle on their own, regardless of their idiosyncratic personal challenges, with uncomfortable demands from fair-minded, respectful adults. In those situations, I am comfortable stepping back. But when a child of mine shows undue distress from treatment by adults in positions of authority at school or in medical settings (or in the neighborhood for that matter) I will be more willing to step in and stand up for my child. I may have come on too strong with Jimmy's teacher, but the boost to my ego in seeing that I could and would take a stand against her on his behalf was exhilarating. Both the intensity of Jimmy's distress at my initial failure to validate his dread of school that day and my realization that in his eyes I'd colluded against him with the teacher he feared have been wake-up calls. Following that episode, I have strengthened my resolve to let my boys know I have their backs. Most of all, I have resolved to avoid any response on my part that smacks of abandonment when either of them manifests distress related to the behavior of authority figures in their lives.

SEE ME AS I WILL

We've just made it through the book project episode when Dorothy Cruickshank, the school counselor at Jimmy's elementary school, calls. An outraged and tearful Jimmy has landed in her office during morning recess. This time it *is* teasing. Jimmy's been done in by name-calling on the playground. The culprit is Freddie, another third-grade boy, who for some time has made a point of taunting Jimmy about his face.

"Is he okay now?" I ask.

"I think so," Dorothy says. "We had a talk. I know he'd like me to punish Freddie. I told him I could do that, but punishing Freddie might just incite him to get even with Jimmy for telling on him. I tried to convince Jimmy there's a cleverer way to handle the name-calling. May I tell you what I'm thinking?"

"I'm all ears," I say.

"I want to work with Jimmy using a book called *Thinking, Changing, Rearranging* by Jill Anderson. It's a kids' book about how to rethink negative thoughts and assumptions that lead to feeling bad about yourself or others."

The book is based on the principles of rational-emotive therapy. The approach would teach Jimmy to interrupt the unexamined thoughts that are triggering victim thinking and emotional upset in reaction to taunting remarks. What if he could duck the insults and reroute his self-defeating thoughts into self-empowering messages? It might make a world of difference in his self-confidence.

"I'd like to do some exercises with Jimmy to help him neutralize the name-calling," Dorothy says. "I believe I can help him think twice before he lets it get to him. And maybe even turn the tables on the teasing. How does that sound to you?"

"I'm all for it," I say. "Since we can't seem to stop the teasing, I'd give anything to help him hold up better to it."

"Okay!" Dorothy's enthusiasm is palpable. "Pick up a copy of the book so you can see what I'm up to."

I buy a copy of *Thinking, Changing, Rearranging*. The concepts are presented in language a kid Jimmy's age can understand, but how in the world, after so many hurtful encounters, can my third-grader find the inner strength to face, let alone turn the tables on, the playground bullies and the demoralizing effect of their derisive remarks?

Several days later, Dorothy calls to report. "I can't wait to tell you what we've been doing," she says. Then she describes their conversation. She asked Jimmy why he thought Freddie might be inclined to call him names.

"As far as Jimmy's concerned," Dorothy says, "Freddie's just plain mean and makes fun of his face to make him cry or go away. If Jimmy's going to handle Freddie's teasing better, he has to think differently about Freddie and about options for responding differently to name-calling."

Dorothy continues. "I suggested that maybe Freddie bullies other kids because he wants them to think he's clever and powerful.

Maybe he's learned that behavior from someone who bullies him. I let Jimmy know that I hope Freddie wises up, because he might be an interesting kid if he wasn't busy teasing. Jimmy wasn't sure about that, but he did seem interested in figuring out what he can do so Freddie doesn't get his kicks out of teasing him." She even intimated that Freddie might begin to see that teasing isn't a good way to impress other kids.

She talked to Jimmy about his part in discouraging Freddie. She made it clear that Jimmy has to give up on wanting Freddie punished and focus instead on learning how not to let Freddie get to him. *He* has to make the decision to let Freddie's hurtful words roll off his back. Then she asked Jimmy to think of some responses to Freddie's name-calling that might turn things around. After playing with several phrases, Jimmy settled on one.

The next time Freddie called him a name, Jimmy shot back, "Hey, Freddie! Do you want to keep on calling me names or do you want to play something?" As Dorothy tells it, Freddie didn't know what to make of Jimmy's reaction. The next day, he approached Jimmy and asked him what he wanted to play.

Dorothy staged another intervention. She arranged for a playground monitor who was suffering from an angry poison oak rash on her forearm to be her co-conspirator. Then Dorothy invited Jimmy to take a walk during recess. She describes the scene to me.

"As we approached the playground monitor, I grimaced and said in a loud voice, 'Oh my gosh! Look at her arm! It sure is ugly, isn't it?'"

Dorothy relates how she screwed her face into an expression of disgust. By her account, Jimmy backed away, surprised at her remarks. But she continued, commenting that the rash sure looked painful. She asked Jimmy what he thought caused the rash, if maybe the lady had burned herself, or was born with it. As she expected, Jimmy did not want to continue the conversation.

"I suggested we ask the monitor what happened to her, but Jimmy shook his head vehemently. I asked him why not?" Dorothy tells me. "I told him I really wanted to know, but Jimmy objected. In a hushed voice, he said he thought asking about her arm would hurt the lady's feelings."

"But I persisted," Dorothy says. "I headed straight over to the monitor. Jimmy stayed rooted to the spot. He looked dismayed as I questioned the monitor, staring and pointing at her arm. After a few minutes, I returned to Jimmy and reported matter-of-factly that the lady had an especially bad reaction to poison oak and that the rash itched like crazy but would heal in time.

"When I asked him if he thought I'd hurt her feelings, he nodded and looked extremely disappointed in me, as though he'd lost his best friend."

I'm thinking, *Of course he did! A blatant display from his trusted counselor of the very behavior that demoralizes him!*

"So let me tell you what I did next," Dorothy says, as though she senses my doubt in her wisdom.

"I said I was surprised that he thought I was being unkind. I told him I didn't mean to hurt the lady's feelings, but I'd better check to be sure. Much to Jimmy's horror, I went back over to the monitor and told her in a voice loud enough for Jimmy to hear that gosh, I hoped I hadn't hurt her feelings by asking about her arm. The monitor said, as she'd been coached to do, that oh, no, she just thought I was curious. She said she was glad I asked instead of just gawking at her. I made sure to tell Jimmy I was glad I'd asked the lady about her rash, because now I understood what had happened to her arm. He didn't say much, but I think he got the point."

Later, Dorothy suggested to Jimmy that maybe when people stare at him or ask questions about his face, they might just be curious the same way she was. She wondered aloud if he was feeling up to helping people learn something about cleft lip, rather than just putting up with their stares and nonsense remarks.

I appreciate the effort Dorothy is making to help Jimmy, but is she being realistic? I mull over what's she's suggesting to Jimmy.

"Letting name-calling roll off his back? Helping others? That seems like a lot to expect," I say.

"I think he's getting the idea that he needn't let name-calling derail him," she says, "or assume people always have mean intentions when they look at his lip or make comments. They may have all kinds of thoughts and feelings and questions, and if he avoids them because he assumes the worst, he misses chances to make friends. When someone *does* tease him, he can tell himself that the problem is the name-caller's shortcoming, not his. It would be great if he could rethink his assumptions and see he has choices about how he reacts and how he manages unwanted attention from others."

"Still," I say, "that's a pretty tall order for an eight-year-old."

"Yes, it is," she says, "but he catches on fast and I think he's up to it. The earlier we tackle it, the better."

Jimmy continues to meet with Dorothy throughout third grade. I hear that he and Freddie are playing together more. What a contrast to a short time earlier when Jimmy would do anything to avoid Freddie.

I'm hopeful that Jimmy's teachers can also help with other recess problems—not just name-calling. I get the sense that Jimmy is rarely chosen for dodgeball teams, and instead is being ignored, and overtly excluded. I bring it up with the head teacher. She reminds me that the policy is to let kids work out their issues among themselves at recess. Teachers are not responsible for recess troubles, and the recess monitor hasn't mentioned kids being unkind to Jimmy. She wonders if Jimmy is exaggerating or just needs a thicker skin. So much for help from that quarter. Jimmy will have to fend for himself.

So, I'm surprised to get a call from Josh Reckord, one of Jimmy's teachers. He caught sight of Jimmy on a frantic dash to the restroom during recess. When Jimmy didn't emerge, Josh investigated. He found Jimmy huddled in a stall in tears. He told Josh about some meanness that had transpired on the playground, more than Jimmy could take that day, something he couldn't turn the tables on.

Oh, no, I think. I want to cry myself.

"I want you to know what I've done," Josh tells me. "I enlisted Jason, a popular and responsible sixth-grader, to be Jimmy's secret playground buddy. If he sees kids picking on Jimmy or that other kids aren't playing with him, Jason will do something about it. Does this sound like an okay plan to you?" I can hardly believe my ears. A teacher who will do something to help? I cannot overstate my gratitude.

Two days later, Josh calls to report on a few of Jason's interventions. He's told several kids to lay off when teasing occurs and has invited Jimmy to join the sixth-graders' games when Jimmy's classmates exclude him.

Jason's invitation is the icing on the cake. Without Josh's suggesting it, he invites Jimmy to his birthday party, the only third-grader to be included. Jimmy comes home from the party all smiles. There is a quiet contentment about him that lasts for days. I call Josh to thank him, as I have many times. His subtle, insightful intervention—arranging for a big brother on the playground—transforms Jimmy's recess experience. In the bargain, Jimmy and Jason form a friendship that extends beyond the playground. Thank God for teachers like Josh, whose sensitivity and commitment to their students prompt them to rearrange circumstances that are hurtful to children in their charge. His actions and Jason's are clear demonstrations of how compassion from others can change how you think about yourself. Years later, I will observe Jimmy as a teen counselor at the YMCA, extending the same big-brother compassion to young children left on the fringe.

In fourth grade, the taunting crops up on the ball field. Jimmy comes home early from his first flag football practice. He bursts through the door, red-faced and sullen, and stomps off to his room.

"What happened?" I ask. "Is practice over early?"

"No," he mutters. "I left because a couple of kids started calling me Bulldozer-Face." *Here we go again*, I think.

This is one of those times I cannot let things lie. Without telling Jimmy, I call Len Johansson, the coach, and in frustration relate Jimmy's story.

"He probably won't want to continue," I say. "The teasing really gets to him. It's just so discouraging."

"Let me handle this," Len says. "Have Jimmy come fifteen minutes early to practice tomorrow so I can give him a little pep talk."

Jimmy musters up his courage and goes early to the next practice. I hover in the kitchen, fearing the door will fling open at any moment with a distraught Jimmy, but an hour, then an hour and a half, pass with no sign of him. I breathe more easily with each passing minute. When he comes home, his uniform is smeared with mud. I'm ecstatic.

"How'd it go?" I ask.

"Great!"

"Any name-calling?"

"Nope! Coach told the team that we had to be good teammates to each other and that if he heard of anyone calling a team member names, even during school, they'd have to do laps." The buoyancy in his voice lifts my spirits.

Just right, I say to myself. Out loud, I say, "What a smart coach!"

"Yeah," Jimmy says. "Before practice he told me he'd heard about a couple of the guys calling me names. He said some guys think it makes them tough. He said I shouldn't let it get me down too much."

The next time I see Coach Johansson, I thank him for nipping the name-calling in the bud. Jimmy plays hard that season and seems to thrive in the team environment Coach Johansson cultivates. He does not talk about it, and I wonder if the *Thinking, Changing, Rearranging* strategies are also at play in helping him figure out how to participate so other kids look past his scarred lip and see him as just another kid, more like them than not.

Later that year, I get a clear indication that Jimmy is thinking and rearranging. He and another third-grader have joined a spring soccer team at another school. I expect Jimmy to encounter more unwanted attention from this new batch of kids. When I pick the boys up from the first practice, I brace myself. But, to my relief, Jimmy bounds off the field, full of energy. During the car ride home, I cannot resist probing.

"Well, how was it?" I peer at him in the rearview mirror.

"Great!" Jimmy pops up off the seat. "They asked me about my face, and you know what I said?"

I catch my breath. He doesn't wait for my answer.

"I told them I was in a car accident up the McKenzie and if they thought my face looked bad, they should see my butt!" Jimmy grins.

I suck in my breath. Jimmy's preposterous story triggers in me an impulse to call him on spinning such a tall tale. But the part of me that longs to see Jimmy take control curbs the scolding.

"What a story!" I manage to say.

"Yeah!" Jimmy says. "They thought it was really neat, like I was a hero or something."

"I bet!" I say, shaking my head in disbelief. But I'm grinning, too. He certainly did "change and rearrange" the facts, but he's also learning he can take charge of conversations about his face.

Dorothy Cruickshank will keep tabs on Jimmy throughout elementary school, and when he's a sixth-grader, she comes up with another idea. She wants my permission to ask Jimmy to help her out with some sensitivity training related to disability at a grade school across town. I will remember the bad taste in my mouth at the thought of Jimmy being on display, but I will listen. Dorothy has had good ideas all along where Jimmy is concerned.

The episode will become etched in my mind, and it replays in my head for years to come.

"Usually," Dorothy says, "I call on a friend who was a thalidomide baby and has no arms. He's done remarkably well managing his disability—has a job, even rides a bicycle with special handlebars. And he does a terrific job talking to kids about his experience with disability, not just the physical challenge, but the social challenge, too—you know, the stares and shocked reactions he gets all the time.

"But," she continues, "he's not available for my class next week, so I'd like to ask Jimmy to do the job."

I shudder. "But he's only a kid!" I say. "I can't imagine that he'll feel comfortable standing up in front of a bunch of strange kids, let alone talk about his cleft lip."

"Maybe he won't want to," Dorothy says, "but I think he will if I prepare him. I'll tell him that the expert I normally invite, the man with no arms, is not available, so I'm asking him to be my guest speaker. I'll tell him I've chosen him because he's the best expert on hurt feelings I know. And kids need to hear what he has to say about name-calling."

"Well, when you put it that way . . ."

"It could be very empowering for him," Dorothy adds.

For me, that's the hook. "Okay," I say.

She goes on to tell me that she will impress upon Jimmy that she's asking him to do a very important job, so important that she's arranging for a driver to chauffeur him to and from Washington School, where the class will be held.

Jimmy agrees to be Dorothy's expert on hurt feelings. I wonder if she's asking too much. What if he buckles under uncomfortable questions?

He comes home from school that day, looking as though he'd shrugged a monkey off his back.

"How'd it go?" I ask.

"Okay." Not much to go on, but his expression tells me it was a good day. I sense he wants to hold sweet feelings of victory close to his chest.

Later, Dorothy tells me that the kids at Washington School were rapt with attention when Jimmy explained his birth defect and how it complicates his life. When he related how he feels when called names, other kids volunteered their own stories about taunting remarks about their glasses, stuttering, being shy or overweight.

Jimmy learns he can talk matter-of-factly about his cleft and more openly about the hurtful effect of name-calling. And he discovers he is not alone. He sees that kids with poor eyesight, buckteeth, excess pounds, or speech impediments have the same challenges, and that some kids of color, lower socioeconomic class, or a minority religion have more to deal with than he does. I'm grateful beyond words to Dorothy, Josh, and Len for engineering these confidence-building experiences for Jimmy. They are helping him take control over how others perceive him and how he perceives himself. And they are helping me see what my son is capable of. They rank right up there with Dr. Hess as professionals who go above and beyond to make a positive difference in Jimmy's life and mine.

Even later, Jim, the name he will prefer as a teen, will show deeper understanding of the range of people's sensitivity (or lack of it), and will exercise greater control over how he reacts to others' interest in his lip, whether benign, curious, or caustic. He will accept that on first encounters, others notice his face is different. He will have learned that if he wants distance from attention, he can assume a don't-mess-with-me manner. If he feels like interacting, he can engage in conversation to make others comfortable, sometimes explaining that his scarred lip is due to a birth defect. And then, there will be times when he is simply too tired to deal with it and he will walk away.

When asked later in life, Kent does not remember Jimmy's cleft coming up in their interactions—not as a topic of curiosity or in moments of conflict. He was aware, however, that Jimmy was teased in elementary school and knew that it had something to do with his cleft. On one occasion, he observed some bigger, stronger boys taunting Jimmy. He sensed Jimmy's pent-up emotions and felt sad that he was unable to help. Afterward, Jimmy expressed to Kent his frustration, anger, and feelings of helplessness. Whenever Jimmy came home from school in a down mood, Kent sensed it had something to do with teasing. He thinks that beginning in elementary school Jimmy began to choose his friends carefully—people who were beyond making an issue of his cleft.

Though it will pain me to realize that he needs to be so attentive to how his appearance affects how others first perceive him, I am relieved to know he can take charge of the impression he leaves them with. He will learn to define himself, rather than be defined by a disability label or others' prejudices toward those who are different. His ability to do all this will make me appreciate even more the thinking, changing, rearranging work that Dorothy did with him back in third grade.

DISH TOWEL DILEMMA

This is not the first time I've stalled at the dish towel display at Payless. I finger a towel I've admired before. I'm drawn to the subtle images of eggplants, grapes, tomatoes, and intertwining vines. It's of mediocre quality, probably incapable of holding up to drying more than a half-dozen dinner plates and two or three pots and pans, but the sale price of $1.99 is right, and a pair of them would certainly add some panache to my kitchen. What's the big deal about spending a few dollars on new dish towels? Certainly, I could justify replacing the worn, drab towels whose ten-plus years of service have taken their toll. But then, the familiar arguments for self-denial arise and assert themselves. The old rags, ratty though they are, still do the job. Who needs colorful dish towels, anyway? They are not a necessity and buying them would amount to pampering myself. No one else at home is fussing about the dish towels. It would be an unnecessary expense, an extravagance. I turn away empty-handed.

My dilemma with dish towels has been plaguing me for months. But my problem goes beyond dish towels. Recently, on the spur of the moment, I snapped up a cranberry-colored blouse on sale at the Emporium. My mood had brightened the moment I caught sight of it, and I envisioned wearing it on an evening out with James. It fit perfectly. Why not? I hadn't bought myself a pretty blouse in ages. But almost immediately after hanging the blouse in the closet, the bubble burst. A litany of self-recriminations played over in my mind. Why did I think I should treat myself to a blouse I didn't need? Just knowing it was there in the closet put me in a foul mood. On its third day in my possession, I returned the blouse, even before I confessed its purchase to James. Another close brush with self-indulgence. What gave me the idea I deserved it in the first place? What makes me think I *don't* deserve new dish towels?

I know deep down that the real issue has nothing to do with the purchase of a dish towel or a blouse. It has to do with my wondering if my desire to go to graduate school is self-indulgent. When I married James in 1967, I turned down an acceptance for a graduate program in French and took a teaching job, happy to do so, to support us during his medical school years. It was understood that as soon as it was feasible, I would take my turn at advanced studies. We had chosen Eugene, Oregon, as a place to settle, not only because the offer to join a group of internist-nephrologists was attractive to James, but also because the University of Oregon offered the opportunity for me to advance my education.

Twelve years have passed since I deferred graduate studies. Now, with James established in a medical practice, the time is ripe, but I'm stopped in my tracks by a growing conviction that graduate school would be a selfish pursuit. As I experienced family life, and in particular, a child with unique medical needs, French literature lost its appeal. I turned my sights in a whole new direction—toward child-rearing and family development. Since becoming Jimmy's mother, I've felt strongly that I needed more than instinct to guide my parenting, particularly since his development might be complicated by having a cleft. I wanted more knowledge about child development and psychology and proven strategies for fostering self-confidence and coping skills in young children. What should a parent be aware of when her child's development is frustrated by repeated surgeries, and altered speech and facial features? What exceptional psychological and social challenges would he encounter, and how should a parent address them? Were there adjustments James and I should make in our parenting? How would our family dynamics be impacted?

Through the Community Education Program at the University of Oregon, I take a few courses in child development and parent guidance and begin investigating the master's program in counseling psychology. As I come to grips with the enormous time commitment it would take, graduate education seems more and more out of my reach. I feel increasingly unable to justify taking that kind of time from my parenting responsibilities, particularly where Jimmy is concerned. But the longing persists, and I struggle to reconcile the conflict in my mind. One moment, a voice in my head scolds, *How could you possible justify cheating your children?* A moment later, another chides, *What about you? What about your dreams? You're giving up too easily!* The tug-of-war in my mind does not abate.

Maybe talking to other parents of children with clefts would help. I convince the social worker at the Crippled Children's Services Center in Eugene (now a regional clinic of the Oregon Health and Science University's Child Development and Rehabilitation Center) to form a support group for parents of children receiving services at the cleft palate clinic. Only two mothers accept his invitation, but the three of us form a strong bond and help one another think through practical and emotional issues. Finally, I'm among moms who don't need an explanation of my worries about Jimmy, don't shy away from talk of personal vulnerability, and understand the dilemma in making time for themselves when it might mean robbing time from a child with exceptional needs.

Within the safe environment of the support group, I wrestle with my indecision. How would I manage to have meaningful time with James and the boys? I would need to be flexible enough to find classes during the hours the boys were in school and also accommodate the demands of James's rigid and time-consuming work schedule. Attending classes would introduce another scheduling hassle, decreasing my availability at home. My time for family would be even more strained and limited.

Besides the practical issue of fitting graduate studies into a busy family life, there's the emotional tug. I had not factored in the overwhelming pull of my love for James and the boys. I worry that distance will develop between me and my children, me and James. How will I feel if I miss too many precious moments? Or if I am not available when one of them could use my help, a hug, a smile, or a corrective intervention? How will they feel? Will they turn away from me as an anchor in their lives? Do I really want to risk straining my relationships with them? As I acknowledge that close connections with my children and husband are vital to my happiness, as is my sense of responsibility, the plans for further education seem more and more preposterous.

After months of stewing with no resolution, I decide to seek personal counseling. I find Jude. The conversation starts with Jimmy, the challenges, and my confusion about how best to help him. I lament not making enough time for Kent. I acknowledge that it's tough sometimes with so much solo parenting. I describe my daily routine, currently devoted largely to family. I confess how often I blow fuses, how stuck I feel, my difficulty getting out of bed in the morning, my reluctance to burden James by asking for help with household matters, let alone with personal problems. To be honest, I tell her, I feel bad about my mothering, especially for not being as much help to Jimmy as he needs. I cry a lot, and I ask her for help to come to terms with giving up graduate school and to stop feeling so sorry for myself. Through it all, Jude listens, empathizes, and validates. She remarks how laced with guilt my thinking is and wonders what it would be like if I could think things through without guilt. She waits for me to compose myself.

Jude coaxes me to examine my shortcomings with more kindness and through a more thoughtful lens. Dr. Hess's words from nine years ago come to mind. He told me then not to be so hard on myself. As if following his cue, Jude says I need to learn to be kind to myself. Gradually, I'm able to remind myself how much I've cared and how hard I've tried. Eventually, I cut myself slack for my failings, knowing that I will continue to do the best I know how at home, and that just may be good enough.

I begin to see my conviction of unworthiness as self-inflicted punishment for not being able to make life easier for Jimmy and for not living up to the ideal I had in my youth of the kind of wife and parent I wanted to be. Depriving myself of graduate studies, and even of small pleasures, has become a way of punishing myself for my failings.

"What little treat could you give yourself in the next week, whether you think you deserve it or not?" Jude asks.

The answer comes slowly.

"Maybe a dish towel," I say.

"Dish towel?" Jude cannot mask her surprise.

I describe the months of indecision about buying a new dish towel.

"Okay," Jude says so emphatically she startles me. "Before the next session, I want you to buy yourself two new dish towels."

"Two?"

"Yes. Two!"

"I guess I can do that," I say, feeling a tinge of excitement.

Two days later, I'm standing once again before the dish towel display at Payless. The vegetable-adorned dish towels are still in stock, still on sale, and as inviting as ever. With no hesitation, I pick two off the rack. Then a dish towel sporting an assortment of kitchen utensils along its borders catches my eye. I grab a couple of those, too, and head down the aisle with a swing in my step and not one twinge of guilt. The good feelings last through the week and beyond.

Over time, Jude helps me challenge the self-defeating thoughts that are sabotaging me. Perhaps I *can* find enough time in the day for both family and personal pursuits. It even seems reasonable now to ask James to recommit to our earlier plan and help make graduate school possible for me.

Jude and her husband, Jerry, a psychiatrist, offer a couples session to talk about the demands my attending graduate school will put on James, our marriage, and the family. I disclose my fear that asking for time away from home and help with household tasks and parenting will put an undue burden on James. True to his generous nature, James offers to support me by doing the weekly grocery shopping and to arrange his call schedule so he can be home one night a week, allowing me to attend an evening class.

Jerry asks James if he has any worries about my attending graduate school.

I am stunned when James discloses that he is not worried about being burdened with housework and childcare, but that I will find life at home with him less appealing than the life and people I will discover in graduate school.

"I'm gone a lot," he says, "and often tired and preoccupied with patients' needs when I am home. That can't be much fun for her."

I listen in disbelief. I reassure him my devotion to him and our family has never been in question. Quite the opposite.

I wish it had dawned on me to seek counseling in Jimmy's first year of life. Why did it not occur then to the doctors and teachers to refer me to a counselor rather than gloss over my concerns? Why had I allowed them to tell me how to think, rather than think for myself? Perhaps I would not have been so stuck all these nine years. Perhaps I could have managed better the dark thoughts that have been dragging me down. But now I'm freeing myself of those tangles. James and I negotiate a division of household chores and parenting tasks and I get used to the idea of claiming time for myself.

Within a few months' time, I'm taking courses on child development as a community education student at the University of Oregon. Outside of class, I study on my own from used university-level textbooks on psychology and parenting. What pleasure to use my mind and find myself moving toward a goal that a short time ago seemed unattainable. I begin to imagine a career as a counselor who works with parents of children with disabilities.

Every so often the oh-so-familiar thoughts of self-indulgence and unworthiness break through my resolve, bent on sabotage. That's when I grab one of the dish towels from Payless, a potent reminder of the moment I realized I could afford to be good to myself. I snap it several times and banish the intruding thoughts. I know now how to keep them at bay.

Torchons

Never was a sudden sound so hopeful
'round the table of her farm-kitchen birthplace
as the snap of her mother's dish towels.

Later, grim the words of professionals—
until she would hold close her son's clefted face.
Never were his quiet sounds so hopeful!

Yet the years made her dreams forgettable.
When yearning for her littérature française
while walking past a sale on dish towels,

she pondered a life of lost potential.
Perhaps family was her entire fate.
Never was her inner voice less hopeful.

These echoes led her to seeking counsel
to redream herself into a new embrace.
But first she snatched up those two dish towels

and stood tall at her own kitchen table
with all her doubts and recovered her grace
from within the sudden sound so hopeful
of the snap of her own new dish towels.

UNTETHERING

Jimmy appears in the kitchen dressed in swim shorts and announces that he wants me to drive him to the neighborhood swimming pool.

"I need a ride, Mom. You can come too, can't you?"

My shoulders square off for an encounter. "I'm a little busy just now. Why don't you ride your bike?" I continue washing the vegetables I'm preparing for dinner. For more than a week, I've been urging Jimmy, now nine years old, to go to the neighborhood pool by himself. As if he senses that my hesitation indicates reluctance, he lays it on thicker.

"It's too hot to ride my bike. C'mon, Mom!"

I know what's really going on. He wants me to be around in case other kids make him too uncomfortable. Jimmy is more than capable of riding his bike to the pool but is not always up to facing the unknowns of the pool scene. What if he doesn't find a familiar friend to play with or is ignored by the kids he knows? What if someone makes a remark, points, or stares at his lip? Will he be able to put to use the thinking, changing, rearranging skills he learned from Dorothy? If I'm along, he knows I'll be as attuned as he is to the social vibes and will not argue if he says abruptly, as he has several times, "Let's go home."

I'm torn each time this scenario unfolds. When I'm there to rescue him, Jimmy's not figuring out how to deal with the uncomfortable attention that occurs routinely in his life. In my mother's heart, I want to spare him painful encounters, but every bit of common sense I possess tells me I need to push him to be tough enough to weather the remarks and the hurtful stares.

"Okay," I say. "But no more than an hour. Kent will be coming home from Mike's house about then, so I need to be home." Once again, I've caved in to my worry that Jimmy needs a safety net.

At the pool, Jimmy leads me to two lounge chairs, where we settle in. Immediately, he opens the book he has brought and holds it up so it shields his scarred lip from view. He looks around and spots Percy, one of the boys who has picked on him. Percy eyes Jimmy for a moment, takes me in, then turns back to another boy whom he invites to jump into the pool.

"I don't want to stay," says Jimmy moments later. He closes his book, picks up his towel, and heads for the exit before I can utter a word. I know better than to press him in the midst of a situation he wants to escape. In the car, I ask what changed his mind.

"I just didn't want to stay." He's looking away from me and out the window. At home, he disappears into the family room and occupies himself with his Legos. In the kitchen, I chop onions with fury. Damn the Percys of the world! Damn my inability to help Jimmy deal with them. Has he forgotten what Dorothy taught him? Or is it just too much?

The accumulation of instances of tough interactions with other kids weighs on my mind. The name-calling became routine in second grade, and on many mornings, Jimmy balked before heading to school. Now between third and fourth grade, Jimmy often opts to play by himself at home or with his dependable friend Seth. He has learned from a savvy school counselor how to handle unwanted attention, but routinely avoids situations where he might have to deal with it. I get it that I serve as a safety net. I also believe it's my job to help him face these situations, but the thought of his being made the brunt of other kids' insensitivity and bullying too often compels me to jump into rescue mode.

For several days, the swimming pool scenario repeats itself: Jimmy asks for a ride, I suggest he ride his bike, he objects for one reason or another, I resist for one or two rounds, heave a sigh, and drive him. Some days there are familiar, friendly peers and he joins the normal horseplay. On those days, he acts as though I am not there, but I'm quite certain he counts on my sticking around just in case. I toy with the idea of telling him I have to leave, but I'm afraid to upset the equilibrium he has found. I know I should be loosening the tether. By making things easy for him, I am surely getting in his way. But then, by leaving him on his own, would I be throwing him to the wolves?

I decide to consult my counselor. She agrees that I need to relax and let Jimmy figure out more on his own. My hanging out on the edge of his life is probably sending the message that I expect him to falter. She schedules a private session with him. Over a friendly game of checkers, Jimmy owns up to having a few problems going to the pool, and in the same breath, tells her he wishes his mom didn't worry so much about him.

That clinches it. I have to get out of Jimmy's way and give him the impression I think he can handle himself without me. But can I let go?

The moment of reckoning presents itself on a blazing hot day in mid-August.

Jimmy appears in the kitchen in his swimming shorts with a towel over his shoulder. "Hey, Mom, I need a ride to the pool."

I don't answer right away. I resolve to follow the script I've developed for this situation. "You'll need to go on your bike, honey," I say as I busy myself at the sink. "I have things to do here."

"I can't," Jimmy counters with a groan. "It's too hot."

"I think you can manage on your bike today."

"You're really going to make me push my bike up our hill?" He sounds incredulous.

"It won't be too bad if you cut through the woods from the middle school."

"Why can't you just give me a ride? You're not doing anything."

"You can do it," I say. "I'm going to stay here."

There's a moment of silence. I scrub some carrots, grab the cutting board and a knife, and focus on chopping them into uniform quarter-inch pieces.

Behind me, Jimmy fumes. "I can't believe you won't give me a ride! You're the meanest mom I know! I just won't go, then. Thanks a lot!" He turns and stomps down the stairs to the family room.

I grip the sink, take deep breaths, and start counting to 500 in silence, as I promised the counselor I would do. *1, 2, 3, 4, 5 . . .* I will not coax. I will not scold. I will not tell him all the ways he can make it work. I will not think about all the good reasons why Jimmy deserves a ride, or how much better it would feel in this moment to make life a little kinder for him. He remains in the family room for a good ten minutes. I'm still gripping the sink and holding my ground, though I'm beginning to soften. *395, 396, 397 . . .*

Then I hear him on the stairs.

"Are you serious, Mom? Are you really not going to give me a ride to the pool?"

Here it comes again. I steady myself for a new assault. *451, 452, 453 . . .*

"Yes, I'm serious," I say. "I'm not going to give you a ride today."

He stops on the landing by the door to the front patio where he has a good view of my back at the kitchen sink. I stand firm, teeth clenched.

I hear the door open. I look around in time to see Jimmy leave and close the door behind him. Through the window, I see him pick up his bike and wheel it through the gate. It could be my imagination, but I swear he is humming a tune. I watch, suspended, as he gets on his bike and pedals off toward the pool. *497, 498, 499, 500! Thank you, Lord!* I collapse against the sink and uncoil. I let the tether slip away. I feel so light I could levitate. In my mind's eye I see Jimmy on his bike, lifting off the ground as he flies free of the tether we've both had trouble letting go of, ready to take on by himself whatever awaits him at the pool.

WHAT DO I KNOW?

Nine-and-a-half-year-old Jimmy emerges red-faced and sullen from the orthodontist's office. His cheeks are wet. I take his hand and quickly lead him out of the office and out of earshot. I kneel before him and put a hand on his shoulder.

"What's the matter, Jimmy? What happened?"

"Dr. Sanders is too mean to be a doctor, Mom," Jimmy says through tears. "He didn't have to shove me."

"Shove you? What for?"

"I thought I was choking and tried to sit up and he yelled at me and shoved me back down."

In a flash of memory, I see myself withering years ago under the anger of Dr. Gray during a pediatric visit. Not today!

Behavior like this from professionals involved in Jimmy's treatment is a huge dilemma for me. I still shudder whenever I think how Dr. Gray yelled and slapped two-and-a-half-year-old Jimmy when Jimmy kicked and screamed after receiving a painful tine test injection. Once again, a doctor's lack of restraint leaves Jimmy and me in shreds. Who comes away from a tongue-lashing and rough handling feeling upbeat? Does Dr. Sanders know or care how hard he makes it for Jimmy to face the next appointment? How anxious I will be about bringing him to see a doctor he fears? I know Dr. Sanders's display of temper is bad form, and I want to complain. But criticizing a doctor's behavior requires that I ignore the strong messages from my childhood that dictate deference to authority, particularly teachers and doctors, no matter how they treat you. For too long, this ingrained injunction has caused me to hold in check my opinions and feelings in situations where doctors have been hard on us. I also fear, pragmatically speaking, that complaining to Dr. Sanders about his harsh treatment of Jimmy will alienate him. Do I want to risk that? He is critical to the work needed on Jimmy's cleft palate. But I know I cannot ignore his harsh treatment of my son.

To be sure, James and I are grateful for the knowledge and skill highly trained specialists bring to repairing Jimmy's complicated cleft palate anomalies, but I am disappointed in their inattention to other trials we experience. Jimmy's severe cleft palate has dealt us challenges on many levels for years and will continue to do so. At first, I expected the medical community, so prepared to take on the structural issues of Jimmy's cleft, to also provide guidance and encouragement to help us cope with other care issues. I thought we would be treated holistically, that the mental and social factors of our situation were being considered, and that doctors would anticipate Jimmy's adjustment problems and any difficulties I would have caring for a child with a complicated cleft. I didn't realize for years that medical specialists, for the most part, were interested exclusively in structural repair. Or that most pediatricians were attending primarily to physical, not emotional and mental, health issues.

My expectation that medical care would be encompassing and supportive was naïve. I should have realized that right away. No one warned me that I would have such a hard time looking at ten-day-old Jimmy's post-surgery face. No medical service checked in on us those weeks at home after that first operation. Had there been instructions on feeding a baby with no palate and a cleft lip still open on one side while the other side was healing from surgery, I surely would have done a better job and been spared bouts of anxiety as I tried to feed and soothe Jimmy.

I could have used a "good for you" from Dr. DeWitt for the effort I was making to introduce Jimmy to vocal sounds, knowing that language development would be a particular difficulty down the road. Instead, the surgeon told me I was wasting my time.

It would have been reinforcing had he recognized my attention to Jimmy's care needs, rather than ignore me, when I made sure to wean Jimmy from his bottle so he would recover more quickly from palate surgery at seventeen months.

"How did you know to wean him?" asked the discharge nurse.

I told her I learned from a mother whose bottle-fed fifteen-month-old son required an extended and very frustrating in-hospital recovery after surgery because of inadequate hydration.

"Ah, yes," the nurse said. "Kids go home much sooner when they can take fluids from a cup."

"Wouldn't it be simple for the doctor to hand out instructions about that?" I asked.

She shrugged.

At the same time, Dr. DeWitt did not value my willingness to stay by Jimmy's bedside throughout the day and night during recovery to soothe him when he awoke fearful and crying.

Instead, when he found me nearly asleep, my head resting on the bed and my hand on Jimmy's tummy, the surgeon was displeased.

"Go home and get some sleep," Dr. DeWitt scolded. "Let the nurses take care of him. Besides, he won't remember you were here."

When Jimmy had surgery at age four, I wish the surgical team had prepared me to be of use in Jimmy's recovery and that they had granted my request for a psychological consult on how four-year-olds weather cleft lip and palate surgery. I might have known to prepare Jimmy to see bruises and stitches on his face. I could have invented a hero story, perhaps describing a courageous little boy who fought off an attack dog and then had to contend with a bloodied face and big, black stitches in his lip for a whole month.

"And, my brave little boy," I might have said, "that's how your face will look after lip surgery. It takes courage to face a mean dog and to have surgery."

Maybe I could have had Jimmy draw before-and-after pictures. I could have talked about how long the bruises would last. If Jimmy had anticipated the effect of surgery, perhaps he would not have reacted with such shock and dismay at viewing his face after that operation. I was not prepared for his anguish or the anger he turned on me.

"You lied to me," he cried and threw the mirror at me. "You told me they were fixing my lip!" I felt immediate sorrow and outrage at myself, but more so at the medical team. Surely, someone on the surgical staff knew how four-year-olds react to their bruised faces after surgery and could have prepared both Jimmy and me to cope with his swollen and stitched-up face. Why had they not prepared us? I still don't know. Were they simply not attuned, or did they not see it as their responsibility? I do know that after that surgery, there was a disturbing, new distance between Jimmy and me and that for a long time, he would seem more wary of my intentions.

I cannot fully explain why I looked for so long to the medical community for comprehensive support and for invitations to be included in Jimmy's care plans. Or why I didn't get the picture after encountering so many comments discounting my efforts and interest in being a constructive force in attending to Jimmy's cleft-related needs. For whatever reason, I assumed too much.

These doctors' comments were no doubt well intended, calculated to dispel my "mother" worries and urge me to leave the important decisions to them. Whatever their intentions, relegating me to an inactive role only inflamed my anxiety and further discouraged me. I was feeling strongly that I wanted—needed—to participate in Jimmy's treatment, and yet, how could I trust my own sense of things when my concerns were so often swept aside? I left many encounters with doctors feeling unheard, misunderstood, invalidated, and unimportant. I grew increasingly unsure of myself and believed I was misguided, unqualified to bring up concerns or be of any use in addressing difficulties presented by Jimmy's cleft. I felt like a schoolchild told she'd failed important tests for which she'd invested her best thinking and effort. I never thought to challenge what seems now like patronizing behavior, the kind that robs you of confidence and a sense of your own power.

It was well into Jimmy's elementary school years when I realized I'd had misplaced expectations, not only for reassurance and emotional support, but also for recognition as an important player in shaping treatment plans for Jimmy's cleft. I began to rethink my assumptions about the medical community and the extent to which medical providers could meet my needs or include me in their arena. I thought, back in 1970, that Dr. Hess's sensitivity to my coping and his insistence on the importance of my role in Jimmy's well-being was the rule, but it proved to be the exception.

So, for the first nine years of Jimmy's life, I relied mostly on my own half-developed strategies, my muddled instincts, and trial and error to support Jimmy through feedings, surgeries, and dental and orthodontic manipulations, as well as the hassles from peers. All the while, I weathered privately the emotional toll from witnessing his ordeals and not knowing how to draw the attention of his medical providers to my concerns. I muscled through the heartache and hard feelings of inadequacy the best I could.

Things came to a head when Jimmy's misery from playground teasing in second grade seemed too much. It became clear to me then that we needed help, not from medical doctors but from mental health professionals. I mentioned my concern to Jimmy's doctors. They mollified me. It dawned on me that if I wanted help for Jimmy's or my distress, I had to take matters into my own hands.

It was a red-letter day when I stuck to my guns and insisted that Jimmy needed a counselor who could help him deal with the distress from recess teasing. Dr. Manny Lotito was the skilled and sensitive school district counselor who met with James and me first. Dr. Lotito had no trouble understanding that playground taunts and bullying had a negative impact on Jimmy's self-image. Or that I, myself, would benefit from counseling. He met with Jimmy after school one day a week for several months, working to bolster Jimmy's morale and self-esteem. Over milkshakes, Jimmy told Dr. Lotito he thought the first and only thing teachers and classmates noticed about him was his scarred lip. I would eventually seek a counselor for myself, but the fact that I'd been able to advocate successfully for our needs had already boosted my morale.

I knew there would be more meetings with medical doctors who would not be interested in my point of view or would discount issues I raised. But I was gaining confidence in my ability to insist on being heard. I would no longer accept advice that missed the mark. I vowed never again to leave doctors' visits disappointed in myself for allowing myself to be overruled when I expressed concern about Jimmy's or my own well-being.

For the record, I wish Jimmy's doctors had wanted to know what I knew about him. He was so much more than a child who needed cleft repair, orthodontia, specialized dental care, speech therapy, or vaccinations. He was a boy who functioned for most of the time like any other boy his age. He went to school, sought friends and engaged in hobbies, played soccer, flag football, and T-ball, and was a speed demon on the ski slopes. He fed the dog, who was devoted to him, and did a modicum of chores. He enjoyed family games and outings and was not shy about arguing with his parents. He shared the playroom with his younger brother, whom he didn't hesitate to boss around. He was intense when he built ten-foot-long communities from blocks and Legos, or when elaborately painting miniature lead fantasy figures for which he constructed dioramas. He lost himself for hours in books with tales of heroes who overcame adversity. If his doctors had taken time to understand his temperament, they might have had more success winning his cooperation. If they had shown more interest in him as a whole person, they might have earned his trust and dispelled his fear of them.

I wish his care providers had asked me what I knew about how Jimmy's cleft affected his daily routines, self-concept, and mood. For example, he couldn't manage foods that required biting with front teeth or excessive chewing. He had tubes in his ears because of frequent ear infections and because of the tubes, he was not supposed to put his head under water in the tub or at the pool. He could not whistle, blow out candles on his birthday cake, or give a bedtime kiss because his cleft lip made it impossible. He had to put up with the constant discomfort of a spanner installed in his mouth to prevent the maxilla from collapsing inward and which also interfered with speech, already difficult enough.

All this and more complicated his days. I knew the jumble of feelings he brought home from a rough day at school. Teasing and playground hassles took a toll on his emotions and self-esteem. And yet, I knew he kept putting himself out there, persisting, participating in school, hobbies, and sports as though his cleft were not in the picture.

I also knew I was on solid ground those times I questioned doctors. I felt justified when I challenged the resident at Stanford's Children's Hospital when he diagnosed four-year-old Jimmy with attention deficit hyperactivity disorder (ADHD). Jimmy had wiggled and squirmed and escaped the exam room, exasperating the bevy of doctors examining him after the emergency lip repair performed a few days earlier at Castle Air Force Base. I protested the diagnosis and demanded that the social worker enter a note in the medical chart stating that the mother disagreed, that I saw Jimmy's flight from the exam room as a manifestation not of ADHD but of his determination to escape an uncomfortable situation. To substantiate my challenge to the ADHD diagnosis, I described the sustained, focused attention Jimmy displayed at home when engaged in reading, drawing, and building with blocks. When Jimmy was ten, I resisted the speech therapist's objections, insisting it was best for Jimmy to take a break from speech therapy because of the unwanted attention it caused when he was called out of class over the loudspeaker.

What should be even more relevant to the doctors, orthodontists, dentists, and speech therapists is that Jimmy's appointments, many of which entail submission to unpleasant, even painful, manipulations, are still hard for him even on the best of days. During many procedures, he retreats into a stoicism that masks whatever dread or fear he feels.

Sometimes, I imagine assembling all his care providers in a room and reminding them, nicely of course, of the power they wield. I would tell them that their bedside manner makes a world of difference to Jimmy's experience in their offices and how he views them and himself. A frown, harsh word, or sharp command can leave him feeling coerced, bullied, and fearful that the doctor cares only about getting his procedure done and not at all about him or the pain involved. If doctors speak only of his "problem," Jimmy then sees himself as a problem or a bother. When he comes away from appointments crying or depressed because of something that transpired during a procedure, I have a very discouraged child (their patient) on my hands, and a lot of work talking him into facing the next appointment. On the other hand, a kind word, interest in Jimmy beyond the cleft, or perhaps an acknowledgment that treatment is no fun can go a long way toward earning his trust and his believing he is more to them than a cleft palate case.

I would tell my audience about Dr. Ernest Kaplan, the surgeon whose compassionate bedside manner and coaching dispelled four-year-old Jimmy's fears and allowed the doctor to quickly remove sutures from Jimmy's lip. By contrast, that same year, Jimmy was distressed and combative when a surgical resident whose manner was officious, abrupt, and impersonal tried to remove stitches from his lip. It is clear to me that Dr. Kaplan's treatment was more efficient and less traumatizing to Jimmy because Dr. Kaplan took time to relate personally to his child patient. He cared that Jimmy get through the procedure with as little discomfort as possible. He took time to gain Jimmy's trust.

Okay. So, I know things about Jimmy that should matter to doctors, and I have knowledge I'm dying to impart about the impact—both negative and positive—of doctors' bedside manner, but how do I get them to listen? I have no professional degree. I am just a mother. I remind myself, though, that six years ago, with James's help, I spoke my mind to Dr. Gray, and that recently, I took on Jimmy's teacher without hesitation over a homework assignment gone bad. Surely, I can find the gumption to make my voice heard in medical settings. This is something I must do if I'm to make a positive difference for my child and for myself.

I was primed to act when Jimmy emerged from Dr. Sanders's office in distress. There is no way I will not have a word today with the doctor. I tell Jimmy to wait in the car and I march back inside. In full view and hearing of all those waiting and working in that office, I ask to speak with the doctor.

"My son came out of this office crying," I say loud enough for all to hear. The receptionist drops her smile.

"Apparently, Dr. Sanders was rough on Jimmy. I need to talk to him."

The receptionist-turned-guard-dog stares me down. "The doctor cannot be interrupted when he is with a patient," she says with authority.

"Well, then, make me an appointment to speak with him privately within the next few days, please."

Back in the car, Jimmy is staring out the back window. He has the look of a punished child.

"I'm sorry, Jimmy. That should never have happened." He says nothing. I doubt he has much confidence that I can improve the situation. I'm not sure I can, either, but I do know better than to leave him in such a dejected state of mind.

"I think we both could use a milkshake," I say.

At Wendy's, we each order a large shake and sit down by a window. I search for a way to make sense to Jimmy of why seeing Dr. Sanders is necessary.

"You know, Jimmy, neither one of us is happy with how Dr. Sanders treated you today." He concentrates on his milkshake. "But we do need him to continue work on your braces." Jimmy's face darkens. "Sometimes the person whose skills you need to do a job has a lousy way with people. You know, poor social skills." Jimmy is well aware of the meaning of social skills, as he receives a grade for them three times a year on his report card. Jimmy shrugs. "For example, Dad and I take our car to the best car mechanic we know, even though he's a grouch. We need our car to run well, but we don't have to be friends with the mechanic." I watch Jimmy as he works on his milkshake, and I wonder if I'm helping.

"So, Jimmy, let's say we give the orthodontist a passing grade for his orthodontic skills. What should we give him for social skills?"

"An F!" he says without hesitation. A spark of energy flashes in his eyes.

"I agree. He's flunking social skills for sure. Let's hope he improves on the next visit." Jimmy's face relaxes just enough for me to concentrate on my own milkshake.

At home, alone in my room, I vent the sorrow, hurt, and anger I feel at seeing Jimmy leave yet another appointment feeling he's been punished for doing something wrong. I don't know if I can undo the damage, but I know the doctor was too harsh and I know what I must do.

When we meet, I'm hoping Dr. Sanders will acknowledge he'd been too rough on Jimmy, that he'll promise to make Jimmy's experience in his office less daunting in the future. He does not. Instead, he defends his policy of making children mind his instructions and asserts that he has no qualms about using physical restraint if needed. He goes on to imply that we are lucky he's taken Jimmy on as a patient, as he doubts any other orthodontist in town would do so.

He's right about that, but I'm here to talk about the negative impact of his behavior on Jimmy.

"But Dr. Sanders . . ." I hold steady. "You must know that Jimmy has gone through a lot with so many surgeries and so much orthodontia. Appointments are very hard on him. And now that you've been so angry with him, he dreads seeing you again."

Dr. Sanders blinks.

"We both know he has to continue orthodontia, even though he doesn't want to. Can't you make it easier on him?"

He says nothing.

"I'll be coming into the treatment room with him at his next appointment," I say as I rise to leave. "That's the only way I can get him here."

"That's not necessary."

"I think it is," I reply.

At Jimmy's next appointment, I sit quietly to the side. Dr. Sanders glances my way before turning to Jimmy.

"I apologize for scaring you at your last appointment. I'm sorry I pushed you."

Jimmy looks at him, nods, closes his eyes, and waits for the exam to begin.

The appointment proceeds smoothly. The doctor talks to Jimmy in a matter-of-fact voice as he works. No harsh words. No threats.

On our way home, Jimmy and I stop again at Wendy's to soothe our nerves over milkshakes.

"So, Jimmy, how would you grade Dr. Sanders today on social skills?"

He grinned. "About a B-plus."

"That sounds about right," I say.

What matters most to me is that Jimmy left the orthodontist's office without tears, his head held a little higher. I stand a little taller, too, ever more confident that I know a thing or two about what Jimmy needs from professionals besides their expertise. And I now know that I can speak up when I need to, for Jimmy's sake and for mine.

JAMES: OBLIGATIONS

Throughout four moves during the seven years between Jimmy's birth and when we landed in Eugene in 1977, my trajectory as a physician-in-training and compulsory military service dictated where our family lived. Barbara accepted these moves as necessary to the life we were building together, even though these frequent relocations also meant discontinuity in Jimmy's care and her career as a French teacher, as well as reintroductions to new neighbors, classmates, and medical providers.

In August 1973, six weeks before I entered the Air Force in Merced, California, we were blessed with the birth of our son Kent. We'd had no way of knowing—as prenatal ultrasound was not yet available—if our baby was healthy in utero. On the night of Kent's birth, we felt even more unsettled when we learned in the delivery room that our labor and delivery room nurse was the same one who had attended us during Jimmy's birth in Cleveland. Furthermore, Barbara's obstetrician was unavailable during her labor, a repeat of her labor situation in Cleveland. Were these bad omens? Indeed, Barbara's account of Kent's birth and the frightening follow-up are detailed in the chapter titled "Boomerang Years," at the beginning of Part Two.

Our deployment to the West Coast was emotionally difficult for our parents in Ohio and Maine. But the next two years were a welcome intermission between periods of medical training. They allowed us to strengthen our family bonds. I served on base as a medical officer practicing internal medicine for a large population of mostly retired military families. This was my first job as a doctor in a non-supervised role, and I loved it. I gathered additional experience by moonlighting for a busy internist at a community hospital intensive care unit in the town of Merced, and I grew increasingly confident practicing my profession.

I had more time off than before. With Jimmy and our infant Kent in tow, we frequently traveled throughout California and Oregon. In our secondhand mini-motor home, Jimmy and I slept together in a cramped bunk over the cab, while Kent slept in a daybed in the nook next to the mini-fridge, and Barbara on a bed that converted from the dining table. Barbara and I took some time away together during my leaves, and enjoyed new friendships at home. I was able to provide childcare so Barbara could attend woodworking classes where she happily built bookshelves, a terrarium coffee table, toys, and an enormous easel for Jimmy.

Barbara managed most of the frontline interactions with Jimmy's provider team based at Stanford's Children's Hospital, a three-hour drive from our home but the closest university hospital with a highly regarded plastic surgery program. Barbara and I had hoped for a seamless transition of care for Jimmy, so we were not prepared for the surgeon's suggestion that he had different and preferred approaches to repairing a cleft lip and palate from what surgeons in Cleveland had done. Barbara demonstrated increasing confidence as Jimmy's advocate during interactions with the team at Stanford. She voiced her objections to orthodontia out of concern for subjecting Jimmy to another series of interventions that were not essential at that point. While I initially embraced the recommendations of the expert medical authorities, I respected Barbara's concerns as well, knowing they were based on the authority of an experienced and reflective mother. I understood that her position was in the best interest of our family. Her objection to a surgical resident's diagnosis of ADHD and insistence on entering her own opinion in Jimmy's medical chart was likely an unprecedented action at the time, particularly in a profession where a traditional hierarchy often did not seek out or permit a mother to record her observations and opinions in a medical record.

We moved back to Rochester in late 1975 and I completed my nephrology (kidney disease) fellowship over the next two years. By 1977, I thought I knew everything there was to know about the kidney (except why we had two of them) and I was ready to launch my career as a practitioner. Barbara and I agreed about priorities for location, which, if well enough thought out, would provide a permanent home for our family. After multiple on-site visits to job opportunities around the country, I felt the best offer awaited me in Eugene, Oregon. Barbara reminded me that we had agreed that she had to give final approval before *our* decision was finalized. After visiting Eugene, she announced that Eugene suited her as much as it did me, especially because it offered the University of Oregon, an ideal place for her to pursue postgraduate education at some point.

Eugene was a great place to raise our two boys and for each of us to develop successful careers. I joined two other nephrologists/internists in an independent specialty group and worked hard to establish a reputation and to build a successful practice. I worked long hours but came home nearly every night, though often not in time for dinner, and I was always home at least two out of three weekends. Barbara still dealt with the issues Jimmy faced on the playground, in class, with new neighbors, and in professional offices. She advocated for Jimmy with increasing determination and tackled self-doubts. Over time I watched Barbara's self-criticism turn into a resolve to actively participate in Jimmy's care plans.

Barbara's professional pursuit took a new path. When she began to discuss how her personal activism might evolve into a career, I applauded her taking this step. Her enrollment in graduate school meant I had to assume more responsibility at home. Besides doing more laundry and washing dishes, I did the grocery shopping on my day off. I made arrangements with my partners to be free by 6:30 every Wednesday evening for several semesters to be with the boys so Barbara could attend required classes. It was an adjustment for both of us. My free time was reduced, and Barbara felt guilty about spending less time at home, especially when the boys gave me a hard time. Eventually, we hit a comfortable stride and I discovered a benefit I had not expected. As my time with the boys increased, they sought me out more often and I experienced fathering in a way I had not enjoyed before. This development created more balance in our parenting roles, and I enjoyed increased time with the boys.

To My Doctors

Hold the boy down!

You are important, you remind us.
You know better than we do
what should be done next and why
whatever has been done to date

was not done well, why you'll do better,
if only we would stop questioning
and trust you to proceed with
the procedure you want to try.

Remove the mother from the room.
She cannot comprehend
what her son really needs.

To be fair, this wasn't every one of you,
and back then—though not so long ago—
was a different time.
But by my records and experience,

this remains a common attitude.
Perhaps seven out of ten of you
doubt our story is really true, or that you
even fit this description. Maybe eight.

His case is quite complex,
more than I have ever dealt with,
but I'm up for it.

And why would you see yourself as this?
We are all indoctrinated to believe—even you—
that ancillary harm is forgiven
when doctors are earnest.

But sometimes the harm is hidden and deep.
I know, I know, it's still "unintentional,"
but all so avoidable if you'd just remember
our expectations are always greater than yours.

His lip will look much better
once we get this right,
we promise.

If you harbor any uncertainty
about the positive outcomes,
learn to navigate the promises
to save the child from drowning in hopes.

If you're worried for the mother
then prepare her to be worried.
She has already overcome
more than you care to know.

Well, we did our best . . .
He'll heal and someone can
try again.

Ok, look, I only remember a few of you
as actual assholes, and most of you
as just interested in my cleft as a case file
and your own opportunity. Forgiven. Done.

But all of you made an impression
on my mother—too few as inspiration,
too many as opposition, but all
as her motivation. For that, I thank you.

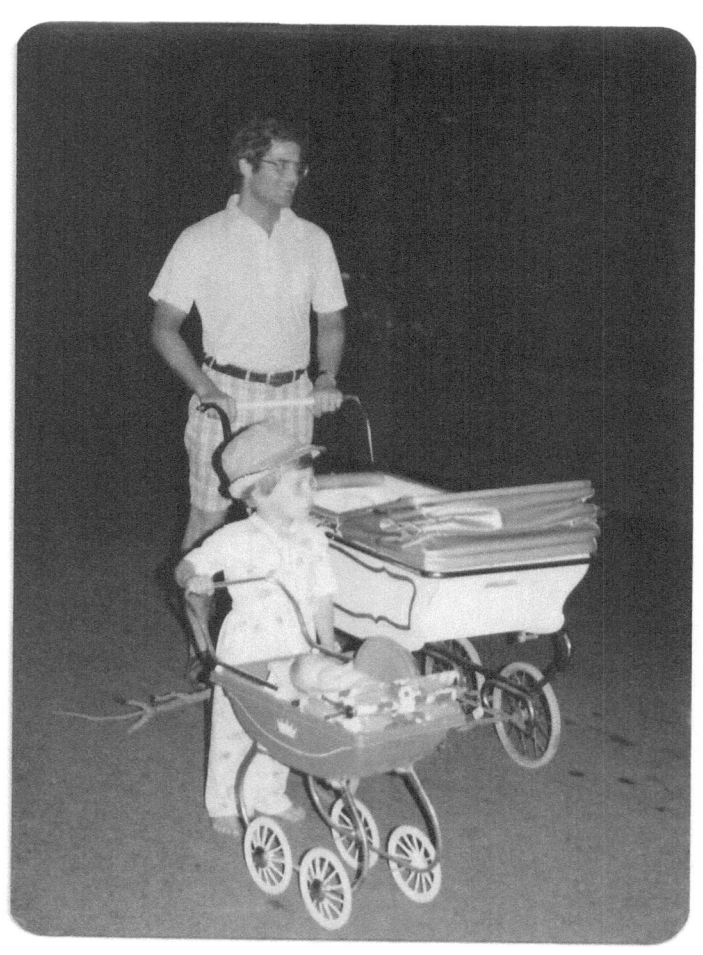

Jimmy, age three, and James take their "babies" for an evening stroll.

First family trip in the camper van. Jimmy, three, and Kent, three months old.

Jimmy, three and a half, and Kent, six months old, with James and Barbara.

PART THREE:
1980–1988

THE BIG QUESTION

I've asked myself the question a million times and now it comes at me like a slap in the face from fourteen-year-old Jim.

"What did you do to cause this, Mom?" He points to his upper lip marked by scars from five surgeries—three to close the bilateral clefts and two to repair scars. "You must have done something. This doesn't just happen to someone." His look, half-accusatory, half-pleading, stops me in my tracks.

I catch my breath. The question is huge, and I pray I don't mangle the answer.

From the moment I laid eyes on my newborn baby with his missing palate and large gaps on both sides of his upper jaw and lip, I've searched for the answer. Multiple doctors showed up at my bedside that first sobering day with encouraging words about the fixability of cleft lips and palates, but no one ventured a hypothesis of why this happened to my child. Why my baby? Why me?

My questioning began immediately. When Dr. Lowrey, my obstetrician, tried to console me by saying that in the lab, white mice developed cleft lips and palates at the drop of a pin, let's just say I was not consoled. Indeed, I became even more unsettled. When Dr. Lowrey recommended I think immediately about having a second child, I did not say to the good doctor what I was thinking: *Are you crazy?* I was more persuaded by the theory circulating at the time that mothers were the carriers of the abnormal gene that caused clefts and that male children were more likely to be affected than female. James found no instances of clefts in his family, but my mother remembered a male cousin with what may have been a cleft.

"It was never talked about," she said. "So, I can't be certain."

I remember the large gap and funny-looking nub between the two front teeth of my upper jaw when I was young. The nub was removed early on and braces corrected the gap when I was around twelve. Though James and others reminded me there could be other causes, I heard plenty to implicate my genes.

I would learn later that geneticists discovered that genes from the father can also contribute to cleft palate malformation. Future research would identify other variables causing craniofacial anomalies, but in the early 1970s, despite the vacuum of knowledge that existed, there was a strong suggestion that the mother's genes were the most likely suspect. This was sobering enough but I also wondered if I had done something during pregnancy to have caused Jimmy's cleft. Over the years I pondered the possibilities. Stress? Too many late nights grading French essays? Too many stairs to our third-floor walk-up apartment? Too many aspirins?

The most haunting questions arose from a sense that I was being punished for past transgressions. No doubt my upbringing by staunch New England Protestants had something to do with my feeling that I was paying for acts of unkindness, untruths, small-minded and self-aggrandizing behavior committed earlier in my life. I spent many prickly moments examining my past behavior: the inventory of snarky impulses and snotty remarks that had crossed my mind and lips over the years, fibs I'd told to keep out of trouble or preserve my reputation, instances where I had behaved in an unbecomingly ambitious way. And the list kept growing. I could find ample cause for my deserving a lesson in humility. The notion that I had done something to bring this complication to my child's life gnawed at me.

Though his father and I had answers about the cause of ABO incompatibility that had complicated both Jimmy's and Kent's first days of life, hard evidence for the cause of Jimmy's cleft remained unknown. James accepted this.

During Jimmy's early years, James asked repeatedly in a gentle voice meant to comfort me, "Does the cause really matter?" I envied his ability to take it all in stride.

But I could not. I continued to fester about the cause of Jimmy's cleft, aided and abetted by the parade of self-appointed diagnosticians—the grandmotherly lady in the window seat of the airplane, for example, who leaned over her husband to inquire with syrupy kindness if I had dropped my little boy when he was an infant. My first inclination was to reply, "No, I threw him against the wall," but instead, I maintained a benign expression and explained that no, he was born with a cleft lip. Nor did I appreciate the inebriated dentist at a cocktail party who puffed up and opined in a booming voice that it was my genes. People offered opinions at rest stops, on playgrounds, and on the street. Many had relatives, or knew someone, or knew someone who knew someone, with one kind of cleft or another. A grandmother in our neighborhood invited me in for a chat, wanting to know if Jimmy's cleft came from my side of the family or James's. It turned out that her grandson had been born with a cleft and she assured me that in her case the bad genes had most definitely not come from *her* side of the family.

Later, when supernumerary (extra) teeth emerged in Kent's hard palate and required oral surgery to be removed, I became further convinced that my genes put my offspring at risk for malformations of the mouth. Doctors were no longer so quick to say that Jimmy's cleft lip and palate were a fluke. In a text on early childhood development, I read about the potential of drugs, alcohol, nicotine, and caffeine for causing birth defects and added the occasional glasses of wine and daily coffee I'd ingested during pregnancy to the growing list of possible causes for which I could take responsibility.

Little wonder I developed an inferiority complex. I had produced a baby with a birth defect in a culture where perfect children were idealized. A counseling psychology professor of mine delivered a lecture on inferiority complexes. He argued that an inferiority complex is not inherent. We do not come into the world with one. Nor is it rooted in reality, but rather, is a product of norms and values embedded in our brain by our culture and family. We use benchmark criteria from these norms and values to evaluate our self-worth. If we don't achieve the benchmarks, we assess ourselves as inferior. But, since we are thinking organisms with the capacity to make choices, we can choose *not* to embrace cultural benchmarks as a way of measuring self-worth. We can detach ourselves from societal norms and standards that leave us feeling inferior. It's simply a matter of un-psyching ourselves.

What if you have an actual physical defect, like abnormal genes that cause birth defects? They *are* real, not a product of one's mind or culture. Wouldn't it be psychologically healthy to just accept that I'm inferior in the genes department? Just as I am inferior to talented musicians with regard to producing music? Why not spend less time trying to talk myself around my inferior genes and instead simply talk about them as matter-of-factly as I talk about inherited hair color and height? As I struggled to take the sting out of the word "inferiority," I moved a lot closer to thinking about flawed genes without feeling so diminished.

And now, on a quiet evening at home with a fire warming our front room, teenage Jim asks what I'd done to cause his cleft. His questions at age three were out of curiosity, wanting to know why his lip was different. After feeling shocked and upset with his post-surgery appearance at age four, he rarely, if ever, asked about his lip or palate.

And now, this pointed question. It could have undone me, but somehow it didn't.

"What makes you ask?" I resist defending myself, or admitting guilt, and stay with his question.

"In biology class, we are learning about how babies of drug users often have birth defects. Did you use drugs, Mom?"

A strange calm comes over me as I field Jim's sharp, line-drive question. I call up with surprising confidence the mother part of me that has come to terms with the probability of the cause.

My voice is steady and sure. "If you're talking about drugs like pot, cocaine, or heroin, I did not." His piercing look holds me in place. "But I did use aspirin and cold medicines." He waits.

"I've been asking myself the same question since the day you were born, Jim. I've asked doctors and read books, and depending on the expert, the answer changes. One year it's caffeine, then it's alcohol and drugs. And yes, I did drink a lot of coffee and a glass of wine now and then. And even though there have been no instances of cleft palate in our families that anyone can remember for sure, my best guess is that it's a problem with my genes." I tell him about the gap between my front teeth that required orthodontia and about the extra teeth in Kent's palate. "So, that's the best answer I can give you—my genes are most likely responsible for your cleft problems." I look straight at him. "And I'm more sorry than I can say."

Our eyes lock. I want what I say next to hit with full force. "But you need to know something more. You were a planned-for and wanted child. Your dad and I love you very much and I wouldn't trade you for the world."

We stay that way for a long moment and then Jim quietly leaves the room. James, who has been sitting frozen on the sofa, comes to life.

"Honey, that must have been devastating."

"No," I say, "it wasn't." I feel a sudden lightness, an unburdening.

"I didn't realize until this moment that I've been needing this question for years. It's a relief to answer it. At least now, Jim will not blame himself for being born with a cleft. I don't mind that he may blame me. Better me than himself."

I may never discover a better answer, but this one brings a peace of mind I've not felt before.

To Questions Without Answers

You draw us forward, teasing what we understand,
smirking as we only find more questions.

You don't resist our guesses, our science, the writings
we pass around to keep from falling down so

deep in the myths we need for why hard things happen,
why a cleft on this child, why this life for this mother.

Yet, you never reveal resolution. You enable us
to conceive of a God both deliberate and mocking.

You allow us to imagine that sway over our circumstances
might be just one more revelation ahead, and so we dream

of catching you that we might breathe again and move on,
all of us together. Yet there you go still smirking, singing

it could be this, it could be that, it all could be, could be
for no reason at all, at all, there could be no reason at all.

Perhaps I Have a Cleft Because

I am the blessed, the chosen one, as in ancient times.
My mother drank just a bit too much during pregnancy.
I am cursed for the sins of forgotten ancestors.
My mother smoked just a bit too much.
I did a terrible thing in a past life.
My mother ate too much spicy food.
My parents' lives were easy, so they had this coming.
My mother exercised too much, or too little.
A couple links of genetic code did what they were
    supposed to do.
God hates me.
A couple links of genetic code awoke from a long slumber.
God hates my mother.
A couple links of genetic code unlinked.
God knew I wouldn't be a big believer and clefted me early.
I needed an excuse to push back on the world.
God was preparing my path.
I needed a challenge, a reason, a foundation.
God doesn't exist.
All the above, in some way.
None of the above, but something else.

In the dimming of the evening in my bedroom as a teen, as the world slowed to shadow and all things found their quiet, my tongue traced the smooth cleft in the dark of the roof of my mouth and I began settling into acceptance of my mysteries.

SOLO

I cut Jim off in mid-sentence. "No, I'm just not comfortable with the thought of a long bike trip by yourself." My son heaves an impatient sigh. His face reddens and clouds over. "Why don't you find out if there's a bike trip offered at the Y this summer?" I suggest.

"That's not the same, Mom! I want to do this on my own."

"But you're only fifteen! That's too young to be taking a trip alone. It'd be much safer if you traveled with someone, even just one other person."

Jim turns and stomps out of the kitchen. "I'm almost sixteen, and I can take care of myself!" His voice rises. "You don't understand! You just don't understand."

He's got that right! Why on earth would I permit him to take off by himself on a long-distance bike ride? And where did he get such an idea? On the one hand, I'm thrilled that Jim has such an intrepid spirit. It has served him well. It seems to trump any timidity born from experiences with unpleasant reactions to his cleft. It gives him the boost he needs to take on the world. On the other hand, Jim's penchant for risk-taking and disregard for safety have put me in a panic since he was a toddler.

He was only two when he started breaking free from me in department stores. I'd spend a half hour searching for him up and down aisles, enlisting clerks to assist me. Often, I'd find him hiding inside a rack of clothing. I had to resort to a halter and tether to keep control of him.

Between the ages of three and five, Jimmy became notorious for disappearing on camping trips, off to explore on his own as soon as we parked the camper. When he was six, he darted away from us toward the parking garage at a fireworks show and got lost in the throngs of people exiting along a narrow pedestrian bridge. We had to wait until the crowd cleared to find him, praying all the while that he had not fallen off the upper-story passageway onto the concrete below, or into the river on the other side of the lawn where we had been picnicking, or worst of all, kidnapped.

Once, when he was ten, he took off on his own at the mall and didn't return. Was he lost? Kidnapped? More likely, he was on a lark, having the time of his life. I had his name called over the mall's loudspeaker. "We have a lost boy. Would Jimmy Walker please come to the star at the center of the mall to find his mother?" I hoped the message would embarrass him enough to make him think twice about disappearing on me in public places. When he appeared, he glowered at me. "I was not lost. I knew exactly where I was."

"But I didn't! And that's the problem!" I hoped my willingness to consider him lost would cure him from going off on his own. Fat chance! Although I grew to expect Jimmy's attempts to escape parental oversight, each episode left me feeling derelict for not keeping a closer eye on my child.

Jimmy (we still called him Jimmy then) was thirteen when we took a family trip to Boston. He defiantly insisted that he be allowed to ride the MBTA alone to Boston Garden, the large sports arena we'd visited earlier in the week. Despite our reservations, we gave in, fingers crossed. He set out, armed with the hotel's address and enough money for a phone call and cab fare. He returned, head held high, with a Boston Bruins hockey puck in hand. He discovered each day something else he needed from the sports store at the Garden and by the time we headed home, he had an impressive collection of hockey pucks, a cap, and a T-shirt. His dad and I managed our angst back at the hotel during Jimmy's Boston adventuring, sticking close to the phone and expecting any minute to have to rescue a lost boy. But he returned safe and exuberant each time. Each foray on the MBTA sent the boy's self-confidence soaring and helped James and me see that, given the opportunity, he could manage himself in the world. On none of these adventures had he mentioned his cleft being a worry, but was it? If he had to endure stares or remarks, he handled them on his own.

My obsession for safety has continued to sabotage my efforts to embrace Jim's current fierce desire for independence and the risks it entails. I can't count the times I've warned of danger and implored Jim to take fewer risks, if not for his sake, then for mine. His father takes Jim's risk-taking behavior in stride better than I do.

"He's an adventurous kid," he says. "It's not all that bad to take risks." When I give it more thought, I have to admit I'd rather see Jim stick his neck out than shy away from new and challenging experiences.

But a solo bike trip that no mother I know would sanction? Surely, his father will find this too risky for a son who has not yet turned sixteen, but instead James seems intrigued. *He's blind to the dangers*, I think to myself. Two days pass without mention of the bike adventure and I allow myself to believe that my objections have persuaded Jim to abandon the idea. Summer is several months away, and surely, he'll have forgotten about this preposterous bike ride by then.

He catches me a couple of days later when I'm trapped in the kitchen preparing dinner. "Mom, I'm serious about this bike trip. You gotta let me do it. I don't see what you're so scared about. I'm not some little kid who doesn't know how to take care of himself."

I clench my teeth. "Jim, it's just too dangerous. You'd be in places where you don't know anyone. What if you got hurt? How would you get help? I'm sorry, I can't say yes to this. I might be more open to the idea if you found even one person to take the trip with you."

"Mom, you're missing the point! I want to go alone!" Again, Jim storms off. Am I being too cautious? After all, he's always on his bike, goes all over town on it. But more than four hundred miles by himself? Just the thought makes my stomach muscles tighten. Lurking somewhere is the shadow of a deeper worry. Would his cleft scars draw attention from unsavory types along the way? I shudder and push the thoughts away. I just have to hold the line, I tell myself, and in time he'll give up.

Two more days pass. As if on cue, Jim enters the kitchen while I'm at the stove. "Look, Mom, I get it that you're worried." *Good*, I'm thinking. *He gets it!* I am not prepared for the endgame he pulls on me. "This is really important to me, Mom. What do I have to do for you to consider letting me go on this bike ride by myself?"

His perfectly reasonable question shatters my defenses. I was anticipating a concession, not a call to reason. I want to respond accordingly.

"That's a fair question," I say, impressed in spite of my dismay with the mature nature of his overture. "Let me think about it." For the remainder of the time it takes to get dinner on the table, I ponder the criteria for safety I will ask Jim to satisfy before I will give my blessing to his scheme to head off by himself on this solo bicycle trip. They will be conditions I'm half hoping he will find impossible to meet.

When I present my list of requirements, I steady myself, bracing for an explosion. Jim studies the page. "Okay," he says and leaves the room with an expression of determination that surprises me.

In the following months, Jim sets about satisfying each one of my conditions. He enrolls in a bicycle maintenance class at Lane Community College and starts saving money so he can come up with half the funds needed for a new bicycle, tent, bike bags, tools, and travel expenses. He no longer refuses odd jobs at home, and he seeks work through his wrestling coach, who owns a construction company. He consults with the owner of the bike shop to develop a safety plan, should he find himself having to stop for the night in unexpected places. He learns that small-town police are not the people to ask for help, as they may be leery of a stranger passing through. Better to seek advice at the fire station. For a trial run, Jim joins a group on a weekend bike trip to the coast and back. He agrees to schedule his trip in conjunction with a Y-sponsored group bike trip in the San Juan Islands. After the San Juans trip, he will head off on his own to travel by ferry to Vancouver, British Columbia, where he plans to stay with the family of a girl he has met through Y-sponsored youth retreats. Together they will take in Expo 86. He allows me to contact Mrs. Farmer, the girl's mother, and she assures me she has spoken to Jim and will be delighted to have him as a guest for his several days in Vancouver. He maps out his itinerary from Vancouver to Eugene, some 425 miles, and gives me a copy. Except for a few unavoidable hours on the streets of Seattle, he chooses back roads in Washington State and Route 101 along the Oregon coast. He plans overnight stops at state parks, all estimated to have manageable distances between them for a reasonable day's ride. And he promises to call me every day by 10:30 p.m. so I can sleep at night.

It dawns on me that I no longer have any basis for denying Jim his bike adventure. I talk myself out of the lingering fears the best

I can. I adopt a mantra that I repeat every day and will continue to repeat during his bike ride. *If something bad happens to Jim on this trip, at least I can say I let him do life his way.* I begin to believe in my heart of hearts that this adventure represents more to Jim than a bike ride. Has he developed a specific plan to prove to himself that he will not let his cleft limit him? Does he simply want to get away? It seems more that he craves an experience to discover his capability to go it alone. If overcoming cleft issues plays any part in his quest, I do not hear about it and this fortifies me. Other parents have stories of teenagers pushing for more independence, but the mothers I talk to are quick to say a solo bike trip of this magnitude would be more than they could handle.

"You're not going to allow it, are you?" one asks.

"I wouldn't consent to something so dangerous," says another.

The idea of such an adventure excites a father. "I wish I'd done something like that when I was his age," he says. James gets behind the idea, too.

Jim successfully tackles each item on my list of requirements. His excitement grows and I become more reconciled to the notion that the bike trip is inevitable. Eventually, I find myself overseeing the operation as Jim prepares his gear and himself for the great adventure, and on the appointed day, I watch with a forced smile as the bus departs from the Y. On the day I know Jim and his bicycle are traversing the San Juan Strait by ferry toward the Farmers' home in Vancouver, I invoke my mantra to quiet my nerves. I count the minutes until 10:30 p.m. when he will be calling to tell me he has arrived safely. When no call comes at the appointed time, I'm beset with mea culpas. By eleven o'clock I'm pacing the floor in a cold sweat. At 11:15, I place a call to the Farmer home. No answer. I repeat the call several times and still no answer. Finally, at midnight, the phone rings.

"Hi, Mom, it's me." I collapse with relief.

"Where are you? Are you okay? Why the heck didn't you call earlier?" I'm on the verge of delivering a you-call-on-time-or-else scolding when he interrupts.

"The Farmers aren't home."

"What? You've got to be kidding me! I talked to Mrs. Farmer about this and she said nothing about not being home when you got there!"

"I've been sitting on their porch since nine o'clock. I heard the phone ringing inside the house and knew it had to be you. So, I went to the neighbors' house and told them the situation. They let me use their phone and said I could put my tent up in their backyard for the night."

"Thank goodness! But what will you do tomorrow?"

He isn't sure, but he will call me in the morning. Which he does. The Farmers arrived home shortly after midnight. Seems they'd forgotten Jim's arrival date. I stifle the scathing commentary on the Farmers and focus instead on Jim's steady voice. Things are back on track and I can breathe more easily.

Over the next ten days, we receive nightly reports as Jim calls from various points on his route. He bikes along the Seattle waterfront without being crunched by a semi or taxicab. Often, he abandons his itinerary as his distance recalculations or fancies dictate. Usually, he lands comfortably in campgrounds and reports that other campers are welcoming. On one occasion some nearby campers share their dinner with him. We are concerned the night he calls and we hear thundering traffic on the highway in the background. We celebrate his good judgment the night he tells us he's about to move from the beachside campsite he'd chosen because a dozen or more Hells Angels appeared on the scene and were tearing up the nearby beach with their Harleys.

But I'm not so sure about his judgment the night he calls from the home of a couple who offered him a bed for the night.

"How did you end up at someone's house?" I inquire as visions of ne'er-do-wells spring to mind.

Jim explains. He'd arrived in a small town and spied an open lot next to a restaurant and asked the restaurant manager if he could set up his tent in the vacant lot for the night. The manager said he'd have to ask the owner. Before long, a man in his sixties drove up and introduced himself as the restaurant owner. Within minutes, the man invited Jim to come to his house for a hot meal and to spend the night in a regular bed.

"Are you safe? What happened to the plan of asking help from the firefighters?"

"There's no fire station here, Mom."

Red flags are popping up left and right in my mind. "Who are these people? Are you sure they're not up to no good? Where are you sleeping? Can you get out of there in a hurry if you need to?" *Is that a chuckle I hear on the other end of the phone?*

"Mom, I'm fine. You'd really like the Grants. They have grown sons who took bicycle trips when they were my age, so they thought it would be fun to meet me. They fed me a great meal and we've been talking."

"But where are you sleeping?"

"In their family room on a fold-out bed."

"Is there a door in that room? If you had to, could you exit the room easily?"

"Yes, Mom. Not to worry."

But I do. Needlessly, it turns out. The Grants are of course lovely, generous people and eventually, I'm happy Jim didn't allow my suspicions to ruin his time with them. It also occurs to me that the Grants were taking a risk on a stranger, too.

As the projected end of Jim's trip nears, I'm buoyed by the thought that he will soon be safely home. A good night's sleep appears to be on the horizon. On the eve of his scheduled return, he calls from the coastal town of Florence, only sixty miles away. I am giddy with relief and from his high spirits. But then . . .

"I'm going to extend my trip another two days. I'm going on to Reedsport and I'll come back to Eugene on the Smith River Road."

"Really?" I'm not thrilled, but what could I say? His excitement trumps the insipid objections that come to mind.

"I won't be calling in, but you don't need to worry. I'm okay on my own."

"We'll see you when you get here," I reply, aware as I speak that I truly feel no fear for his safety. Instead, I'm uplifted by his accomplishment and the exuberance in his voice.

Two days later, after his epic twelve-day bike ride, Jim rides up to the front door. He's bronzed from his days in the sun, more muscular than the almost-sixteen-year-old who left home not so many days before. His bicycle sports both a Canadian and an American flag on the front fender. As I rush down the steps to greet him, he raises his arms in a triumphant gesture. His eyes blaze, telling me that he has conquered a giant.

It hits me that in addition to riding high, Jim is also riding free. He has shed the tether I was reluctant to let go of. Though I feel a loss in his pulling away, I know deep down it's just what he needs to be doing. I am bursting with gratitude when he strides up the steps with a confidence I've not seen before. This is the independent spirit and ability to separate from his parents that I've prayed for. A weight lifts from my shoulders. Excessive worry over all this has dogged me for the past months. Now, in an instant, it evaporates into thin air. I now know with certainty that Jim can manage himself in the world and that his cleft will not limit his options.

In the days that follow, I feel as though I've completed a momentous feat of my own. As Jim breaks free of the tether I've held too tight for too long, I drop my end of the tether with a sense of relief. I feel a new sense of freedom, perhaps equal to Jim's.

In the space left free from worry, I relive the years of raising Jim to this point. I sense more than ever that our efforts to become authorities and spokespersons in the sixteen-year struggle with his cleft have culminated in victory. It has been a matter of choosing ourselves, over and over again, as the most important voices to listen to. And yet, I cannot let go of the knowledge that many of the hardest times could have been less daunting. I've no doubt that we would have had an easier time if there had been greater emotional support and stronger relationships with professionals. The more I think about it, the more restless I become to do something about it, not just stew about it. How can I make a positive difference for parents and kids with needs like ours? I know I can't rest until I think of something.

Phone Calls from a Bike Trip

One of my mother's fondest fear-filled memories is my solo bike trip from Vancouver, Canada, to Eugene in the mid-eighties. She's resistant but has been trying to let go of me for years. I'm young and privileged yet coming-of-age stories need some sharp edge to be of any use. Her final insistence is that I call her from wherever I end the day, every day.

On a stretch of campground in the San Juans I leave my YMCA group for a ferry to Vancouver to visit the World's Fair and then meet a girl. Her parents forget I'm coming, so does the girl. I'm locked out of their house, my first night's shelter. I call my mother from their neighbor's house. She's horrified, then thankful. I realize this will be a long trip for her.

On a stretch of already narrow back lane near Oak Harbor, I'm almost run off the road by a pickup blaring a horn and I'm struck by my distance from anything familiar. I curse the driver. Later, as I'm setting up camp in a dark side-yard, I'm taken in by the hospitality of strangers; they say blessings for me as we all hold hands. I'm living in a parable. I call my mother from their kitchen phone. Again, she's horrified, then thankful. I have invented a new style of mother torture.

On a stretch of curving state highway through central Washington, the meadows are spotted with wildflowers spreading unhurriedly to a rise of trees, then on to fading mountains in a high horizon. On the other side of the road, a lush forest deepens into green-black old-growth. The way is idyllic like this for miles. I laugh out loud several times. I'm inside a cliché of "meadows spotted with wildflowers" and "deep dark forest," but here I am, it is real, I'm fairly certain. For a couple of hours this goes on forever. I tell my mother. She believes me, she always has.

On a stretch of river beach in Rainier, I relax into the evening looking back at the night-lit Lewis and Clark Bridge, realizing everything will be okay. I've already decided to head to the coast tomorrow instead of Portland. There's nothing I cannot now do. Real bikers show up and turn roaring doughnuts on the street-lit sand, relaxing in their own way. I observe fear as a choice, perhaps for the first time. I tell my mother this story, she takes it as well as can be expected.

On a stretch of impossibly straight road just off the Oregon coast, bounded at each far end by coast-wooded hills, I'm set to resume after another flat tire and realize a silence has settled in, a wide stillness. No cars or RVs approach from either direction, no engine echo or bird call hangs in the air. Even the wind is holding its breath, which never happens here. I wait for something, it seems I need to wait, it seems this place has been waiting for me. The blue of the sky and the heat of the sun are the purest of themselves I've ever known. The moment stretches open and invites me to stay. I do not remember how I leave. I tell my mother about the black bears at the campground instead.

On a stretch of the curving, cliff-cut coast highway Oregon is famous for, the southbound biking line is squeezed against a guardrail above the sea or against a fringe of pavement interrupting the fall of a ravine. The wind is either with you or against you, pushing on every available surface. When the wind is with you, the day is glorious. The ocean is a pulsing whisper I almost understand. I tell my mother about the ocean endlessly by my side.

On a stretch of highway shoulder outside Reedsport, I study the map. The route back to Eugene is marked, but the way south beckons like a girl from another country who might love me. I have the sudden thought I could disappear into a fresh history. There is a rightness to both paths rooted in the center of my being. A few years later I would be sitting on the boulders of Gibraltar and consider signing on to a freight vessel with this thought. Many years later, before my son, before my first marriage, I would be heading home on an interstate completely clear of traffic and consider driving into the distance with this thought. Even now, this thought sometimes rises like an abrupt storm offering to alter the course of my life. If you have lived, you are familiar with this thought. I never tell my mother this.

I still have the photo of me, burn-tanned and smiling, with the blue bike fully geared, in front of my parents' house. My stance says I'm already looking forward to catching up with my yet-young forever friends. My mother insists something has changed about me. Perhaps she's looking at me from somewhere she's never stood before. Perhaps I'm standing there as if I've just arrived. I forget if I say anything to my mother in that moment.

CROSSING LINES

"Three-day suspension." My heart sinks as Wilma White's words register. Wilma is the high school's vice-principal and disciplinary officer. I've had occasion to hear her voice before on several auto phone calls intended for parents: "Your student was absent in class today," or "Your student was late for class today." I've missed many of her calls because when the boys get home before I do, they intercept her messages. Wilma is notorious for her diligence in notifying parents when students cross a line. She also seems to relish delivering penalties for rule infractions. To challenge her authority would be a risky move.

"Mrs. Conway handed in a pink slip today citing Jim for insubordination," Wilma intones with all the solemnity of a high court judge. "That calls for an automatic three-day suspension starting immediately." After a pause, she adds in an upbeat voice, "but he's allowed to do his assignments while he's suspended. So, his grades shouldn't suffer."

This is not good news, of course, but Jim does fit the profile of a kid who could rile a teacher prone to heavy-handed rule enforcement.

His willingness to step over the line to defy my authority has motivated me to find creative ways to get him to say yes—well, maybe not quite *yes*. Rather than order him to bed when he refused to go as a young child, I simply turned out the lights and went to bed myself. I learned to reward compliant behavior as much as I could instead of threatening punishment. I worked hard to check my emotions and neutralize my tone of voice.

He was not above defying other adults either. When he was ten, James and I left him and Kent in the care of Nora Maxwell, with whom we occasionally exchanged weekend childcare. Within an hour of our arrival at the hotel in San Francisco, I got a call from my friend Judy, who informed me that Jimmy had had a run-in with Nora and had returned to our house, using our hidden house key to enter. He'd called Cathy, our emergency contact for the boys, to let her know about the situation.

"She bosses me around too much," Jimmy said when I called him. It took several more phone calls and some doing to negotiate a face-saving truce between Jimmy and Nora. Eventually, Nora softened, Jimmy agreed to return to her house, and James and I could continue our weekend in San Francisco.

As a high school student, Jim has consistently made the point that he can think for himself and applies himself to schoolwork according to his interests. I remember reacting to his C in typing.

"Is typing difficult?" I asked.

"No," he said, looking me steadily in the eye, "but a C is fine with me, because I only want to be an average typist."

"But it affects your GPA . . ." I could not help saying.

"I know," he said with an indulgent smile. "Don't worry, Mom, I will live with the consequences of my choices." I was dead in the water.

Jim demonstrated more than once that he was not a conventional student. He surprised both James and me when he dropped the advanced placement literature course and opted to replace it with an independent course in creative writing. Later, he balked at applying to college, protesting what he thought was a rigged application process advantaging students whose parents had connections or other resources. Eventually, he connected with a small college whose program in creative writing intrigued him enough to pique his interest. He ended up successfully applying to the University of Redlands, which is in California.

Jim, currently in his final high school semester, has been coasting with other seniors toward graduation, but now, it appears he's hit a snag by crossing the line with a teacher.

I take a deep breath. "What exactly did he do?" I ask Wilma.

"Mrs. Conway says he was loitering in the hall by his locker."

"And . . . ?" I wait for further explanation. Loitering alone does not constitute insubordination, I'm thinking. "So, did he say something disrespectful to Mrs. Conway?" I'm ready to believe he might have.

"No, I don't see that here in the complaint."

"Did he make some kind of face?" I know well Jim's ability to communicate a you-are-so-ridiculous comment with his eyes. If Mrs. Conway was the recipient of what I call his "stink eye" expression, I can imagine that she felt disrespected.

"No. He doesn't appear to have shown any disrespect."

"I don't quite see the grounds for insubordination," I counter. "I need to talk with Jim and hear his side of the story. I'll call you back tomorrow."

At home, an hour later, Jim is out of sorts.

"What happened with Mrs. Conway?"

"I was just finishing my math homework at my locker." His words sizzle. "I don't know what her problem was. Two other teachers passed by me and didn't say anything at all."

"Did you talk back to her?"

"No!" His eyes flash.

"You didn't give her the stink eye, did you?"

"No, Mom! All I said was 'This will just take a minute.' Then she said, 'All right, then, I'm reporting you for insubordination.' Honest, Mom, that's it."

His story matched Wilma's. "But you're suspended for three days! You must have done something more than not move fast enough!"

"I didn't. And what about the teachers who went by me and didn't say a word? Maybe they thought it was a good thing that I was doing my homework! Just my bad luck Ole Bag Conway came by."

By now I'm feeling incensed as well and have a burning desire to take on Wilma White and Mrs. Conway. Even Kent recalls that Wilma seemed to have it in for Jimmy specifically.

I've never wanted to be a parent-from-hell, but I can't ignore this. Was there something more at play? A teacher with a bias? Something that provoked Jim to be noncompliant?

"I'm going to speak to Wilma about this. Is that okay with you?"

"Yeah," he says. I can tell he feels he has no one else to turn to.

I phone Wilma the next day, the first day of Jim's suspension.

"I've had a conversation with Jim and his story lines up with yours," I say. "He understands that he broke a school rule, and that he deserves some kind of penalty."

"Of course," Wilma says. I imagine she's hoping I want to avoid a fuss.

"But I've got to tell you, Wilma, I'm having a lot of trouble with this suspension. First of all, I sure hope Jim doesn't learn from this how easy it would be to get a few days off from school. He just needs to sit by his locker doing homework and refuse to jump to attention when a teacher asks him to move on!"

"But there's a rule." She hesitates. The defender of justice in me takes charge of my side of the conversation.

"I know about the loitering rule, but I object to the heaviness of the penalty. Wouldn't a simple detention better fit the offense? This would be like your losing three days of work for parking your car on a yellow no-parking strip. Wouldn't that penalty seem excessive? Furthermore, it's common knowledge among the students that some kids get off lightly, and that's one of the reasons Jim's feeling frustrated by such a severe penalty . . . as am I."

"I'm sorry about all that, but I have to respond to a report of insubordination from a teacher." The enforcer in Wilma holds firm.

"I can't accept this as it stands," I say. "I don't think Mrs. Conway has made a good enough case for a three-day suspension. I'm asking now that Mrs. Conway give more detail about exactly why she decided Jim's behavior warranted a three-day-suspension."

I am not prepared for the "explanation" from Mrs. Conway that arrives in the mail a few days later. She has filled in the pink slip beyond the word *Insubordination*. What she writes stuns me. There is no description of Jim's behavior. Instead, she writes "Just because Jim has special needs does not mean he can expect special treatment." I hear disdain in her words.

Special needs? Special treatment? Jim reads Mrs. Conway's explanation. He winces, tosses the pink slip on the floor, and turns away.

What a low blow! Jim's cleft condition had nothing whatsoever to do with his decision to do homework by his locker or to move too slowly in response to Mrs. Conway's command. Yet, Mrs. Conway has used this to beef up her defense for heavy-handedness. As though Jim expects special treatment because he has a cleft! As though he needs to be brought down a peg or two! Well, she certainly has succeeded in bringing him down—and me with him.

Within seconds, outrage sweeps away my surprise. It's no longer an issue of loitering and suspension. It's now an issue of her singling Jim out for some kind of lesson she thinks kids with "special needs" need to learn. This teacher has implied that because of his cleft, Jim expects special treatment. She has made an issue of his cleft when it has no relevance to the behavior in question. On the other side of the room, Jim sinks into the sofa.

"I'm going to demand a face-to-face conversation with Mrs. Conway, and I want Principal Jones and Wilma in the room," I say, barely containing my fury. "She should not get away with this kind of comment, or her high-and-mighty attitude."

"Please don't, Mom. It will just make things worse."

"But Jim, this is so wrong!"

"No, Mom, I don't want you to do any more."

I take a deep breath and choke back words of protest. I do not want to let it go, but I remind myself that this is about what Jim needs, not my indignation.

"Okay," I say. "But if you change your mind, I'd be more than happy to give that woman a piece of my mind."

"I know, Mom. But you've done enough. Besides, it won't make any difference."

It breaks my heart to see him looking so defeated. I'd been happy to see his insistence on fair treatment a few days earlier, but now, with the cut of Mrs. Conway's remark, his resolve has vanished.

"Do you mind if, at least, I write a letter to Mr. Jones and Wilma about the inconsistency of rule enforcement?" I have to do something.

He shrugs. "That'd be okay, I guess." He resists my effort to give him a hug.

It infuriates and saddens me that a teacher tosses Jim into the disability pigeonhole in such a stigmatizing manner, implying that he expected exemption from school rules because of his cleft lip. It's disheartening that a teacher makes "special needs" an issue when it has no bearing. Jim says no more about the unfairness of the suspension. He seems to be dealing with a far greater issue now.

The day following my discouraging conversation with Jim, I write the letter to Mr. Jones and Wilma White detailing my concerns about inconsistent rule enforcement and penalties, noting that penalties appear to vary depending on the temperament of individual teachers. I offer to help form and participate on a committee of parents and school personnel to improve the discipline policies and enforcement practices so that students may feel the system is just. I receive a boilerplate reply thanking me for my concern, but nothing more comes of my proposal. Nor do I hear another peep from Wilma or Mrs. Conway about the pink slip remarks—no further explanation, no acknowledgment, no apology. They are willing to let Mrs. Conway's demeaning remark remain on the record.

Jim serves out his three-day suspension without further complaint. He refuses to talk about it, and I do not ask, choosing rightly or wrongly to let it be. He isolates himself for a while, as he usually does after upsetting incidents like this. I step back. I sense, too, that my anger and sadness place an additional weight on his shoulders.

I do not know how to soothe the recurring hurt, his or mine. I'm as defenseless as he is against this kind of stigmatization. In my head, I unleash my fury and imagine reading the riot act to Mrs. Conway, Wilma, and the entire school administration. I fantasize that they feel chastened and Mrs. Conway promises to refrain from shaming and belittling comments. Though there are no further grounds for addressing Mrs. Conway's inappropriate comments, it might have been possible a few years later. In the 1990s, federal laws that mandated more equitable treatment of students with disability drew attention to stigmatizing practices in school systems. Teachers like Mrs. Conway would be obligated to reconsider their pejorative treatment of students like Jim, and particularly those with more serious challenges.

It is some consolation that Edie Anderson, Jim's chemistry teacher, has also raised a big stink with Wilma White about the three-day suspension. Edie calls to tell me about it. She ranted at Wilma for putting Jim on suspension for so little reason, describing him as a basically well-behaved, serious student. Edie is perturbed in part because she has to do extra work to get Jim's homework to him, but mostly she thinks Mrs. Conway should be curbed. Edie has become my heroine of the hour.

I remain disturbed by the incident. I hate feeling helpless when stigmatizing remarks are leveled at Jim. Even though I doubt people like Mrs. Conway will change, I know I must find a way to speak up. I am realizing yet again that I cannot live with myself if I remain passive when teachers or other adults play the disability card in ways that disempower Jim, or myself, for that matter. I hope I have the backbone in the future to challenge authority figures who misuse power. I know I could have, would have, done more this time. I let it go because Jim asked me to, but I resolve to venture further across lines in the future should the need arise. I trust we will both find ways to defend ourselves against abuse of authority.

ESSENTIAL CREDENTIALS

I resolve to find a way to make things better for kids and parents like me, parents who too often feel rudderless within the medical and educational systems, parents who too often find themselves and their kids hurting and left to their own devices after encounters with doctors or teachers. The incident with Mrs. Conway has given me new incentive to complete goals I envisioned several years ago.

In 1980, with James's full support, I had plunged into graduate studies in counseling psychology at the University of Oregon with the goal of becoming a counselor to parents like myself, in particular to young parents. Nine years into mothering Jimmy and grappling on my own with difficult feelings, I discovered the benefits of personal counseling and came to believe that if I had been steered earlier in Jim's life toward counseling therapy, I might have been better able to manage the bumps in the road that often frustrated young Jim's and my journey. There had to be many parents who could use counseling support as they coped with the demands of parenting a child with disability. This gap in counseling services begged for attention and I began to believe it was a gap I could fill. Being a mother with notches in my belt wasn't enough. I needed professional credentials. A master's degree would accomplish that.

I was discouraged to discover that little existed in counselor training courses to help me develop strategies for helping parents where disability of a child was a major stressor. I had taken basic coursework in early childhood development, parent guidance, and various theories of counseling, but found no coursework dealing with the social and psychological challenges for children with disability, or for their parents and siblings. In one parent guidance course, I inquired about adapting counseling strategies to address parenting children who are challenged by disability.

"Wouldn't a counselor need to take into consideration the unique circumstances of parenting a child with disability when providing parenting guidance?" I asked.

"No" was the reply. "The principles of child guidance are the same."

"But aren't there family-specific adjustments and emotional factors at play for these parents and children? Considerations for siblings?"

"That shouldn't make a difference in the parenting approach," said the professor.

Wrong, I said to myself, but I didn't bring it up again.

It was equally disconcerting to become aware of the prevailing mutual distrust that prevented medical and mental health professionals from working collaboratively. Medical doctors seemed unwilling to endorse counseling as a serious treatment for depression and anxiety because counseling efficacy had not been tested by the rigors of scientific methodology. Besides, there were medications to deal with mental and emotional distress. At the same time, professors and students in the counseling psychology program regularly made cynical remarks about the medical doctors, assuming they would exclude counseling as an option for treating distressed patients. I could not help expressing my consternation to one professor whose derisive remarks to the class about doctors seemed only to reinforce the polarization.

"Why do we spend so much time being so negative about doctors?" I blurted. "Shouldn't we be working to overcome the disconnect between medical professionals and mental health providers? How is this mutual disdain helping patients who need the services of both?" I left the classroom in protest, flustered, and upset.

Things took a turn for the better midway through my master's studies. I presented myself to Dr. Diane Bricker, head of the Early Intervention Program in the Special Education Department at the university. Her program trained special educators in classrooms where half of the young children under three years of age had a disability. I asked if I might develop a parent support group as a practicum. I believed such a group would benefit parents of the young children with disabilities who were enrolled in the early education classrooms.

Dr. Bricker agreed to my proposal. I reserved the building's comfortable lounge area. One morning a week during class time, I offered parents free doughnuts and coffee in the lounge. The parents were reserved at first, but soon they were comfortable enough to open up. They talked about the impact on their lives of having a child with disability—tension with their partners, siblings whose needs were being neglected, family members' and friends' insensitivity, feeling awkward in public, financial burdens. They seemed to feel less alone learning that they experienced similar troubling thoughts and feelings and that these were normal reactions to their circumstances. They spoke of worrying whether their child was getting help that would make a difference.

I learned quickly that parents had many questions and few answers. In the group they vented about worries from their personal and family lives—relationships, finances, parenting their child in the Early Intervention Program, and siblings. Their complaints about teachers or their child's Individualized Education Plan (IEP) were born from anxiety about whether their children were getting the help they most needed. They wanted to have a say more often and hear more frequent progress reports. I encouraged them to raise questions with teachers and to brainstorm with the group about constructive ways to present issues to teachers.

I met regularly with Dr. Bricker and provided reports as requested. She approved, and the parent group flourished. In ensuing terms of working with parent groups, I adapted strategies from my training in individual and family counseling to the specific needs of parents of young children with disability. It was rewarding to see that whatever reluctance these parents may have had in seeking help from a counselor, fearing it would imply stigmatizing neediness, it soon disappeared. In addition to talking over coffee and doughnuts during parent group sessions, many parents sought me out for personal and couples counseling. It helped that I was also a parent of a child with disability. It gave me credibility far more potent than a professional degree. The parents trusted that I intrinsically understood their heartaches, frustration, and worries. And I saw how much I had in common with them. I heard familiar themes in their stories of struggle that strengthened my conviction that counseling support for parents with their specific life experiences was important.

Dr. Bricker invited me to help her write an application for federal funds to support and engage parents. Our proposal was successful, and the grant we were awarded provided funds to pay parents for their time in the classroom learning to assist teachers. In the process, parents learned important skills to aid their child's development. Parents and teachers learned to work together. Soon, I was working with parents and the local chapter of ARC, the Association for

Retarded Citizens (later renamed The Arc), to create a parent support network. We developed a training program to teach listening and support skills to parents of older children with disability. These parents then provided support to parents of newborns with a disability similar to their child's.

As my graduate studies progressed, I set my sights on earning additional credentials—a doctorate and a psychologist license—that would give me greater credibility in professional circles. Imagine my being addressed as Dr. Walker! As a graduate student, I took advantage of opportunities to speak to special educators about the need for supportive services for parents and the inclusion of parents in discussions about their child's care.

I made efforts in my community, too. I discussed with a medical doctor friend how important it is that pediatricians more routinely refer parents to counseling resources.

"That makes sense," he said, "but frankly, doctors are plenty busy taking care of the child who is their primary patient. We don't have time to attend to parents' needs, too."

"But referrals to counselors could not be all that demanding, could they?" I asked.

"No," he replied kindly, "but it just isn't on our agenda."

But it should be, I thought.

His candor simply underscored for me the existing difficulties. Given my own experience and what I was hearing, it seemed doctors did not yet consider mental health counseling for parents as a meaningful complement to medical treatment. How many parents were assuming their doctors would provide the support they needed? Were parents hitting dead ends, as I had, when they disclosed to a doctor emotional or mental distress, their own or their child's? Did they feel informed and confident enough to make a specific request for, perhaps even insist on, a referral to mental health services?

When I first worked with special educators, I was struck by how little it occurred to them as well to consider referring a parent to a counselor. They were concerned but at a loss when a parent expressed despair about a failing marriage, mentioned lack of gas money, disclosed feelings of inadequacy in managing their child's disability, directed anger at providers, or showed signs of exhaustion and mental illness. Though highly trained in teaching children challenged by disability to achieve optimal levels of functioning, educators were not trained to help parents cope. Nor was it normal practice to refer parents to counseling services. The educators I encountered devoted enormous time to evaluating a child's development, describing problems, devising treatment plans, informing parents of all of this and in some cases, as at the Early Intervention Program, training parents in skills to promote their child's development. While this was critically important, I felt frustrated that treatment plans seemed to be formulated with little input from parents. What behaviors were most important to the child's functioning at home? Often, parents knew ways to work with their child that might have been instructive to teachers. Wouldn't teachers have benefited from knowing these? What about focusing efforts on behaviors that were priorities for parents, which might include improving parent-child relationships, getting their child to mind their instructions, achieving easy bedtimes, establishing compliance with hygiene routines, or finding friends to play with?

Educators of young children with disability also emphasized the importance of positive interactions between the mother and the young child, citing the benefit to the child's development.

"What about the mother?" I broke in. "She's developing, too, especially if she's new to mothering a child with disability. Reinforcement from positive interactions with her child is important to her development too, isn't it?" Over time, teachers in the Early

Intervention Program warmed to my perspective on parents and gladly referred parents for personal counseling and participation in the parent support group I was facilitating.

I hoped my goal of combining counseling psychology and special education studies would make sense to the faculty of the Counseling Psychology Department. While meeting requirements for degrees in counseling psych, I was also earning credits as a graduate teaching fellow in Dr. Bricker's Early Intervention Program. At least one professor in the Counseling Psychology Program didn't see the point of my spending so much time in the special education area.

"What does special education have to do with counseling psychology?" he asked. By now this myopic perspective did not surprise me. Nor did it dissuade me.

"My professional goal is to counsel families who have a child with disability," I reminded him. "I'm convinced that counseling for them needs to be tailored to their unique needs and there's no coursework in the Counseling Psych Department that addresses this. Dr. Bricker is allowing me to experience a special education environment and giving me the opportunity to develop a counseling approach for this parent population. It's absolutely in line with my professional goals."

He shrugged. "That's a lot of coursework that doesn't count toward your degree."

On that point, he was right. I was accruing quite a few credits for coursework in special education that did not satisfy requirements for my degree in counseling psych, but I was glad to have them. They gave me both access to the population of parents I was interested in working with and close contact with special educators with whom I wanted to gain credibility.

I continued cobbling together a program of study combining coursework and practicums in counseling psych and special education. With tongue in cheek, I hung the name plaque James had given me for Christmas on my office door at the Clinical Services building on campus. It read "Barbara R. Walker, W.M.T.B." Often I heard voices outside the door, puzzling over this strange professional designation. When someone asked what the initials W.M.T.B. stood for, I stifled a smile and told them: "Wife and Mother of Two Boys."

"It's a joke, then," they were apt to say.

"Not at all. Most of what I know about children and family comes from being a wife and mother." My name plaque may not have had academic weight, but it was a way of acknowledging all that I'd learned from life.

My work with Dr. Bricker, as well as training in counseling psychology, inspired my studies and research. Like my master's thesis, my doctoral dissertation dealt with parent-professional communication and partnerships. Dr. George Singer, a researcher in Oregon Research Institute's Special Education division, generously supported my dissertation work and my interest in promoting more sensitive and productive communication between parents and pediatricians and special educators. As Dr. Bricker had earlier, he asked me to write articles for publications of which he was the editor. He encouraged me to give presentations at national special education conferences. Together we produced a role-play video to demonstrate to pediatricians the difference between ineffective interactions with parents and interactions that foster collaboration. I was invited to conduct trainings on communication and collaboration skills for both professionals and parents, always emphasizing the importance of parent perspectives and the vital role parents can play as partners in determining meaningful treatment outcomes.

Dr. Ann Turnbull, a national figure in the world of parent advocacy and legal rights for people with disability, invited me to sit on a panel of parents at a conference for special educators and parents. She thanked me for speaking candidly about the wishes, thoughts, and feelings parents hold back. "Educators need to know more about parents' experiences and be more sensitive to their perspective," she said. Ann Turnbull's words told me I was on course.

It was not easy to bare my soul in public and plead for greater understanding from professionals. But as I spoke more and more in this vein, I became encouraged by the response. Audiences were attentive not only to what I had to say from a professional point of view but also, and more personally gratifying, what I said from my parent perspective. I pointed to my firsthand experiences in multiple medical settings over at least eighteen years, experiences that informed my assessment of professional behavior toward parents. I spoke candidly about the powerful influence professionals have on parent morale.

I described specific examples of professionals who made the road difficult and others who smoothed the way. I described the exceptional attention to parents I'd observed on the hospital ward by the staff of a cardiac surgeon at Stanford. He believed that when parents are involved and given counseling on presurgical and postsurgical care, the child's recovery is easier and surgical outcomes are maximized.

As I near the end of my graduate work, I remain intent on earning my professional credentials and reaching those professionals who, for whatever reason—lack of training, busy schedules, disinterest, excessive specialization—have not made engaging parents part of their treatment plan. These credentials will give me credibility with doctors, lawyers, and teachers who need to know I speak from more than just personal experience. But the credential that will always give me the most credibility with parents is the title W.M.T.B.—Wife and Mother of Two Boys.

Forever Friends

Oh, you boys and girls of high school, how little we knew then
    but the world
of clichés as we climbed on the theme-park ride of youth,
    despite everything
that mattered happening everywhere else in the eighties,
    except high school
being the thing happening to us, mattering to everyone else
    except us
being told the goal was just to finish so we could move on to
    what came next.
Surely you all noticed my cleft lip?
Surely you all chose to embrace me anyway
among the friends you brought with you
from your cool elementary school or the even cooler
    middle school,
those whose first secrets you had already forgotten,
those who angled for lunch period and lockers close by—
where I wanted to be, close by some new others
who wanted to be close by me,
not for pity, not because my mother arranged it, not
    because of chance.
Oh, how desperate I must have been!
And then to be taken in by all you hallway-lingering friends
hopping to U.P. for a smoke before after-lunch period
and later to the kegger up the hill fast arranging
who were the drivers or the high riders.
Oh, the drives! In pairs, and groups, all of us, and
Each a gift of time we gave each other—remember?
Up around the Butte, back down Fox Hollow at speed,

or descending Fairmount Boulevard, after midnight,
no headlights, whooping through the firs, chill night gasping,
our heads through the sunroof, popping curbs between mailboxes.
Or out east and back to Marcola, Lowell, or out west to Crow,
or a half-day to the coast just to see coast, and the blue of the sky.
Not even talking, just grinning, just gracing each other
with presence and not a single other desire.
Surely you noticed my cleft
and didn't care, and still don't even today
as we roar past the fifty-year milepost, still smiling
like wild childs on the edge of being set loose,
who know the world now is more unknown than ever,
yet is familiar, and waiting, waiting like a friend
who loves remembering when it all began,
when all that mattered was just being seen
for the first time as a real person
in the same struggle to figure shit out,
becoming aware we didn't have to
figure this all out alone
ever again.

Ode to Sport

I

Tired of lush horizons of the mind, the Muses inspired sports
    for us to seek and excel in physical arts,
        not just through virtues of labor,
            or the landscapes of a lover,
or the whims of war, but through a singular personal choosing
    to submit to risk our one body, our one name,
        our muscle, mind and strength of heart,
            all for self and hometown glory,
all toward victory, all for adulation!

The calling to sport is many a child's first play far from the hearth,
    to test themselves, and even more among others,
        where excuses are rejected
            and all cleft or homebound troubles
are relieved through earning respect by giving sweat to
    shared purpose
    pursuing honest success or honest defeat,
        each so equally guaranteed,
            and neither fully understood
or usefully employed but in close company.

The effort spent is the reward. What separations a child brings
are divinely in such callings slowly bridged.

II

I've played at many rough games that put my fragile face
    in danger,
        none more than wrestling, yet only there I found—
            from the dank, padded practice rooms,
                dense with fresh bleach and heavy air
wherein I broke my hand punching a wall, and my ankle
    was snapped
        by the eldest Culp, and I sparred ardent teammates:
            Ari, Asa, Simcha, my peer—
                a path through fear of such dangers,
a measure of confidence to last a lifetime.

I was solid enough in meets across the Oregon valleys.
    My tally forgotten, a few visions linger
        from the wide, high gymnasiums
            under lights and hollering crowds
wherein I struggled with leg-riders from Lowell and never beat
    Stenger of Thurston, but won twice in Cottage Grove,
        once a breath from tipping the scale,
            the other against a man-beast
after moving up to better the match for all.

Only these memories remain. I may not have wrestled with
    great skill,
but from wrestling cultivated great pride.

III

As surely as sport yields the extent of personal potential,
    so too does sport connect across generations
        in ways beyond the family,
            with coaches in bonds just as tight:
Henry, built like a truck, grinning mid-throw, heart as big as any;
    Sean, who drilled us hard, but was hardest on himself;
        George, who provided to each one
            within our need just enough space
to give each day to bringing our best as wrestlers

and a lifetime to serving others as a means to know ourselves.
    To him I owe much of my finished character,
        and some of the marks on the world
            I've yet to leave or undertake.
In these later days, I grapple more with words and no more
    with men.
        As my body grows thick and my mind looks inward,
            my gratitude to sport endures–
                that for all the divine reasons
for my cleft, nothing remains beyond my resolve.

We each are given challenges. If we seek to meet them in triumph,
all we do is leave everything on the mat.

MY NAME IS . . .

Seventeen-year-old Jim lies on his back on the exam table in a corner of the large room. He has been ushered there by an ever-so-considerate gray-haired social worker responsible for setting up patients for case presentation. To pass time, she asks him questions about himself. Sure enough, as Jim predicted, only seconds pass before she eyes his team jacket and asks about his varsity letter. Earlier, in the parking lot, I asked Jim why he was donning the heavy team jacket on such a warm June day.

"It gives them something to talk to me about," he answered. "It's less awkward this way."

The medical people attending this evaluation are having trouble talking to me, too. The twenty or so doctors and residents show no interest in me as I approach the presiding doctor at the head of the large conference table.

"I'm Barbara Walker, Jim's mother," I say as I hand him the chart I've brought from the orthodontist.

"Didn't Dr. Walker come?" The doctor in charge peers around me over his glasses.

"No, he couldn't come." I square my shoulders. "But I can answer any questions."

"Oh." He sighs. "Well, I'm disappointed. I was expecting to discuss the medical issues with your husband." With no further word, he turns his attention to the medical case file in front of him.

"I'm also quite aware of the medical issues involved," I say. "And I can discuss them with you."

With not so much as another glance in my direction, the doctor launches into his presentation.

"This is a particularly complicated cleft," he begins.

Not a patient with a cleft, not Jim Walker, but a "complicated cleft."

I'm left standing there, the sidelined mother. It's a treatment I've come to expect. The social worker appears and invites me in a whisper to follow her to the waiting room.

"You can have a cup of coffee while you wait."

"I'll stay here. I want to listen." She hesitates, retreats a bit, but hovers nearby.

After a lengthy discussion of the particulars of the "cleft case" before them, those assembled, most of whom are in white coats, trail behind the visiting consultant as he moves from the conference table toward the X-ray viewing boxes mounted on one wall. The consultant is a plastic surgeon with expertise in craniofacial anomalies and has been called upon to advise Jim's medical team how best to tackle reconstruction of his still-not-repaired palate and upper jaw.

I follow the white coats to the X-ray viewing boxes. Again, the social worker materializes at my elbow. "I think it's best you wait outside," she says. Her insistence verges on urgency. It seems to be her job to keep me preoccupied. The consultant and several others turn toward me. I understand from the looks leveled at me that I am intruding inside a privileged circle.

"I only want to listen," I say. "I want to hear what you think about addressing Jim's cleft repair."

Silence.

"I won't interfere." I smile and step to the back.

The consultant turns back to the X-rays. The others follow suit. He points to several areas on the X-rays of Jim's mouth, pinpointing the problems and rendering opinions on the surgical repairs required. Jim remains in the flat-on-his-back position assigned to him on the exam table, excluded from this vital discussion about how to make his jaw and palate whole, even though he is obviously old enough to understand and participate, even though *he* is the one most affected by their decisions.

After fifteen minutes of commentary, the consultant strides to the exam table, scanning the medical chart in his hands. The assembled white coats follow en masse. They lean in and peer down at Jim, hovering over him.

I do not follow to the exam table. I already know what will happen there. The expert will direct a bright light into Jim's mouth, push his tongue down with a tongue depressor, and probe and scrutinize every nook and cranny—the clefts in both sides of his upper jaw, the floating piece of jaw left suspended and vulnerable at the front of his mouth between the two clefts, and the sizable fistula (opening) remaining at the front of his hard palate. They will hem and haw about how to close all the gaps. The assembled surgeons and dental specialists will lament the number of missing teeth and ponder about how to construct bridges and eventually supply implanted teeth that will allow this patient to chew and control food properly.

"So this is the cleft palate in question," the consultant begins. He has stationed himself at the head of the exam table and reaches for Jim's mouth without making eye contact.

"Open," he commands.

Jim turns his head toward the consultant and without opening his mouth, looks up at him.

From a distance, I wince and manage the stew of humiliation, indignation, and anger that wells up in reaction to such impersonal treatment. I've lost count of similar encounters over the course of Jim's seventeen years. I've come to expect, if not to accept, that as "the mother," I should remain silent.

For the most part, my desire to be accepted by specialists as a critical party in my son's treatment has been unfulfilled, beginning with the surgeon who performed the lip and palate repairs in Jimmy's infancy and toddler years. Dr. DeWitt implied that I was out of my league when I thought I could work with Jimmy at home on his speech. He advised me to just concentrate on being a good mother. Wouldn't a "good mother" want to play an important role in resolving her child's medical problems?

As a young mother and for years afterward, I took Dr. DeWitt's words as a general directive to leave the cleft-related work to the experts. But after years of caring for Jimmy, cleft and all, I dared to believe I could be helpful in discussions with specialists about his speech, orthodontic, dental, and surgical needs. However, my experience as his mother did not hold much weight in professional settings. This rankled me and I itched to do something about it. When Jimmy was ten, I announced that I wanted to attend the conference at the end of a two-day evaluation. The doctor in charge paused.

"Mothers don't normally attend," he said. "It's a medical conference."

"But I need to hear what everyone thinks," I said.

"I'll make a note of that." He did not refuse my request.

I made the rounds with Jimmy to visit the various professionals on the evaluation team. The orthodontist challenged me.

"I understand you want to attend the post-evaluation conference."

"Yes, I'm looking forward to it."

"Well, it's really not appropriate for a mother to attend. In fact, it's a problem." He leveled a pointed look at me. I had the feeling he had me pegged as a mother he could put in her place.

I bristled. "Why is that?"

"If you're there, we can't speak candidly about the medical issues."

"Why not?"

"We'll be discussing issues with previous treatment."

I reflected for a moment. It seemed he was worried I might be a mother looking for a lawsuit opportunity.

I gathered my thoughts. I would not accommodate this man's displeasure at my wanting to attend the post-evaluation conference.

"How about this?" I said. "I'll excuse myself from the part of the meeting where you all review the treatment history and critique the work of Jimmy's previous providers, and I'll attend only the part where you summarize your assessments and make recommendations for the next steps in his treatment."

"That's not a parent's job! It's ours!" he snapped. His face flushed. "Don't you think the doctors should decide what happens next?"

I kept my calm. "It's *my* job to understand what you doctors are recommending. And it's *my job*—mine and Jimmy's father's—to decide which recommendations to act on. I don't mean to offend you, but as Jimmy's mother, I consider myself a consumer of services with some choice."

"I think we're done here." The orthodontist stood and turned away.

I was happy to leave. The encounter had shaken me, but at least I did not let myself be dismissed as just "the mother."

The post-evaluation conference at this visit presented additional challenges. A social worker convened the meeting. She announced that the case that day involved a ten-year-old boy with a cleft palate. No name. Just a case. Before turning the meeting over to the medical team, she said in a cautionary tone, "The mother is in the room." Apparently, my name wasn't germane either. She pointed to where I was seated against the wall. Heads turned. I smiled and waved, hoping to convey friendly intentions.

I took notes on the proceedings. All the while, Jimmy was required to lie still on an exam table on the far side of the room. From time to time during the session, various experts left the conference table to examine his mouth. He lay quietly and submitted to the various probings.

At one point, an oral surgeon took the floor and reported with enthusiasm the paper he had recently given at a medical conference on implanted teeth. At the time, transplanting teeth was a new procedure still in an experimental phase.

"It's similar to transplanting a potted plant," he opined. Furthermore, he thought it would be a good idea for this case, given the number of missing teeth.

I raised my hand. "I have a question."

Heads turned in my direction, eyebrows shot up. The mother has a question?!

"How many of these tooth implants have been performed at this medical center?"

The oral surgeon shuffled his papers. "Well, ah, only one to date."

"And what do you estimate to be the rejection rate?"

He hesitated and then replied quietly, "About fifty percent."

"Then I don't think we're interested in this for Jimmy at this time. We'll wait until the procedure has been perfected."

There was an awkward silence and a few mutterings around the table before someone brought the room back to order. I may have been out of order, but, by George, I made it clear that as Jimmy's mother I *would* have a voice in discussions about my son's medical treatment.

When the meeting ended, several attendees clustered around the exam table where Jimmy lay. He looked at the ceiling, hands folded over his stomach. As the experts leaned over him, he dutifully opened his mouth so they could peer inside. Others at the meeting chatted in groups or shuffled out of the room and I was left standing along the wall.

A doctor, older than the others, made his way toward me. I braced myself for a prickly encounter, but the friendly expression on his face disarmed me. He introduced himself as the surgeon on Jimmy's case and shook my hand.

"Mrs. Walker, let me ask you something," he said. "We've been discussing the need for scar revision on the left side of Jimmy's lip, the one affected by the accident when he was four. It could be smoothed out quite a bit. But I want to know from you if he's having social adjustment problems because of his scar. If he's getting teased a lot, it might help to do a repair now. Many parents push for it because of teasing. But, as you know, surgery is a difficult ordeal for a ten-year-old, and if he's managing well socially, it can wait. He'll need at least one revision on that lip as he grows, and for sure before he leaves home at eighteen."

He paused, eyebrows raised, a questioning look on his face.

I was stunned! Did I hear correctly? He used Jimmy's name and addressed me by name! He was asking my opinion about how Jimmy's cleft was affecting his life! This surgeon was breaking the mold.

"It has to be what his parents think is best for him," he added.

In less than a minute, this surgeon made me feel valued as part of the team. He let me know that my participation in decisions about Jimmy's treatment mattered. Did my speaking up at the conference lead him to understand I needed to be considered? That it was better to involve me than ignore me?

Jimmy and I left the clinic in the late afternoon of the second day. As we drove back to Eugene, I was lost in thought about all that had transpired. Jimmy's voice from the back seat was barely audible.

"I'm just a bunch of problems, aren't I, Mom?"

"Why do you say that?"

"My problems . . . that's all they talked about. They don't even know my name." His voice cracked.

My heart sank.

"We need a milkshake," I said. I pulled off at the next exit.

"Feels yucky, doesn't it? Having to let them stick their hands and tongue depressors in your mouth over and over. That's their job, Jimmy, to understand the problem with your cleft and figure out how to fix it. It's too bad they only talk about problems and don't take time to get to know you and all the neat things about you."

He works on his milkshake in silence.

"Remember how we talked about our car mechanic?" I say. "We go to him to fix problems, not to talk about how great our car is."

We took our time sipping our milkshakes. We also took time to rate the social skills of each of the professionals we'd encountered over the past two days. The kind surgeon got an A, and the orthodontist got an F.

That was seven years ago. Now, at age seventeen, Jim continues to need the expertise of skilled specialists like this consultant to address his cleft problems. The caring surgeon of seven years ago has long since retired. Now he seems like a mirage as I do my best to hold my own against the not-so-subtle efforts to keep me on the perimeter of this discussion. No one addresses me or Jim by name or inquires about our concerns. I can handle it, but I worry about how Jim will fare in this face-to-face encounter with the aloof consultant from LA. I've seen his spirits nosedive when doctors treat him as just another item on their docket. Often, he simply closes his eyes and withdraws. As I watch, fearing the worst, the consultant bends over for a closer look, and extends his gloved, skilled surgeon's fingers toward Jimmy's mouth.

"Open," he says.

Jimmy extends his right hand toward the surgeon.

"Hello," he says. His tone of voice is as firm as the consultant's. "I'm Jim Walker. What's your name?"

Memory Study 2

Open, please . . . wider . . . wider, good . . .

I shut my eyes before they turn on the exam light.
I don't need to see their shadowed heads floating

as I try not to taste the thick soap on their fingers
or the tang from the metal picks, the small round mirrors.

Close . . . open again . . . close . . . open and wide . . .
A history of poor attention . . . close . . . open, good . . .

They lean over one by one, then one by one again.
I know two of them, and the rest know me as a case file.

Yes, this whole area of instability . . . close . . .
And open . . . no, the mother is outside . . . close, please . . .

I tune out, on the brink of sleep, as usual. They're the doctors.
I'm a tricky cleft in a teenager, a worthy problem to gather around.

These really are the most comfortable chairs ever conceived,
so easy for sleep to slip the mind from time and tune it all out.

Open, open . . . see there, the anterior . . . open wider . . .
Open . . . suction please, good . . . open wider . . .

The specialist wiggles the last incisors and both upper canines,
mumbling into the chasm behind the premaxillary segment.

The dentist asks what people want for lunch.
A surgeon digging in the gums says he doesn't really care.

Good, open wider . . . close . . . open . . . stay open . . .

No questions will be directed at me. They are the doctors.
They have a few molds, photos, a few options to discuss,
    and anyway

Close . . . open . . . close . . . open, please . . .

Sometimes I still find submission the easiest choice
not to be what you are for a little while.

Close . . . open . . . close . . . open, more . . .
Close . . . open . . . now hold . . . hold right there . . .

HOW TO LIVE WITH MYSELF

I'm caught off guard. My day has been uneventful, and I've come home early from work. James's call changes that. The distress in his voice sets me instantly on edge. He's just had a conversation with Mrs. Romaine, the high school counselor. According to Mrs. Romaine, Jim walked out of school a couple of hours ago in a distraught state. Something in his reaction to a conversation with his friend Diana caused Diana to alert the school counselors that she thought Jim might harm himself. When Mrs. Romaine questioned him in a hallway among students changing classes, Jim reacted with frustration. She then called him to her office, where she and another counselor questioned him further. He didn't want to discuss anything, stood up, and walked out of the building. Mrs. Romaine interrupted James at work to inform him of the urgent situation. Jim failed to show up for wrestling practice after school, which is further cause for concern.

I can hear the alarm in James's voice. "Did he come home?"

"He's not here." My voice wavers. "I don't know what upset him or where he is, but there's a note from him on the kitchen counter. It says, 'Don't worry about me. I need some time.'"

"I feel awful," James continues. "Mrs. Romaine said Jim told her he didn't talk much to us about what worries him, and she implied that our poor communication with him was a big part of his problem."

Oh, great! A double punch. Not only is Jim in a wretched state, but we are to blame. I've been here before: Jim often balks in a session with a doctor, an orthodontist, a speech therapist, a teacher, or a counselor, and they imply that we could be doing more to make him more cooperative.

I try to sound steady. "Honey, let's not fall into that trap. Whatever upset our son today happened at school. Besides, we both know Jim has always held his cards tight to his chest despite our best efforts. Let's not let Mrs. Romaine make this our failure."

"Still . . ."

"I know." My voice cracks. "Let's not beat ourselves up. Let's just hope Jim works his way through this. I'll call as soon as I learn anything."

As soon as I hang up, my chest tightens. My heart races. Jim's senior year had been going well, but something hit him hard today. My first thought—like a knee-jerk reaction—is that Jim's cleft has something to do with it. If not his cleft, then what? A remark from Diana? Something that transpired in the counselor's office? Whatever triggered Jim, thoughts of the worst-case scenario give me the chills. What if Jim doesn't work his way through this?

I remind myself that in many respects Jim is like other teens who are known to have extreme reactions to frustrations, upsetting interactions, or situations they perceive as unfair or humiliating. I know mood swings are par for the course for most teenagers, but to run off by himself . . . that is not usual. I can't deflect memories of times when Jim has had thoughts that made me worry about his despair. I have read his stories for class assignments and found scraps of writing left in his room. His writing often reveals a sense of futility—that no matter the effort, desire, and hope you invest, you cannot ensure your own success and happiness. Nor can others.

The story he wrote when he was ten jumps to mind. The assignment was to write about an experience on the moon. In Jim's story, he was an astronaut whose lunar rover broke down one hundred yards from the mother ship. With heroic effort he made his way back to the mother ship with only a minute of oxygen left. Step by excruciating step, he clambered in slow motion over the rock-strewn surface, fighting exhaustion, fully aware of the oxygen ebbing away second by second. Struggling, he crawled inside the mother ship's hatch. His oxygen was depleted. The crew rushed to rescue him but by the time they had sealed and oxygenated the hatch and pulled Jim's helmet off, he was dead. They had not gotten to him in time. Even though he'd done all he could, others had not been able to get him to safety. He needed others, but they had not been able to save him. Where did these tragic ideas of futility come from? TV shows? Books? His imagination? His temperament? Or, as I couldn't help thinking, from feeling demoralized by unwanted and hurtful reactions to his cleft? I shudder.

I'm caught in a spiral of indecision and emotion. Knowing this situation would throw any dedicated parent into a similar state doesn't relieve my torment. Would other parents sit tight and not get on the phone and call every person who might know where their child is, get in their car and drive around to every place in town that child might have gone? I try to calm myself and to ignore the fear and guilt-inducing thoughts.

I return over and over to Jim's note and read it aloud—"Don't worry about me. I need some time." I want the words to sink in and steady me, drown out the heckling voices that shame me for not searching for him. I anchor on Jim's request for time. Hasn't he told me, in so many words, he can and is working through his dilemma? Isn't he telling me I can trust him to know what he needs to do?

I recall that in contrast to stories he wrote that were laced with futility, Jim also devoured books where heroes overcome daunting odds for their survival and emerge triumphant. I think of his solid relationships with adults who mentor him. I hope he is drawing on lessons from these role models. I hope he reminds himself of the many friends he cares for and who care for him.

I choose to sit still and wait. I hope I can live with this choice.

Living with choices has been fundamental to my idea of myself. One of the strongest beliefs I developed during my upbringing was that I needed to be my own counsel and be responsible for my choices. At home at night as a teenager, I often turned to a poem by Edgar A. Guest taped on the wall over my bed. The words resonate with messages I heard often from my parents. The first six lines had become a mantra and served me well when I had difficult decisions to make.

> *"I have to live with myself and so*
> *I want to be fit for myself to know.*
> *I want to be able as days go by,*
> *Always to look myself straight in the eye;*
> *I don't want to stand with the setting sun*
> *And hate myself for the things I have done."*
>
> —*From "Myself" by Edgar A. Guest*

I came into adulthood believing I knew how to have a clear conscience at the end of the day. Because I had been raised to think before and after about the effects of my actions and had followed most of the rules laid out by parents and teachers, I believed I would be richly rewarded in my lifetime. I perceived my marriage to James as one such reward—a rich one indeed—and anticipated that having a family would be another. Then, with Jimmy's birth and all that followed, I felt as though the contract I'd made with fate—that if I were ethical and lived by the rules, I would be rewarded—had been a fantasy. Living by the rules was not paying off. I felt punished. What had I done to deserve the heartache of having a child needing painful surgeries just to be able to eat and speak without unusual difficulty? And even now, good intentions were not enough. I was willing to do what it would take to minimize the ordeals we faced but, no matter how hard I tried to do the right thing, or how much time I put in, I couldn't help feeling I was failing to provide what my boys, and Jim in particular, needed and deserved from me. My ineffectiveness exhausted me. Some days I threw my hands up in defeat. Sometimes, I refused to think about how Jim's day was going.

Now, once again, I find myself searching for a compass point. Unanswered questions, indecision, and emotional turmoil leave me spinning. Time passes with no word from Jim. The counselor's words of concern for Jim's safety and our failure to communicate with him echo in my head. The cacophony of critical voices comes alive, harping that I am shirking my responsibility. I pace the room. What if the day turns out badly?

Then, the lines of Guest's poem come to mind. I ask myself what I can do right now to be able to live with myself, however the day turns out. I read Jim's note again—"Don't worry about me. I need some time."

Over the din of critical voices rises another one, strong and steady, urging me to trust Jim to find his way. With this thought I steel myself and conjure up reassuring thoughts. Jim has fortitude. Hasn't he grown stronger and surer of himself as he has tackled school and athletics and met goals he's set for himself, like the arduous bike trip? Of course he prefers, would probably demand, to manage this distress on his own. The more he's done without parental assistance these days, the more satisfied he seems with life. His cleft has seemed less and less an issue and no longer appears to cause hesitation in his decision-making or impediments to his social life. And perhaps most important of all, I want to believe in, and want him to know I believe in, his ability to make wise decisions, especially now that he's about to leave home.

I remind myself that this is not the first time I've made a choice to sit on the sidelines worrying about Jim being in harm's way. The long solo bike trip tested my stamina for days. On other occasions I've managed to give him room to figure out how to manage challenges on his own, and I suspect there have been many times I'm not aware of when Jim has successfully worked himself out of dark holes. In my rational mind, I trust Jim will discover, without the help of his highly invested mother, how to work through his troubles today.

I take a deep breath and continue to sit with my choice to wait it out.

I remain in this cocoon of self-preserving thoughts and suspended panic for what seems like hours. I do not think of preparing dinner, or whether there will be homework to monitor, or plans I need to make for tomorrow. I am only partially aware that Kent has come home from school. I do not wonder when James will come home. And then, I hear the exterior door on the landing open and close, then footsteps descending the stairs and heading toward Jim's bedroom. I take a deep breath and return to a mobile state. I feel warmth in my veins. I dial James's office.

"He's home."

A few minutes later, I venture downstairs and knock lightly on Jim's bedroom door.

"Yeah?" His voice is sullen.

He's standing by his bed, turned away from me. I hug him from behind and feel his body relax. We stay that way a long moment.

"Thanks for the note." I gave him an extra squeeze.

I do not ask him what happened. I doubt he will tell. I may never know what went wrong for him at school today—if Diana said something that brought him low, if Mrs. Romaine pushed him to a boiling point, or if he was upset with himself for being vulnerable once again to what others say. I *do* know that this boy who is having a tougher-than-usual day, who rarely discloses feelings to anyone, and who Mrs. Romaine said could not talk to his parents took the trouble to leave me a note, reassuring me that he was not in harm's way. His note was the antidote I needed to resist Mrs. Romaine's insinuation of dire outcomes and communication failure at home and to quell my fears about Jim's safety. I was able to mute the defeating voices in my head that called for a rescue response and instead put my trust in Jim's message. It was a difficult choice, but in the end, I'm convinced that giving him the time and space he needed to find his own way through his troubles was the right thing to do.

I go to my bathroom to freshen up. After splashing cold water on my face, I gaze at my reflection in the mirror. My face shows the wear and tear of the last few hours, but I'm able to look myself square in the eye without flinching. I can live with the choice I made today.

Cupid's Broken Bow

After the surgery at seventeen, lip still swollen, I remember
pacing the basement, the dull brownness of the walls, of small talk,
of the ebbs of light—all tired of the effort to remain here.

The promises this time had been inspiring—filling out the upper lip,
connecting the orbicularis oris, restoring cupid's bow—as promises
    should be.
Only in their breaking is there any truth worth knowing.

We've all been given broken promises. Then we lean over
    the dark edge
looking for an out. The call of the future fades, also tired
    of the effort,
restless for some sudden release from the long-drawn waiting.
    I remember

becoming a deep inhale of myself. Then I let go of being repaired
    and beautiful,
of being loved, of being kissed like a teenager. As the swelling
    receded
and my upper lip remained a flat whitened smear, the world
    released

and I flew.

LETTING GO

Jim is tight-lipped and somber this early morning in late August 1988. He has exchanged brief, tight hugs with his dad and Kent, who now wave a last goodbye as I back the loaded van out of the driveway. James's eyes are moist and he's pursing his lips, emotions written all over his face. Kent furrows his brow as though he's figuring out how to think about his brother's departure. They each make an effort to wish Jim a hearty send-off, but their goodbyes are solemn rather than robust. I grip the wheel and set my jaw, committed to my task. It's a big day for all of us.

"Well, here we go," I say, hoping to elicit a hint of excitement from Jim. "Hope we haven't forgotten anything." Jim has been far from diligent in packing.

"I'll be fine." His reply is barely audible. I take a deep breath as we turn up 30th Avenue and toward I-5. We are bound for the University of Redlands, a long two days' drive to Southern California, where Jim will be starting college. I sneak a peek at him in the passenger's seat. He is looking straight ahead, stone-faced. I have no idea what he is thinking or feeling about what lies ahead, or behind, for that matter. His mood is no doubt dampened because the injury sustained to his right arm in a car accident two weeks ago prevents him from participating in the driving. Whatever his disposition, I am determined to deliver this boy to his dorm room at Redlands. I've put aside for now concerns about still-needed attention to his cleft and think instead about the milestone this trip represents for both of us: Jim is leaving home and I will be letting go of him.

Over the last few months Jim has been steadily pulling away, spending less time with family, more time out with friends, and refusing to tell us where he was going and with whom. I could practically lip-sync his responses to my routine questions.

"What are your plans tonight?" I'd ask.

"Going out."

"Where?"

"Out and about."

"With whom?"

"Friends."

"Anyone I know?"

"Nope."

"Guess I'll have to trust you. You know the rules."

"Yup."

"You need to wake me and breathe in my face when you come home."

He would sigh.

"Okay." I let loose a hefty sigh of my own. "Have a good time and be safe."

To which he signed off with "Sure, Mom."

I was in no way reassured, but I also knew that in a few weeks, I'd have no role in monitoring his activities. Jim's mishaps and displays of defiance this past summer have rattled me, especially the car accident two weeks ago. He'd fallen asleep and rolled our Volkswagen

Rabbit on I-5 after picking up a friend from a late-night flight at the Portland airport. Fortunately, no one was seriously injured, but it rankled me that I didn't even know he'd driven to Portland. This and his impatience with parental rules, unexplained overnight absences, and general chafing against parental surveillance I chalked up to typical teen behavior at this important juncture in life. I also saw Jim's restlessness and increased urge for independence as a typical teenager's way of telling his parents he was ready to leave home.

In truth, I was pleased he was engaging in last-summer escapades. For the most part, I liked seeing him claim his independence. My bruised feelings when he pushed me away did not last long. I could take all the rejecting gestures in stride because they signaled that cleft issues were not a distraction, and that Jim has developed the self-confidence he needed to make the break from us.

One particularly intense interaction between Jim and me stands out. He was steamed about having to ask me for transportation because the Rabbit had been totaled in the accident. His sarcasm as we tried to negotiate his ride for the next day drew a sharp reprimand from his father. Jim reacted with an emotional outburst. In an anguished tone of voice, he declared that we didn't understand him, never had, and never would. I could handle hearing that we didn't understand him. He'd made that claim plenty of times and I couldn't disagree.

"I don't fit in this family," he said through tears. "I'm not like you two and Kent. I want different things." That remark stung, but it was not news. There had been many indications that Jim was restless with our conventional middle-class lifestyle.

His father and I sat stone-still, nerves tensed, expecting more. I braced myself for a blast of recriminations. *Here it comes*, I thought. *All the ways I've failed him. Just stay calm and hear him out. Steel your nerves.* Among my biggest fears were that he would say I hadn't been there for him, that my going back to school had been hard on him, that I didn't care, that I was a horrible mom, that he hated me.

"And you never trusted me." His tone was blistering, but I didn't wince. That was a fair assessment, too, and one I knew my friends routinely heard from their teenagers. I had indeed often raised trust as an issue and even now felt justified in having done so. If these were his chief complaints, if there were none about not loving him or how I dealt with cleft issues, I was home pain- and guilt-free.

"Give me an instance," I said, hoping his example would be one I could manage.

"On prom night, you removed all the liquor from the house." I gave an inward sigh of relief. This was a softball.

"You're right. You were having friends over for the night and we felt we shouldn't have alcohol in the house." I paused. "We *did* give you total control of the house that night," I reminded him. "You must admit *that* required some trust on our part."

Jim was silent, still smoldering. I took advantage of the lull.

"I've got to tell you, Jim, I get it that you wanted us to trust you with more freedom and choice and that you feel I, especially, have held too tight a leash. Maybe I worried about you more than I needed to, but honestly, you wanted to do so many things that were outside my comfort zone. You scared me senseless with some of the risks you took. All I can say is that I bent over backwards for you as far as I could without breaking. I'm sorry if you felt misunderstood and hemmed in. I honestly gave as much leeway as I could and still live with myself."

I waited for another shoe to drop, but it didn't. I hadn't mentioned how his vulnerability due to his cleft was ever present on my mind and neither had he.

James sat quietly, a pained expression on his face. Jim's upset must have been hard for him, but I think he was more fearful that

Jim's verbal lashing would leave me in tatters. It did not. I had not been accused of the failures I most feared. And, perhaps even more importantly, Jim's outburst had given me an opportunity to reveal myself as the mother I tried to be, to defend unapologetically the constraints I'd imposed. I was willing to clash over it if it meant keeping him mindful of being responsible and keeping out of harm's way. I was doing my job. As I spoke in my defense, my mind was clear, and I stated my case with heart and head perfectly aligned. It felt as though I'd been rehearsing for this moment for a long time. For the peace of mind that followed I was enormously grateful.

And now, as we put miles between ourselves and home, I wonder if his sleeping such long hours in the back seat is due to fatigue from the trauma of the accident, the last two weeks of hell-raising, a way to avoid me and my questions, or all of the above. Perhaps this pulling into a shell is the best way for him to deal privately with whatever is on his mind. With each mile, I feel more keenly the distance growing between us.

I might feel better if I were convinced college was what Jim wanted. Hadn't he declared at the end of his junior year that he wasn't so sure he was interested in college? He had also flirted with enlisting in the military. I was terrified at the thought that either of my sons would end up one day in some hopeless combat situation. When I expressed my dismay to a physician friend, he assured me that the military would reject Jim because of his cleft.

"Think about it. The military won't want to incur the medical expense of the surgeries he still needs and will probably think he'd miss too much active-duty time while recovering."

This awareness was bittersweet. I did not like to think about Jim suffering yet another rejection because of his cleft, but I can't deny my relief upon hearing these words. Indeed, after the initial interview, Jim heard nothing more from the recruiter. He kept whatever he thought to himself, and we knew nothing about why his investigation into the military came to a halt. His father and I did not probe, keeping our relief to ourselves.

Moreover, the direction he is taking now toward college was proposed by Redlands, not by Jim. To lift my spirits on the long drive to Redlands, I remind myself of all the times Jim has made good decisions for himself, many without our guidance—undertaking the solo bike trip, becoming a teen counselor and participant in leadership activities with the YMCA, joining a Junior Achievement program, engaging in wrestling and football. Hadn't he earned respectable grades and SAT scores and that honorable mention his senior year with the National Endowment for the Arts that led to the invitation to apply to Redlands?

At long last we arrive on the Redlands campus, which is teeming with incoming freshmen. Jim is not thrilled to have me tagging along but allows me to see his dorm room. It's hard to imagine how two souls will share the limited space. To make matters worse, his roommate, Calvin, has grabbed the side of the room with windows and plugged his appliances into all the available electrical outlets, all of which darkens Jim's mood. He appears eager for me to be on my way, to handle this situation without me worrying in the background.

Despite his objections, I insist on staying for the dinner planned for incoming freshmen and their parents. To be honest, I'm more than curious to see how Jim will blend in. We seat ourselves with a dozen students and parents at an assigned table on the main quad. Dinner proceeds with polite conversation among parents as students fidget and eye one another and the presiding professor, their freshman advisor. The professor eventually turns the conversation to a discussion of *The Tao of Pooh* by Benjamin Hoff, the required reading for incoming freshmen and college staff. The ice has not yet broken, and the professor has little success eliciting comments from the students, who are focusing their attention instead on their plates.

I catch my breath as Jim turns toward the professor, meets his eye, then raises his hand. The professor glances at Jim's name badge.

"Yes, Jim?"

I come to attention. Jim has come out of his shell! I do not discern whether he's making a comment or raising a question, but the professor brightens. I do not pay attention to what the professor says in reply. I only know that he and Jim are conversing about the meaning of a particular passage in the book. I am entranced as I watch this exchange. I do not know if this comes naturally for Jim, born out of his sensitivity to the passage, or if he has to screw up all the courage he has to open his mouth. Is he intent on establishing himself as a serious student, or just saying what's on his mind? This is the boy who has worried about what others will make of his facial scars, his slightly altered speech, and who has been known to shy away from public scrutiny, especially from strangers! But here he is engaging the professor mano-a-mano. He appears confident in what he thinks and speaks with conviction. He seems to be altogether in his element. I want to jump out of my seat and applaud. This is the sign I need—seeing Jim take to this college environment. He is clearly diving in, cleft be damned, and right before my eyes. *Thank you, Lord.*

When I say a final goodbye to Jim a little later, I cannot prevent the catch in my throat and the tears that well up.

"Mom, please don't cry."

I take him by the shoulders and look squarely into his eyes. "This is a big moment, Jim. I'm full of all kinds of feelings and they're all good. These are happy tears. Please know I hope this turns out to be what you want." I muster a smile. "And remember to have fun."

He allows me one last hug.

"I love you," I whisper.

"I know," he says.

I turn away and blow a kiss, then make my way to the van as Jim heads back to the dorm and all that he has to contend with in that roommate.

Mission accomplished! I whisper to myself. I plan to steal away and revel in this victory. But then, as I am driving back to the motel in the solitude of the van, I'm overcome with a deep consuming pain in my chest that takes my breath away. It is as though something vital has been cut out of my insides. Involuntarily, I let loose a wail so violent that I pull over to the curb until it subsides. I let the tears flow, unable to stem pent-up emotions I cannot name. Back in the motel, I try to make sense of this visceral upheaval. Apparently, letting go of Jim involves more for me than saying, "Goodbye, and have fun." Who knew letting go would be so physically painful? I am stunned and realize what a momentous event this leave-taking is for me, much harder than for Jim, I'm hoping.

By the time I arrive home after two days of Books on Tape and bouts of self-talk, I have come to terms with my feelings. I continue to succumb for a while, as any parent might, to worries about how Jim is adjusting—to the roommate, campus life, and academic challenges. And I also wrestle with concerns unique to him. Would the scars on his lip cause unwanted attention? Would he be able to connect with specialists near Redlands skilled enough to help him with cleft care needs? In time I also put these worries on the back burner. I resolve to entrust Jim to his own devices and to believe he has what it takes to make the most of the many opportunities ahead of him.

Jim's absence leaves a hole for sure, but the gut-wrenching pain I felt the day I handed him off to Redlands has eased. I recall the pain of Jim's delivery at birth. I hadn't anticipated as intense a pain then, either, but I now understand such pains to be inevitable in parenting—in our wanting, loving, and investing the best we have to give, and then letting our child go.

Jim, age twelve. Serious about football. Eugene, OR.

Jim, barely sixteen, triumphant after bike trip from Vancouver, BC, to Eugene, OR.

Jim with Barbara, Kent, and James. Ready for high school graduation, 1988.

PART FOUR:
1988-2021

TRANSITIONS

Back in Eugene, I shift gears. With Jim at Redlands, I coast a while. Adjusting to the change in family composition, I take a fresh look at what's on the road ahead. James's busy practice and increasing responsibilities in the medical community take up much of his time. I now turn more attention on Kent and will soon shift back into high gear at the U of O, forging ahead with graduate studies.

At the same time, Jim is never off our radar. James and I wonder how he is adjusting, knowing that the first year away from home is often a difficult transition. How much should his father and I make cleft issues a part of our infrequent phone conversations, particularly since Jim seems intent on putting these issues aside? Though at arm's length, we decide to keep treading lightly, wondering aloud on phone calls if Jim has followed up with the orthodontic referral his Eugene surgeon made. We do not press, even though unfinished work on his cleft weighs on us. We realize Jim needs to be in charge now and understand why he would want to defer cleft palate issues, which could certainly throw a monkey wrench into his first year at college.

When we talk, we listen for clues that might tell us how he is adjusting. Does he like his courses? His professors? How is he faring with his roommate? Surely, he would be willing to grumble about Calvin, whose self-indulgent, blasé devil-may-care attitude is the antithesis to Jim's minimalist, everything-matters modus operandi. But Jim rarely mentions Calvin and reveals little of the irritation I witnessed when he first encountered him. Jim gives brief responses to questions about his activities, studies, classmates, and professors. He does let us read his English compositions and the positive feedback from his English professor, the same one he connected with on *The Tao of Pooh*. We glean enough here and there to know that Jim is engaged and finding college worthwhile.

Meanwhile, it's hard to believe that fifteen-year-old Kent, who began life in the NICU with a serious ABO blood condition, is now a robust teenager. He is tackling his courses, playing football, and horsing around regularly with a rambunctious group of friends. Having learned the ropes with Jim, I am more adept at keeping an eye out and managing the typical as well as the blindsiding challenges teens are apt to throw at their parents.

My worries that Kent has been disadvantaged as the sibling of a brother with a disability are dissipating as I see Kent mature. Whatever complications our family circumstances have dealt him, he now shows the willingness and ability to take on the world. He is elated in 1990 with early acceptance in the fall of his senior year into the business program at the University of Colorado. We are still not sure if the nature of the academic program or the nearby ski slopes held greater appeal. He makes a decision that will take him away from home and high school friends, as did his brother, a healthy indication, I believe, that he wants to make his own way.

When I deliver him to his freshman dorm room in September 1991, I have an eerie déjà vu, a sharp memory of Jim's first day on campus three years earlier—an equally problematic roommate who puts us both in an edgy mood. Like his brother, he urges me to trust he can figure that situation out on his own. As we say goodbye at that oh-so-poignant and heartrending moment of leave-taking, it's stiff-upper-lip time for both of us. I thought I'd be better able to steel myself, having survived the wrenching letting go of Jim at Redlands. Is there a mother anywhere who, while celebrating her child's momentous first step into their own separate adult life, has not also felt a visceral pain? As I did when Jim left home, I have a week or so of a funk and fret about Kent's transition. And as with Jim, he weathers the first term and finds a comfort zone.

As Kent takes on his freshman year of college, Jim is entering his senior year at Redlands, where he is majoring in creative writing and computer science. He is focused on an emerging mapping technology, learning skills that will serve him well later in his career.

Jim made one attempt during his time at Redlands to attend to cleft palate concerns. We were relieved when he agreed in his junior year to have an orthodontic evaluation. Perhaps his cleft became easier to think about after his experience in a Speech and Audiology class he took as an elective. He may have taken the class because it was an easy A, given how much he already knew about speech problems related to a cleft. In any case, his expertise was obvious to both professor and students, many of whom were professionals working in clinics serving children with cleft palates. In a phone call with us, Jim related that one of the professionals-in-training asked him to speak to the parents of children at her clinic.

"I told them they should talk to you, Mom," he said. "You could tell them plenty."

Little did he know how validating that comment was.

On his own, Jim traveled to Riverside, about twenty miles from campus, to meet with the recommended orthodontist. We were disappointed, but should not have been surprised, to learn that Jim's encounter with the orthodontist was a fiasco. The orthodontist recoiled upon examining Jim's mouth, picked up the phone, and in front of Jim, chastised the referring surgeon in Eugene for sending him a patient with a complicated cleft mouth, a problem he had no idea how to fix. I was furious, but helpless when I heard in Jim's voice how demoralizing that interaction was. Yet another setback that would make the next appointment all the more difficult to contemplate. We did not have the heart to ask him to seek alternative orthodontists in the area.

Jim graduates in spring 1992. On graduation day, he is energized and upbeat as we mingle with his creative writing mentor and fraternity brothers. His plans are uncertain except that he wants to take a break from education. At twenty-two, he is itching for a road-trip adventure. Kent is immersed in college life in Boulder, Colorado. The boys are still in transition, still figuring out their life goals. At home, James has become even busier with his medical practice.

And now, I have homed in on the goal that seemed a mirage twelve years ago. After more than a decade of graduate studies, thesis and dissertation, and licensing, I dive into a career as a counseling psychologist.

ON HIS OWN

We kept mum our concerns about what Jim planned to do next with his life now that he had graduated from college. He did not look for employment or pursue higher education. Nor did he show interest in taking on cleft issues. He was hankering for a cross-country road trip. While his father and I celebrated his adventurous spirit and apparent sense of freedom from cleft worries, we remained mindful that more orthodontic work and surgery would be necessary. Jim converted our ten-year-old Beauville van into living quarters and packed it with a few clothes, construction tools, and books. At his request, I made curtains for the van windows so he could have privacy when he wanted it. On a bright fall day Jim set off with his friend Josh toward Texas. He decided to extend a stopover in Austin and took a job as a roofer. Not the career step I'd imagined after his college education.

"Oh," I managed. "Not what you planned, though."

"No, but most of the crew is Spanish-speaking, so I'm practicing my Spanish a lot, and I enjoy hanging out with these guys. A new perspective on life." Cleft concerns seemed far from his mind, an awareness that tapped on my worry button.

Jim lived in his van and made do. I tried not to think about the privations of his living situation, but I did choke up that first Christmas Eve when Jim called from a parking lot phone booth. It pained me to think of him alone in his van at Christmas. He heard the catch in my voice.

"Don't feel bad, Mom," he said brightly. "I'm parked next to a Boy Scout Christmas tree lot and it's very Christmassy."

I searched for the silver lining to this situation. After a couple of days, I found it. If Jim could live happily on his own with so little, he could surely land on his feet anywhere. This thought and a feeling that cleft issues were not currently a problem for him sustained me.

Little did we expect that Austin would be fertile ground for our son. In 1993 he accepted an offer that allowed him to park his van on the Austin ranch of a researcher in sustainable building systems. He would live among the prototypes of electric cars and straw bale houses scattered over the property and share the two-burner electric hot plate in the shed with another resident assistant, an older man who had lived on the ranch for years. In return, Jim would assist the researcher on some of his projects.

During our first visit to the ranch, James and I couldn't disguise our bewilderment. What parents would not have questions upon finding their college-educated son living in a van and cooking his meals in a woodshed? The researcher quickly reminded us that Jim was getting a thorough hands-on education on the ranch, the equivalent of a master's-level internship. The look on Jim's face told me he was right where he wanted to be. He would go on to become an activist for sustainable development within the city of Austin, earn a Master of Regional and Community Planning degree with a focus on sustainability, and eventually land a job at the University of Texas in his chosen field. Medical benefits of this job relieved worries about managing costs of looming surgeries and other specialty treatment related to Jim's cleft repair.

Jim has experienced family life as well. In 2000 he married Scheleen, with whom he shared an intense commitment to environmental and community planning. To everyone's relief, their son, Jimmy Boone, born in 2002, showed no trace of a problematic palate or lip. Although that marriage ended, Jimmy Boone has blossomed into an energetic and enterprising young man. He's been a joy to his father and has grown close to Cathy, whom Jim married in 2015. This relationship has brought immeasurable comfort and happiness into Jim's life. I've never seen him so at ease with himself.

But all this time, the need for more cleft surgery has loomed in the background. During his first few years in Austin, in the nineties, Jim's efforts to find direction from orthodontic and craniofacial specialists were beyond discouraging. A consultant in Dallas seemed uninterested. He referred Jim to a dentist in Austin who appeared baffled by the referral.

"I don't know anything about cleft palates," he stated unabashedly. Jim appreciated the dentist's honesty, and they parted on a friendly note, but it was another discouraging dead end.

Eventually, Jim did connect with an orthodontist in Austin who specialized in clefts. He helped Jim find a craniofacial surgeon and together they discussed a plan that involved orthodontia and eventual jaw and palate reconstruction. Still, years passed with no concrete plans for the surgery everyone knew was necessary.

In 2013, when Jim was forty-three, reconstruction became a matter of urgency. He risked developing painful jaw misalignment unless the left side of his maxilla was moved forward and the gaps in both sides of the maxilla were closed. He mustered his resolve and activated the surgeon and oral specialists, and after much orthodontia and consultation, a Le Fort surgery to reconstruct the upper jaw was scheduled for May 2014. The plan was to move the left side of the maxilla forward, rebuild bone mass in the two gaps in the maxilla, and close the fistula in the front part of the hard palate. However, the surgeon was not able to complete in May all the repairs as planned—too little bone and skin graft material and too little time in one five-hour surgery.

Five months later, Jim underwent a second surgery to complete the work. This operation was as grueling and painful as the first. But to our amazement, Jim came through the second operation with an astonishing ability to control the pain and anxiety within a very short time after more than six hours of surgery, and he stopped pain medication the day following the operation. When I arrived at the ICU where he was recovering, I found him sitting up in bed conversing amicably with a nurse. He'd adopted a cheerful businesslike approach to the entire situation, remarkably at ease with the monitor wired into his cheek to keep track of the blood flow in a newly created blood vessel leading to the surgery site. He attributed much of this new peace of mind to the meditation he and Cathy had practiced, a program designed specifically to help prepare patients for surgery. Though there were several disconcerting glitches during recovery, Jim handled them with more equanimity than I could have imagined.

Weeks later, Jim also took in stride news that the results of the second operation had not yielded the hoped-for results. By now, he seemed to expect less than surgeons envisioned. The bone grafts to the maxilla did not fuse as intended, which meant he was no longer a candidate for tooth implants. I caught myself sliding into a familiar funk and anticipated Jim would do the same. But instead, he turned his attention to what was possible in the future. It was as though he had not held out hope this time for a best-possible outcome and had stopped believing that surgeries would yield an ideal solution. His measured, matter-of-fact posture seemed to signal that this time he was not susceptible to the debilitating thoughts and feelings that had brought him and the rest of us so low after earlier surgeries.

Now he faces additional orthodontic work to give him a full set of teeth via a bridge, but he's in no hurry. Cathy's straightforward support has been key to his equanimity.

"She loves me . . . cleft and all," he says with such certainty that I sense her complete acceptance is something he has not been sure of in previous relationships.

It has been twenty-two years since Jim took off in the Beauville van with no plans in mind but the next destination on the road. Now he is settled into work, family, and community. As I consider the path he has traveled from his earliest years, I see how he has met and triumphed over the adversities his birth condition dealt him. I see that he has relentlessly refused to let his life be defined or shaped by his cleft. On his own since college, he has grown into a thoughtful man who cares deeply about home, community, and the planet, knows what he wants and pursues it with vigor and commitment, who never tires of helping others, who loves well and enjoys the love and respect he receives in kind. He keeps true to his highly ethical principles, whatever the challenges. Today he is reaping the rewards of his determination and effort to shape a life of his own design.

Dallas Specialist

The specialist in Dallas looks at me with an authentic *Is
   this it?* look,
even after hearing my case with all my twenty-odd years
   of indignation
from a previous first-time, last-time visit with a lower specialist
   in Riverside.
I am huffed up after an hour of waiting in the waiting room
   with two kids
with elongated skulls, concave, smooth dough half-pounded,
   half-made
into faces skewed and honest. They were racing plastic snails
   and laughing
in the familiar way all kids do when they find the others who are
   like them. Their mothers
chatting and half-smiling, in the familiar way all mothers do
when they find others grasping at the same self-doubts.
   And here I am
with my bit of not-poorly-repaired cleft palate and a fresh chip on
   my shoulder.
Hoo boy! Slice of humble pie anyone?
Those kids didn't notice me, or if they did, they did not see me.
No memory of me will surface when their own self-pity darkens
   their thoughts.
I had desired to leave the waiting room, not in obvious surrender,
   but in defiance
to mask the surrender. But I didn't, because my teeth are
   falling out now

and it's been years since I cared about my teeth or finishing
    the repairs,
and I am here more as a favor to my parents who do care, who
    have always cared,
who need these repairs finished as a proxy for closure of this
    birth defect
and all that. I explain none of this to the specialist, who leans me
    back in the familiar way
all specialists do when they are done with the pretense of listening
and plucks the left front tooth from my jaw. *This one is dead*
    already, he says,
even after all I've done to convince myself there's yet life there,
yet something worth saving. The tooth clinks in a metal pan.
The specialist straightens up, says, *Come back when you're serious*,
    and leaves.
Hoo boy! Couldn't give any fewer fucks.
But I see it isn't personal. He is flicking the chip off my shoulder,
    hitting a hard reset
in the familiar way doctors always don't intend. And I also see
all I imagine as my life's structure is just my imagination after all.
I see all my many burdens, the weight of dying teeth,
    of being owed
a remaking into any kind of beauty, all swept away in a moment,
and now, with no more imaginary chips to play, here I still am.
    Suddenly
children's laughter from the waiting room reminds me
this is just living.

My Son's Sonogram

I can't comprehend
what the doctor says
is plain to see:
No cleft palate.
I'm still shivering
from nights and days
huddled at the feet
of the old gods.
The doctors told us
to be prepared
for the probabilities
of genetics.

Why would we
knowingly
bring a clefted child
into the world?
Do I really believe
I could do better
than my mother did
with me?

Being born with a cleft
is not as bad now
as it once was, and
I understand any life
welcomed into the world
is a wonder.
I understand the choice

is not mine alone to make
or to live with.
But still, but still, if I could
spare a child, my child,
any more hardship
than life already promises,
why wouldn't I?

Before meeting with the doctor,
in the dim light of morning,
as the world woke from dreaming,
with my tongue lightly resting
in the dark of the roof of my mouth,
my mystery spread black wings.

I wondered if the old gods,
before blessing us
with all the possibilities of light,
hesitated
before blessing us
with all the possibilities of shadow.

Lover
for Cathy

I hid the glass with my soaking dentures. But one morning
you found me rinsing them in the kitchen sink, hunched
over my solitary business. I remember you stepping to me,
placing one hand on my arm holding down my mask of teeth,

the other to my neck, pulling me in for a kiss—oh such a kiss—
your tongue flicking across the soft bulge of pink gums
where my incisors should be, where absence is a constant,
lingering your tongue a moment as long as memory.

My breath caught a bit, and you smiled.
You don't have to put those in if you don't want to. I don't care.
And I so loved you for not caring. Until then, I'd never loved
someone's awareness of my cleft as much as yours right then.

And you turned to make breakfast from eggs and leftovers,
moving easily into the day. A gift of acceptance
for the giver is but a passing moment, yet for the receiver
is like hidden gates thrown wide to a horizon only imagined.

Le Fort

1

Whereby the jaw is cut from the skull
along a natural fracture pattern
discovered in nineteen-oh-one,

allowing the relocation of the jaw
in three dimensions, with options
if grafting is considered viable.

Such surgeries are now common
for correcting mid-face deformities,
with reliable long-term results.

2

I am hopeful for long-term results. I am
choosing to sleep back under the knife.
I am not uncommon in my deformity.

I am a golem of bone and hope. I am
a man of many options. I am still
allowing this. I am allowing this

new intervention with the original rupture
of my jaw, my original state. I am
choosing to be reshaped one more time.

3

They say recovery is six weeks at best
with your jaw wired shut, liquid diet, resting

to allow the packed-in bone to settle,
to round off so your face appears more natural.

They say some people won't recognize you.
They remind you that you chose this, once again.

4

My lover does not care much about any of this.
She loves me because I am more than this.
She walks ahead, beside, behind as she senses.

She is yet new to me, her reactions yet new to my son,
my parents, to all who know me. Yet, she stands at the center.
She makes a six weeks' supply of soup with my mother.

She collects my hopes of a day my face might be finished,
saying in my ear, *Baby, if this is what you want, then
I want it too. I'm here. I'm in this for the long-haul.*

Le Fort, Take 2

1

Whereby the first surgery is less successful
than the doctors had hoped and sections of jaw
couldn't be relocated as far as they desired,

no matter how hard they pulled. However,
once the jaw heals, they can saw it apart again
and shave bone chips from the other hip

to be packed in around a better metal mesh. Plus,
they can still get to what they really need to get to
and transplant nine inches of a major blood vessel

from the thigh into the jawline to feed the new bone
as well as the soft-tissue graft over the palate
that should, at least, close the cleft this time.

They hope they can get it all done this time.
They hope the cleft can be closed, and if so,
they hope this is the last time. Fingers crossed.

2

The thing about choosing to seek closure
is to be committed, as if on an epic quest.
You can't just stop along the way, mid-quest,

tempting as it is to seek quieter adventures. No,
you must believe in each step, you must believe the hardship
is worth surviving, that the end is worth achieving.

Even if you've grown uninspired by your own story,
the lives of others may depend on a resolution,
and so you continue without needing to find yourself any more.

3

My son visits me in recovery,
both of us shy.

I see his love for me shiver and shine
in a new way.

His life depends on me for a moment,
a breath only.

I finish filling the catheter bag
to make him laugh.

4

Dead bone chips
slip through my cleft
for months,
the way popcorn husks
stick in your teeth
sharply.

The surgeon shrugs,
asking how I like
the scars,
how neat they are,
how well sewn
and clean.

Turns out neither surgery
yielded enough
packed bone
to fully close the cleft,
or for implants,
or more hopes.

And so, I am done.
I am done, I
am done.
Let my quest continue
with this beginning
resolved.

On Anger

By a river, long after The Invitation,
my mother continues to insist
I write about anything,
especially and importantly
about all the times I got mad at her
and the anger I am still holding.
(She is sure I still hold anger
against her. I have to be.)

Oh, Mother, the anger is long gone,
I lost it somewhere along the way,
perhaps one night while driving fast
through the black around the Butte,
or perhaps, one day with a woman
who cared about my cleft so little
that all could be forgiven, or perhaps
those angers just released as I lived.

I remember the Native story
about the two wolves in us all,
I imagine the wolf who wants our happiness
is grateful when his brother eats first.

I remember being angry at you, at the world,
at the unfairness of having a clefted face.
But all children have their burdens to wrestle,
and I carry no enduring grudges. Because of you,
dear Mother, because of you, those angers—
turbulent in their moment—eroded away.
Set your concern of angers aside. All is resolved,
all is healed and whole. Be happy now, for me.

TENDING THE FLAME

During that early time of frustration and over the ensuing years of solitary struggle, I developed a growing conviction that things could, should, be easier for mothers in my situation. Despite feelings of powerlessness, a tiny spark of hope ignited in those years, one I would tend and that would become a burning desire to make an issue of the support needs of parents like me.

I became energized when I imagined that I could become a person who could make a positive difference in their lives. That was the flame I needed to nurture. Once I focused on becoming a counselor, I was afire. I worked my way into graduate school armed with unflinching convictions and blazed a trail that combined coursework, research, and training in counseling psychology and special education.

Confident of my mothering credentials, I also earned the credentials that gave me a platform in professional circles. I earned my PhD in 1989 and in 1991 completed the internship and residency hours required to qualify for state licensure as a psychologist. I have been active as an adjunct scientist/researcher in special education at Oregon Research Institute, where I continued to conduct research and lead workshops for parents and professionals interested in collaboration. My work has involved developing curricula for training parents and professionals in communication skills for more collaborative partnerships.

I'm being heard and am finally able to contribute to efforts to improve professional attitudes toward parents and to foster parent-professional collaboration. At the same time, I've established a counseling practice with a special interest in helping parents manage the demands of raising and nurturing a child with disability. All of these activities feed my soul and go a long way toward satisfying the burning need I've felt for years to make a positive difference for these families. My counseling work with parents—validating their perspectives, helping them find their strengths, and coaching them in communication and advocacy skills—has been the most gratifying part of my professional life. It has more than satisfied my burning need to make something count from my trial-and-error journey.

In retrospect, I doubt I would have achieved this sense of fulfillment without the upheaval Jim's cleft issues caused in my life. The turmoil compelled me to examine my values, set new priorities, take up new and often daunting responsibilities, and find purpose. The demands of Jim's care and my personal struggle pointed me toward a cause and a career that have challenged, emboldened, and rewarded me.

The impulse that began as a tiny spark and grew into a burning need to make things better may have flickered and grown weak at times, but it refused to die. It has faithfully lighted the way toward helping my son and me and has fueled my effort to translate what I've learned from my experience into help for others.

JAMES REFLECTS

As I look back, I reflect on how our son's being born with a cleft disorder set Barbara, an expectant mother, and Jimmy, a newborn for whom a normal life was anticipated, on very different trajectories than we envisioned before Jimmy's birth. I see also that key personality traits that took root in each of their childhoods determined how they confronted the challenges that awaited them on these altered paths.

The struggles Jimmy faced in his first three years are beyond his recall. He certainly suffered surgical and emotional trauma, but he rebounded with the help of those closest to him and was able to take part in normal activities of childhood. Our earliest photographs of him from these years reinforce our memories of a smiling, gregarious, playful, and curious little boy. As early as age three, Jimmy showed evidence that the ordeals of treatment did not intimidate him or rob him of his determination to be in charge of himself, no matter the surroundings. He sought minimal direction from us, deciding to study his books in bed well beyond lights-out time or breaking away from our family to explore a forest during camping outings. In his teens and thereafter, he began to follow his own counsel and exercise authority in dealing with various medical providers.

Barbara's path began in the context of growing up in a hard-working farm family in northern Maine, where she developed determination and resilience. I understood her work ethic and unswerving commitment to be successful in college and later to support me through medical school. I trusted her instincts, her capacity to assume responsibility, and her resolve to persevere when tested. As she attests, Barbara sometimes doubted her strength and durability when she faced the frontline trials of early parenting. But she drew, whether consciously or unconsciously, upon strong character traits developed earlier in her life. And she nurtured these traits in Jimmy and in Kent.

The move to Eugene in 1970 held much promise. I could pursue a medical career, Barbara could pursue graduate studies, and the vibrant community offered a healthy environment for raising our boys. But the transition was not without difficulties. The relocation added to the history of disruptions in Jimmy's care, already complicated by three previous moves. This meant encountering different surgical approaches to repairs, and only short-term exposures to medical and other professional care. Although Eugene was home to a sophisticated medical community that included many specialists, there were no medical professionals with extensive experience treating children with cleft disorders. Portland, two hours away, was the closest place where there was a team of experienced professionals organized to assess and treat the multiple needs of our son.

This move also put us at a significant distance from our parents and from the nurturing environments of colleagues, mentors, and physician relatives in Cleveland and Rochester. Within days I was engrossed in my work, but Barbara, who was on her own to settle into a rented condominium with the boys, keenly felt the absence of friends and family. In time we made friends and Barbara felt less isolated.

My usual work schedule encompassed four full weekdays and every third weekend. I was "on call" every third night, which often meant frequent visits to the ER and ICU. This was a rigorous schedule, but it was the only way I understood how to be successful, and I don't remember ever regretting my choice to commit to it. Barbara understood and accepted the demands of my practice, and even during the times when I was most consumed by my work, she rarely complained about my absence or asked me to put my career on pause. For the most part, Barbara supported my efforts to develop a medical practice in much the same way she had supported my internship, residency, and fellowship work. As before, she remained a full-time first responder in all aspects of parenting Jimmy and Kent.

Within several years after moving to Eugene, Barbara acted on her intention to attend graduate school. Her pursuit of a degree in counseling psychology and to establish a professional career was no less thought out or vital to her self-identity than was my career to me. I worried that the requirements of Barbara's career pursuits might destabilize the balance we had established in our parenting roles and in our home life. Would the demands of her studies and subsequent training put new pressure on me, on our marriage, and adversely affect our boys?

There were many adjustments, and we weathered them. Now, with both of us experiencing fulfillment by following chosen careers, our marriage has grown richer and our commitment to each other deeper. I recognize I cannot feel the full weight of the demands of Barbara's mothering, advocacy, graduate studies, and work with parents. Nor can she fully experience the intensity of my work with critically ill patients and their families. We often sparred over the merits of medical versus psychological approaches to wellness. Our lively discussions enhanced rather than troubled our respect for one another, and in important ways helped us be more thoughtful about decisions in our respective work environments and in how we approached Jim's medical needs.

In retrospect, I recognize similar characteristics in the manner in which Jim and Barbara moved along their respective paths during this period—developing tenacity in the face of physical and emotional trauma; progressing from wariness and mistrust of prevailing medical hierarchies to establishing their own authority in planning and implementing interventions; resisting defeat in the face of disappointing outcomes and achieving self-confidence after successful ones; relying on core values of integrity, selflessness, solid work ethic, and inner strength. During this time, Kent developed his own unique personality and arsenal of character strengths. The story of his trajectory merits a separate telling.

I am extremely proud of all three and grateful for the family we have become.

FINDING WORDS

Only Jim can speak the truths of his experience as a child weathering years of cleft palate repairs. Only he can say how our times together as mother and child shaped his becoming the person he is today. Only I can say how the challenges I faced alone and those we faced together altered the course of my life. And now, we have found our voices and words to speak those truths to one another.

When Jim invited me to write "our story," I was initially at a loss for words and reluctant to disclose what mothering him had been like for me. Did I want to admit failures? Lay myself open to criticisms—legitimate or otherwise—of my parenting? Expose myself to lingering anger or his disappointment in me? Could I be honest about my sadness when he had pushed me away and resisted my efforts to comfort him? Could I tell him I wished we had been closer? Communicated better? I feared that writing honestly about our personal struggles would open old wounds for each of us. Would honest talk close or deepen those wounds? Could we find words to reveal hidden personal truths in ways that would bring us closer, or would we fail and grow more distant? I expressed these concerns to Jim. After all, wasn't our relationship relatively stable? I did not want to risk what we had. He assured me he could hear anything I divulged.

Over the years, I had poured my emotions and troubled thoughts onto the pages of journals. Now as I thought of putting words on paper again, several vivid memories of my efforts to find the right words with Jim played like a slideshow in my head.

When he was very young—before he was aware of being different from others or needing fixing—my physical presence and the words all mothers use to reassure small children seemed to comfort him when doctors poked and prodded and performed surgeries on his lip and inside his mouth.

He was three years old when little Jimmy was made aware he was different. A playmate who was simply curious asked him what was wrong with his lip. That question came up later at home. He reached out and touched my lip, furrowed his little brow, and looked at me with great sobriety.

"Why is my lip not like yours and Daddy's and Baby Kent's?" I choked back the lump of accumulated sorrow, worry, and guilt that rose in my throat, kneeled, took little Jimmy gently by the shoulders, and looked squarely into his eyes. As matter-of-factly as I could, I explained how his lip hadn't grown together naturally when he was in my tummy and that doctors had sewn it together. I got a mirror and gently touched his scars.

"These red lines are where the doctors sewed your lip together." Brow still furrowed, Jimmy examined his face in the mirror, putting his hand to his lip. It did not seem to strike him then as anything other than new information about himself. As far as I could tell, our strong-willed, energetic three-year-old continued life as before, happy, and willing to engage anyone who was up for playing. I chose to think I'd managed a decent conversation with him. He seemed satisfied with the answer, but I wondered.

When Jimmy was four, a surgery was scheduled to partially close the large gap in his palate and revise the scar on his lip. His father and I thought we had prepared him by explaining that the surgery was needed to close the hole in his mouth and straighten his lip where one of the scar lines had pulled it crooked. He did not object or question us.

When he came out of surgery, it was a different matter. He asked for a mirror.

"Let me see! Let me see!" he demanded as though he expected a pleasant surprise. He took one look at his bruised and bloody lip full of black sutures and recoiled. He hurled the mirror at me.

"Why did you lie?" he sobbed. "You told me my lip would be fixed!" I realized too late that we had botched it. We could have, should have, done a better job of setting his expectations. No one—not the surgeons, the nurses, his father, or I—had thought to tell him how he would look immediately following the surgery. That there would be swelling, black-and-blue discoloring, dried blood, and ugly sutures, and that it would take a long while to see how surgery had "fixed" his lip. I gasped as he pulled away and cried into his pillow, refusing comfort. Something huge happened between us in that instant. I had a palpable sensation of losing Jimmy's trust that day and wasn't confident I'd ever regain it. From then on, I balked at the thought of talking with him about cleft matters. He seemed more wary of me, more self-protective, putting up a wall to my attempts to engage him in any conversation of a personal nature, particularly about his cleft.

As Jimmy progressed through school, teasing and bullying and the relentless drill of appointments with care providers left no doubt about the full implications of his cleft condition. Too often, he came home from school downhearted, but he said little. I dreaded mentioning playground incidents, upcoming appointments, or reminding him to speak more clearly or brush around the braces on his teeth more carefully. It unnerved me to see how his mood soured when his cleft was the topic of the moment, and I spoke of it only when an appointment was coming up or to encourage compliance with essential treatment recommendations. I felt helpless to make it easier for either of us. Words that might have eased the tension failed me and little meaningful conversation occurred about the whys and wherefores, let alone the stress we were feeling.

In adolescence, Jim, the name he preferred then, withdrew further, and I continued to avoid conversation about his cleft, fearing it would tap into emotions neither of us wanted to reveal. He seemed resigned to medical imperatives; I, to a need to appear strong. I tried to keep hidden from him the intense emotions that flared during and after difficult encounters with professionals, not wanting my distress to add to his worries. The pent-up emotions fermented and often came out sideways. Bickering about table manners, emptying the garbage, homework, or curfew—incidental hot topics between parents and teenagers—seemed infused with deeper frustrations. Never did we attempt conversation about how his cleft issues were affecting us.

In 1987 Jim was seventeen. The surgery to revise the scar that once again distorted his upper lip did not achieve the fix the surgeon predicted. Jim's dad and I pasted on brave faces afterward as we watched Jim manage the pain and disappointment. We witnessed his mood darken over the weeks of lingering bruises and swelling. We postponed his senior picture session and faced the reality of disappointing results. But we did not venture into conversation about the ordeal.

By 2014, I had worked for many years as a counselor helping

parents take on tough communications with their children so they might improve troubled relationships. I knew I had to find words to bridge the distance between us if I wanted a closer relationship with Jim.

I remember well the day the opening came. It was in late May that year, after the first of two surgeries. Jim had learned that the surgeon had been unsuccessful in completing the planned reconstruction of his palate. He had weathered unwelcome comments from friends. He seemed to have fallen into a place of dark thoughts. The news left the rest of us feeling helpless and mired in a jumble of emotions. I hid my tears. I was discouraged and enraged at the same time. How I longed to find words to comfort him and to help us both weather this most recent blow.

What useful thing could I say? Words that first came to mind fell flat. As Jim retreated more and more into himself, I suspected he was blaming himself for expecting too much, for being naïve, and for believing that anything would ever really fix his problem. I harbored similar self-defeating thoughts. How I wished I could talk with him about what was happening to us. But I did my usual thing. I bottled up my jagged thoughts and feelings, not wanting to make matters worse.

I had a good idea why Jim and I have had such difficulty talking about our upheavals before and after surgeries. I'd learned a lot as a psychologist about post-traumatic and acute stress. In our case, it was a matter of having to submit over and over to an all-too-familiar and dreaded painful ordeal, one we felt unable to avoid or discuss. Jim's struggle reminded me of the anxiety and depression manifested in abused children I had worked with in my counseling practice. They, too, were subjected to repetitive predictable experiences in contexts where adults who controlled their lives exposed them to pain they could not avoid. What does an infant make of pain from surgery? How frightening for a toddler, still too young to understand, to submit to operations and the restraints and manipulations during recovery! I had come to believe that the repetition in Jim's early life of painful and frightening ordeals had resulted in a hardwired alarm system deep in his brain that is triggered every time a procedure or surgery is looming, or even discussed. Entering a medical or orthodontic setting, particularly hospitals, must throw him into a hyper-anxious state—even in adulthood.

Add to that the repetition of dashed hopes for the optimal result envisioned by surgeons. In my practice I worked with many teens and adults who had been brave soldiers through painful experiences that did not work out. Their reactions ran a course similar to grief, including deflation, anger, feelings of helplessness, blame of others, and the most insidious of all, self-blame. Depression, even hopelessness, often set in.

But though I had professional insight about Jim's inner turmoil and my own, when he was in the trenches, the psychologist in me stayed home. It was the mother who showed up, burdened by my own fears and sense of powerlessness, and at a loss for words.

All this was on my mind after the first of the two most recent surgeries in 2014, when Jim was forty-four. I felt a burning need to connect with him. I rehearsed the words I wanted to say. I told myself I had to risk the conversation. I banished worries that if I tapped on the sensitive topic of our distress, I would make matters worse for him, and for our relationship. At the same time, I knew I would have a tough time living with myself if I didn't make the effort.

And so, one evening during a family walk in the neighborhood, I ventured out on a limb. I hooked my arm in his and drew him aside.

"You know, Jim, I've noticed how down you seem."

He said something, almost inaudible, about being naïve to think things would work out.

"I heard that last week at the soccer game, a couple of mothers said they thought your face looked better before."

"Yeah," he said. "I didn't need that from friends."

"Doesn't get any easier, does it?"

"And it probably never will."

"Can I share some observations I've made about what we go through?"

He didn't object, so I mused aloud about my theory that there is a connection between his reaction to surgery now and the pain of surgeries when he was very young.

"I've noticed that you go through the same emotional drill every time you have surgery," I said. "I think we both endure a similar kind of hell."

He was listening, so I continued into more uncertain terrain.

"There's something else. My taking you to hospitals and doctors' offices—places that must have seemed like torture chambers to you—must have made it hard for you to trust me. You must have seen me as their accomplice, not your mom. Maybe you even feared me."

He seemed to weigh these words.

"What must it have been like for you when your mother, the one person in the world you should be able to trust to protect you, was the one who took you time and time again to those dreaded places? It's not all that dissimilar to what children of abusive parents experience— your parent shows love one minute, and the next encourages you to cooperate with the people who scare you, even hurt you."

"I've never thought of it in that light." His words were barely a whisper. We walked on quietly arm in arm.

"I have to believe it has made it very hard on our relationship and our ability to talk to each other about it all." We walked in silence, still arm in arm. I felt as though a barrier had lifted. A door was cracking open for conversations we had not had before. He said little, but he wrapped an arm around my shoulder. In turn, I placed my arm around his waist, and we continued without speaking. Something tender passed between us, an acknowledgment of our shared vulnerability in this struggle to maintain strength and equilibrium while facing painful ordeals we cannot responsibly avoid.

When Jim asked me in November after a second disappointing surgery that year what it meant to be his mother, I was floored. It was a question I could not have imagined. Why was he curious then, after all the years of keeping me at bay? What had brought him to that moment? Was it his experience fathering a son of his own? Was it our conversation about traumatic stress five months earlier? New self-confidence from a successful job and happy marriage? Whatever the motivation, I had not seen it coming. He couldn't have known what a Pandora's box he would be opening.

I told him only that it had been the hardest thing I'd ever done, that I wasn't always the kind of mother I wanted to be for him, and that I wasn't sure I wanted to burden him with my emotionally charged memories.

Then came the invitation at Christmas to write a memoir together. With Jim's encouragement, I braved my fears, and we took the plunge together into an honest telling of memories we had not felt safe to share before. We revealed—with hesitancy at first and then more boldly—our most troublesome memories, including those of impasses in our relationship. We let curiosity and desire to better understand each other and to achieve a more open relationship be our guide. We worked at suspending judgment and defensiveness and put aside fears that honest talk about personal truths would hurt or alienate the other. The words flowed. We were stunned and touched by each other's revelations and reacted to them with compassion.

The walls behind which we'd been hiding from one another have crumbled. We now explore with more intense and unapologetic curiosity the landscapes of each other's personal realities. We are no longer shackled by previous misconceptions and hard emotions that sabotage attempts at meaningful conversation. We do not worry that disagreements or inquiries into personal matters will distance us. We laugh more in each other's company. We no longer struggle to find the right words to talk about troubles past or present.

To My Doctors, On Reflection

I struggle with gratitude for you
though I am thankful for the outcomes.

A mirror needs a face to reveal a reflection.

My surgeries are more than most kids—globally—
ever have access to. I recognize the providence.

The heavens are brighter when you're not hungry.

Statistics show starkly how lucky I've been
since birth, in so many ways.

Overcoming hardship hinges on circumstance.

I'm grateful for the state of my cleft today,
and for each of your roles in my evolving.

A voice needs a purpose to say thank you.

Letter to a Clefted Child

None of the circumstances of your birth were ever in your control. From your first moment, you were all you needed. But I know—I remember—the moments the path was hard and I was alone and I could not see how the future would ever be brighter.

You will settle into a relationship with your cleft, as with your own name. At times you will try to disown it, or find only harsh comfort in it, or surrender to how it presents you to the outside world. The world will always and relentlessly respond.

Your family—perhaps even your mother—will do their best to understand what you are experiencing and help. But only your emerging opinion of the rumbled roof of your mouth matters, even though their efforts are earnest and grounded in their love of choosing you.

Your doctors will perform their best and remind you of it constantly, but don't get caught up in their grinning promises. Though you were never broken, be thankful for any early "repairs" of your cleft you were lucky enough to receive. The surgeons will treat you like a project of hope, like a rescue in the aftermath of a disaster. Welcome whatever honest effort they offer, despite the imperfect outcomes, but do not expect them to ever believe they are finished.

Your friends (yes, you'll find deep forever friends) will be the first whose laughter and curiosity feel unconditional and honestly seeking of who you are beyond your cleft. The teasing from others is exhausting, of course—just as storms come and always go, they cast a memory and then fade away.

Your lovers (yes, you'll find those who lick your lips so lightly) will be the first whose intimate desire for you is undeterred by the cleft. This is a bright warm wave sweeping you up as you can't yet imagine.

Claim any surgeries beyond your late teens for your own aesthetic—your self-portrait of connecting muscle, filled-out flesh, drilled-in adornments of teeth. Only you know when to say *I am remade enough. Thank you all, now leave me be.*

There is also much to manage inside yourself, as hunger. Like your tongue, your mind can't help but explore and brood on your cleft, how your burden separates you, makes you involuntarily unique. You may embrace the idea of your uniqueness or you may reject it, as you wish, only you need know. But be watchful of the slow clenching of self-pitying thoughts. (I remain watchful myself.) How you loosen and move through these shadows reverberates into how you move through the world.

Learn to confront mirrors and take in all the distinct differentness of your face—all the details. Don't look for beauty yet; your later lovers will see those layers before you do. For now, just practice not turning away. Repeat to yourself that "normal-looking" is make-believe. Every tree, every bird, every stone, every natural thing is distinct among their own because of their inevitable details. We choose to see these differences with judgment, even you do. (Even I do.) Choosing to see yourself without judgment requires a steady effort.

Learn to stick around for the group photos. Learn how to smile big without revealing teeth or the absence of teeth, and without forcing the upper lip into a more contorted twist. (I have made this my superpower.) How you show up in the record of your life echoes across generations. Be there.

Learn your voice as soon as you feel it. You may hate the sounds your earnest tongue and partial palate cannot make, and hate also the sounds they can make, but this isn't about sound. Your voice evolves in you. (This is my voice, but I am still listening.) Be patient. Tend and nurture your initial whisper into a means of being and expression utterly yours. Trust me.

Learn to place the cleft under stress so you grow stronger. Your life is more immense than the cleft. Some may tell you a cleft leads you down a certain path or, more likely, that a cleft should lead you away from certain risks. Yet this is the life you have been given to do with as you wish. So go out and do, go out further, and come back—always come back again that you may live even more. (I am still learning how to do this.)

As you grow older and learn your own ways, the world will respond in kind and open paths for your choosing, both dark and bright. Only in your mind is your cleft still a question waiting to be answered. Only in your mind is your cleft a mystery worthy of any enduring thought but wonder.

And now, at fifty, writing to you, all I can offer are these few reflections of my childhood, the moments when my cleft consumed my mother and locked up my thoughts with the separations inherent to life—and also the many more moments of creating my place in the world, finding my others, and becoming all I chose to pursue. The measure of your connection to—or separation from—living as you wish begins with how much power you give your cleft.

So, from here, when the cleft swallows you and your dark thoughts swarm, allow them a moment to surge and breathe and flex in the front of your mind. Then thank them as you thank any pain of the body raising caution for the purpose of your survival. Then release them. You do not owe whatever rises from the depths of your cleft any lingering focus.

Now, I know all this sounds corny and overwrought to you, coming from some old dude off the back pages of a book probably handed to you by some well-meaning adult who's trying to help in a way I hope is authentic.

But listen:

You are all you need. Your cleft is as your name. Stand in front of this.

Be grateful for any who take the time to learn it, even your mother.

You are bright. Your cleft neither stakes your path nor mars the way.

Go now. Begrudge nothing and no one. Live fully from *this* moment.

Barbara earns a Ph.D. in Counseling Psychology.

Barbara's first day in private practice.

EPILOGUE

My Father

My father, to this day, will rapidly tap my shoulder—*Jimmy!*
Look, look . . . Look at that chipmunk over there on that stump!
Or we'll be agate hunting at the coast, as we do each visit—
Oh boy, looky here . . . Isn't this one a beaut?
Now show me what you found!

His capacity to still find delight in discovery, in the bird
he's seen four times already that morning,
as it careens wildly onto a feeder, *Jeez, that's cool,*
he'll say to no one, even though we're right there,
also caught up in his raw curiosity with nature.

I learned curiosity from him—fossil-hunting Oregon roadcuts,
scratching for arrowheads on high Washington slopes,
studying his collection of maps about the discovery of continents,
and the butterflies he's caught himself in wonder,
now pinned neatly in frames on the walls.

Even his origin story of being called to practice medicine
after dissecting a frog in middle school is a call-and-response
within a song of men in the world, a song of exploring
what is partially known, a song of handing down devotion
across generations and within our actions as best we may.

Even when he skipped family holidays to take his rounds
at the hospital, to ensure the holidays of others
were not tragic surprises, he was showing his boys
how to respond to the song of being called.
And he hopes, to this day, we both understand.

Dear Brother

We've never been particularly close, then or now.
I think we've known this for a while and not been bothered.

In this exercise of remembering, I found a need for atonement:
I'm sorry I threw you backward through the bay window

in Rochester and that you needed stitches in your foot. I only
intended to pull you headfirst over the couch to the floor.

And the time I pushed baby-doll you in a stroller down a hill.
That was my three-year-old self processing complex feelings.

And the time I slammed an ottoman into your face, I had to
    or else
I wouldn't have won the pillow-fight. I'm sure you understand.

Of course I would have protected you if you needed it.
    I would have
been a big brother if you'd needed one, if I'd been aware

I should have done something back then when we walked
    through the woods
in the dark from school, or in the long evenings, our parents
    far away

upstairs doing their own thing. But you grew strong by yourself.
You became all you needed, and now we don't *need* each other

and that seems just fine for us, doesn't it? Perhaps saddening
from what slim proof others see, yet still fulfilling the sibling bond:

We do not choose each other in the beginning, but from there
we spend a lifetime assembling our own evidence of love.

BEYOND WORDS

This project began as an effort to give one another a candid account of our mother-son experiences dealing with Jim's cleft lip and palate. We learned that though we shared a common history, we remembered events differently or didn't remember at all an event that was pivotal to the other. This was jarring at first and we were tempted to challenge, revive, or correct each other's memories. Like many parents and adult children, we have a past complicated by circumstances beyond our control. There are parents and their adult children who have endured hardships far greater than ours. Others have had easier lives. Either way, many of us would welcome opportunities to smooth out lingering tensions, explain ourselves, feel better understood, and clear up unresolved issues.

Efforts to revive troubling pasts involve tough conversations. Personality, disappointments, anger, sensitivity, defensiveness, the desire to be right, to be seen only in a positive light, unwillingness to forgive or to give the benefit of the doubt—these are some of the factors that come into play and can derail conversations between parents and adult children. To achieve a stronger relationship, both parent and child must feel safe to speak their personal truth in a context of acceptance and love. Each must realize that their individual perspectives on a shared experience are unavoidably different and equally valid. Each is an authority on their own experience and the meaning they assign to events in their lives.

Many parents say they are unwilling to begin an exploration with their adult child into their shared past. Why open old wounds? Why open yourself to criticisms? Why put your child in an uncomfortable situation? Many adult children feel the same way. Our experience tells us that it is possible and that the rewards are immeasurable.

It certainly helped that Jim issued the invitation, signaling that he was interested and ready to hear his mother's personal truths and to reveal his own. I accepted his invitation because I believed Jim's motivation came from genuine curiosity and love. We both understood the risk such an undertaking involves—the probability of dredging up difficult memories, reviving unresolved conflicts, disclosing events that leave one or the other feeling criticized or inadequate. We felt able to manage hard truths that might arise. We knew enough to avoid the common communication saboteurs: the hard "why" questions, finger-pointing "you" statements, and pejorative words, for example. We chose our words carefully and listened with intent to learn. We were committed to exploring, rather than contesting, memories that did not line up with our own. We were able to create a new, shared lens for parts of this project, one that enabled us to interweave our individual memories.

My mother-voice speaks of privately held, often still raw, memories, the ones that reveal vulnerability, have left the deepest marks, and evoke the strongest emotions. My professional voice seeks to explore more deeply my remembered reality and to reassure all parents that their stories deserve a place in the landscape of human experience. Jim's voice reflects on memories and moments from his childhood and teen years that he didn't really want to revisit, as most kids probably don't; yet looking back as an adult, he can own his journey to becoming the man he is today.

The very act of creating a mother-son memoir broadened and deepened our relationship, in ways far more profound than we anticipated. This development became the most treasured part of our writing experience. We became intrigued by how each of us framed and interpreted the circumstances we have inhabited. We welcomed questions and revealed thoughts and feelings in ways that had eluded us before. The act of sharing our truths was liberating. Our trust in one another deepened, allowing us to gain greater compassion for the other's struggles. As we absorbed and reacted to one another's writings, the awareness that we were creating something larger than the sum of its parts energized our work. The benefits to our lives and our relationship continue to accrue. As I recognized the value of my conversations with Jim, I began to engage Kent in similar conversations, inviting him to ask questions about his life in our family and to answer mine. In addition to hearing how it felt to be Jimmy's younger brother, we have been able to talk more openly about my experience being his mother, and his of being my son.

It turns out that my fears about Kent's well-being were unfounded. It appears that our family gave Kent what he needed to make his way in life. He followed a path very different from his brother's, pursued his separate interests, and found and developed his own strengths and talents to become a man of character, accomplished in career and family life.

These endeavors to have candid conversations with my adult children have yielded relationship rewards beyond our expectations. For parents and adult children who are ready to share memories in order to settle unresolved issues from the past, or simply deepen their relationship, these conversations, risky though they may seem, are worth undertaking.

Let Us Be Clear

We understand
a bilateral cleft
is not the heaviest
little godsend.

We understand
many are born into harder facts
than ours, into a world
leveraged against them.

We understand
some children learn themselves
by themselves,
and some mothers are never seen.

But all any of us has to offer
anyone we love
is an attention to sharing
whatever our truths may be

and a commitment to choosing
presence with each other.
In our process we are content
and take nothing for granted.

MEDICAL TERMS

ABO INCOMPATIBILITY

ABO incompatibility, or ABO blood type incompatibility, is a type of illness known as a hemolytic disease of the newborn (HDN). It occurs when the baby's blood type is A, B, or AB and the mother's blood type is O. A person with blood type O has antibodies that attack the red blood cells of type A, B, or AB. Healthy red blood cells are critical for carrying oxygen from the lungs to tissues and organs and carbon dioxide back to the lungs. If a mother's type O blood mixes with her baby's type A, B, or AB blood, her antibodies may attack her baby's red blood cells, causing them to break down. One symptom of ABO incompatibility is jaundice (a yellowish hue to the skin and eyes), which signals the breakdown of red blood cells (hemolysis). Hemolytic anemia is a condition in which there are too few healthy red blood cells to supply adequate oxygen to the newborn's body tissues. If anemic, the baby may have low energy, difficulty feeding, pale skin and eyes, and a fast heart rate and rapid breathing while resting.

To diagnose ABO incompatibility, doctors conduct blood tests to see if the baby is anemic, has blood antibodies from the mother, and has high levels of bilirubin. Bilirubin is an orange-yellow pigment formed in the liver by the breakdown of hemoglobin, protein inside red blood cells that is released into the bloodstream during hemolysis.

Rh factor incompatibility is another type of HDN. Because it occurs more often than ABO incompatibility, screening for Rh factor is more common, allowing treatment during pregnancy.

A mother may have subsequent babies with ABO incompatibility with varying degrees of severity. Not every baby with ABO incompatibility will need treatment. Treatment depends on the level of bilirubin in the baby's blood. When needed, a temporary increase in feedings may help the baby excrete excess bilirubin. If jaundice is more severe, it may be effectively treated by light therapy (phototherapy). With eyes protected by cloth coverings, the baby's skin is exposed to light waves that transform the bilirubin into a substance that can pass through the baby's system. In extreme cases of severe ABO blood incompatibility, the rapid increase of bilirubin may be life-threatening and the baby may need a blood transfusion.

Sources: National Institutes of Health—National Library of Medicine, MedlinePlus (https://medlineplus.gov), Verywell Family (verywellfamily.com).

ATTENTION DEFICIT HYPERACTIVITY DISORDER (ADHD)

Attention Deficit Hyperactivity Disorder (ADHD) is a complex developmental impairment of the brain's ability to focus, plan, and carry out tasks. In the past, ADHD has been misunderstood as a behavior problem, mental illness, or learning disability. It typically first occurs in childhood and may continue into adulthood.

Symptoms vary from individual to individual and may change as an individual ages. Symptoms can be mild, moderate, or severe.

Various medicinal, educational, behavioral, and counseling treatments are recommended to mitigate symptoms. Effectiveness of any modalities varies among individuals. To further complicate treatment effectiveness, psychological, mood, or stressful living situations often co-occur with ADHD.

Source: ADDitude: Inside the ADHD mind (additudemag.com).

CLEFT PALATE

According to the American Academy of Pediatrics (2017), one in every 700 babies is born with a cleft lip, cleft palate, or both. The condition is one of the most common birth defects.

A cleft lip occurs in utero between the fourth and seventh weeks, when the tissue that forms the upper lip does not come together, leaving a gap (cleft) in one (unilateral) or both (bilateral) sides of the lip. A gap may also occur in the upper gum in conjunction with a cleft in the lip. A cleft in the gums interferes with the natural formation of teeth.

A cleft palate occurs when the roof of the mouth does not come together in utero, leaving a gap from behind the middle of the upper gum toward the back of the mouth. The length and width of the cleft can vary, sometimes with a large gap in both the hard palate and soft palate. It is more common for a cleft lip and cleft palate to occur together than just one or the other.

The hard and soft palates make up the roof of the mouth. The hard palate is the bony part that occupies two-thirds of the roof of the mouth and provides structure to support upper gums and to allow space for the tongue to move around. The soft palate is the fleshy muscular part at the back of the roof of the mouth behind the hard palate.

It separates the mouth from the throat and functions to keep food out of the respiratory tract when a person is swallowing or sucking. Both palates are important to swallowing, breathing, and speech. Some children with cleft palate are more prone to ear infections.

Surgery can close the clefts in the lip and palate. Surgery is often done in the baby's first year. In more severe cleft palates, additional operations will be necessary to completely repair the lip and palate. As they grow, children with cleft palates may need dental and orthodontic care and speech therapy.

Sources: Medical News Today (medicalnewstoday.com), American Academy of Pediatrics (healthychildren.org).

LE FORT SURGERY

Rene Le Fort first described predictable fracture patterns of the skull in 1901. Le Fort osteotomy (the surgical cutting of a bone or removal of a piece of bone) is a type of jaw surgery invented over fifty years ago based on these patterns of natural fracturing. This surgery is often used today by maxillofacial surgeons to correct a wide range of dentofacial deformities, most commonly midface deformities. It allows for correction in three dimensions, including advancement, retrusion, elongation, and shortening. In patients with cleft palate, the procedure moves the upper jaw to correct misalignment of the teeth and jaw and palate. Le Fort II is a more rare surgery that moves both the upper jaw and the nose in order to lengthen the nose with coordinated upper jaw movement.

Source: National Center for Biological Information, National Library of Medicine, National Institute for Health, Le Fort I Osteotomy. https://www.ncbi.nlm.nih.gov/pmc/articles/PMC3805729/).

POEM NOTES

TORCHONS

When your mother writes an entire chapter about two dish towels and longing to study French literature, you don't really have a choice to just let that go by, you are obligated to try a response piece in a formal form—such as this villanelle.

ODE TO SPORT

The form is an attempt at a Pindaric ode in structure and content. The reference at the end of the second section is a paraphrase of a Dan Gable quote: "More enduringly than any other sport, wrestling teaches self-control and pride. Some have wrestled without great skill—none have wrestled without pride."

ACKNOWLEDGMENTS

FROM BARBARA WALKER

Words cannot express my gratitude for my husband, James—dedicated physician, caring father, my best friend, and most trusted critic.

I am grateful to members of my writing group—Barbara Engel, Quinton Hallett, Evelyn Hess, and Patty Jacobs—and lifelong friend Felicity Howlett, who have believed in and encouraged my story from the beginning. A special thank-you to Quinton Hallett, whose insight and careful eye helped us put our best story forward, and to Susan Fitzgerald, whose enthusiasm has buoyed me up on the home stretch.

Finally, my profound thanks to my son Jim, who not only invited me to write "our story," but whose respectful curiosity allowed me to speak hard truths.

FROM JIM WALKER

Thank you to Cathy for entering my life in 2012. Your presence, love, and support continue to be an inspiration to me in so many ways.

Thank you to Emily Price Soli for your sharp-eyed, eleventh-hour review of the poems.

We are grateful to have been a finalist in the nonfiction/memoir genre at the 2022 Pacific Northwest Writers Conference. The recognition and the conference experience gave us a needed boost in the publishing journey.

We are thankful to Spike Gillespie, author and memoir coach, for facilitating our very first conversations and helping launch this project in 2015.